Doctoral Education as If People Matter

Critical Issues in the Future of Learning and Teaching

VOLUME 24

The titles published in this series are listed at *brill.com/cifl*

Doctoral Education as If People Matter

Critical Issues for the Future

Edited by

Marie-Louise Österlind, Pam Denicolo and
Britt-Marie Apelgren

TUTA SUB AEGIDE PALLAS · 1683 ·

BRILL

LEIDEN | BOSTON

All chapters in this book have undergone peer review.

The Library of Congress Cataloging-in-Publication Data is available online at https://catalog.loc.gov

Typeface for the Latin, Greek, and Cyrillic scripts: "Brill". See and download: brill.com/brill-typeface.

ISSN 2542-8721
ISBN 978-90-04-52928-1 (paperback)
ISBN 978-90-04-52929-8 (hardback)
ISBN 978-90-04-52930-4 (e-book)

This book is printed on acid-free paper and produced in a sustainable manner.

Printed by Printforce, United Kingdom

Contents

Acknowledgements

Our passion for developing improvements in doctoral education has been both stimulated and sustained by the support of colleagues, friends, and research students worldwide who have also enthusiastically responded to similar challenges and opportunities in the field. We appreciate especially the contributions of those who supplied chapters and advice on our own and we thank them for sharing our journey.

We are also indebted to our publishing colleagues at Brill who have always been ready when required with advice and information and have provided us all with a platform to share our obsessions with the wider academic community.

We would also like to thank the universities that we have been affiliated to over the years for their support of our research and writing.

Most of all, we appreciate the patience and help of our families while we engaged with this project.

Figures and Tables

Figures

Tables

Notes on Contributors

Britt-Marie Apelgren
(PhD) is Professor of Language Education at the University of Gothenburg in Sweden. She has extensive experience in doctoral education. Her main research fields concern teacher cognition, language teaching and learning, language policy, doctoral studies, and leadership in higher education.

Diogo Casanova
(PhD) is the Vice-Rector for Quality and Innovation at the Universidade Aberta. He has experience in leading institutional and international projects related to online learning, teaching and postgraduate education.

Pam Denicolo
(PhD) is Professor Emerita, Reading University, and a chartered psychologist, Academy of Social Sciences Fellow, and honorary pharmacist. She is also an advisor/consultant to universities worldwide on doctoral education. She provides workshops for supervisors and researchers on supervision, examining, research methods, publishing, gaining funding, etc.

Shane Dowle
(PhD) is Senior Continuous Improvement Manager in the Change and Improvement division at University College London. He was previously Head/Deputy Director of the Doctoral College at the University of Surrey and holds a PhD on the topic of doctoral completions.

Dawn Duke
(PhD) is Head of Researcher Development for the Africa Research Excellence Fund (AREF) and leads professional development programmes for early career researchers and academics across Africa, following years of experience running and contributing to doctoral researcher and supervisor development programmes.

Fabiane Garcia
(PhD) is Professor in Education at the Universidade Federal do Amazonas (UFAM). She coordinates the postgraduate programme in Education and has experience in supervising doctoral students to completion.

Martin Gough
(PhD) is variously a doctoral supervisor, researcher and academic developer (including leading on supervisor development), based at the University of Liverpool Centre for Higher Education Studies. He is Co-Convenor of the Society for Research into Higher Education Postgraduate Issues.

Erika Hansson
(PhD) is currently working as a lecturer at Kristianstad University, Sweden. She completed her degree in psychology in 2017, and her areas of interest comprise of disordered eating among boys, bullying among youth, as well as the well-being of doctoral students.

Gillian Houston
(PhD) completed a PhD on the doctoral examination in 2018 and now works as an independent researcher and author. She has supported the UK Council for Graduate Education for many years, as a speaker, board member, chair and vice-chair, now as an Honorary Life Member.

Isabel Huet
(PhD) is Assistant Professor in Education at the Universidade Aberta, an Invited Research Fellow at the University of Hertfordshire, and an Honorary doctoral supervisor at the University of Liverpool. She has experience in designing CPD programmes for doctoral supervisors.

Sverker Lindblad
(PhD) is Professor Emeritus in Education at the University of Gothenburg, researching Education Policy, an area in which he has published extensively. A recent publication is on typecasting in the recruitment of full professor. He is an experienced doctoral supervisor.

Bing Lu
(PhD) is a doctoral researcher in Department Education Studies at University of Warwick She founded the 'Superb-vision network' (SVN) sponsored by Warwick Doctoral College. Her doctoral research investigates how returned doctorate holders conduct doctoral supervision in their home countries.

Alistair McCulloch
(PhD) is Head of Research Education at the University of South Australia. Chair of the QPR conference, in 2017 he was awarded a national 'Australian

Award for University Teaching' for his work in the field of doctoral supervisor development.

Marie-Louise Österlind
(PhD) is Vice Dean and Senior lecturer in Work Psychology at Kristianstad University, Sweden. Her research concerns working conditions and leadership in public sector organisations. She has been a regular board member of The Swedish Association for University Teachers.

Julie Reeves
(PhD) is a Researcher Developer. She contributed to the Vitae 'Researcher Development Framework', was the Capacity Development Co-Investigator for BRECcIA-GCRF, established ReMNet for international research management networking, and is a co-convener of the SRHE Postgraduate Issues Network.

Manuela Schmidt
(PhD) gained her PhD in medical science in 2020 and works currently as a senior lecturer at Linnaeus University and as a postdoc at Jönköping Academy. Her research focuses among others on mental health of university students and various professions.

Matthew Sillence
(PhD) is a researcher developer and Senior Fellow of the Higher Education Academy. Since 2012, he has provided training for postgraduate researchers and professional development courses for supervisors at the University of East Anglia in the United Kingdom.

Gun-Britt Wärvik
(PhD) is Professor in Education at the Department of Education and Special Education, University of Gothenburg. Her research interests concern educational governing, including studies of doctoral education. She is a member of the research group Politics in Education.

CHAPTER 1

Prologue

Doctoral Education as If People Matter

Marie-Louise Österlind, Pam Denicolo and Britt-Marie Apelgren

The impetus to compile and contribute to this book had its origins in the individual work of we three editors, Marie-Louise, Pam, and Britt-Marie, who share an academic passion for improving the experience of the doctorate for all involved in the process. Our work with both national and international colleagues and learned societies has certainly confronted us with the multiplicity of forms of doctoral education extant in the field, yet we have been able to recognise the emergence of common issues, widespread concerns, commonplace frustrations in personal communications, conference debates and in the literature. This is despite, rather than because of, the joy furnished by our own and our students' research activity and our conviction that learning to do research through engagement with doctoral study has the potential to be extremely fulfilling.

Improvement to that experience benefits individuals, institutions, professions and the larger community because engaging with doctoral studies is the prelude to an academic career or the further development of other careers. At the same time, the outcomes of doctoral research contribute considerably, albeit in many different ways, to society at large and to further academic research. Thus, we collaborated to produce a compilation of thoughts and analyses from a wide range of contributors, from diverse disciplines and contexts, about what is challenging and thus needs to be transformed and how that might be achieved in the complex arena of doctoral education.

From amongst the topics that our volunteer authors suggested, we could discern a range of common threads which could serve as sections when structuring the book, although these threads developed and transformed in the process of writing during a time of global disruption. In the end we arranged them into three groups, noting the challenges that impact on all participants in the doctoral process, those that especially concern university staff, and those that mostly trouble doctoral researchers. Those challenges also reveal opportunities for improving the work situations of those concerned. In fact, each chapter covers much ground and several issues, each being akin to one block in a Rubik's cube with links to many others, so their organisation could

 | DOI:10.1163/9789004529304_001

be very different. Nevertheless, in the constantly evolving pandemic context in which we all found ourselves as the writing progressed, our abiding desire has been to have the people involved in doctoral education being the central focus. Each author addresses challenges that either impact all participants or a chosen sub-group in the doctoral work arena and considers ways that these situations could be improved.

However, the pandemic situation has clearly influenced the situations that our authors have written about. Some doctoral-related problems have been exacerbated and others reduced by isolation requirements and the resulting recourse to greater use of technology. Our vulnerabilities as doctoral studies participants have been more clearly exposed while our resilience and creativity has been tested. Readers will find throughout the book references to such issues, but we have chosen not to foreground the pandemic effects; no doubt others will do so. Instead, our authors were free to recognise any new or hidden difficulties and any opportunities revealed by responses to the pandemic.

As you read this book, you will find that doctoral education, like other significant life experiences, is replete with paradoxes, the first being charmingly expressed by the saying: a smooth sea never made an expert surf boarder (or ship's captain, etc.) It is axiomatic that working to discover new knowledge or to support others to do so will be a difficult business. Therefore, any attempts to make the process less daunting will be potentially heir to the frustration of making it, from some perspectives, less 'doctoral'. However, to carry our analogy further, our surfer or ship's captain will be less successful, not more, if they learn their craft during a hurricane rather than on a normally turbulent sea.

Thus, our authors do not seek to mollycoddle participants in the doctoral process; rather, they seek to reduce gratuitous and preventable challenges so to leave only those that are indispensable to developing doctorateness.

1 Overview of Part 1: Challenges and Opportunities for the Key Participants in Doctoral Education

In the first part of this book the focus is on key participants in doctoral education and how governance, conceptual and contextual matters affect not only the doctorate *per se*, but also the characteristics of doctoral research. The four chapters problematise the doctorate as highly regulated and systematised education and research. They explore what challenges and opportunities these present for current and future doctoral researchers and supervisors, and for understanding doctoral education as part of higher education contexts in a globalised world. Examples are given from various geographical contexts (Australia, Brasil, China, Ireland, Portugal, Sweden, and the UK). However, the issues are global, since the provided references demonstrate testimony of trends found and researched internationally. These chapters acknowledge that doctoral education, being part of the continuous restructuring and evolution of higher education as a whole, has suffered much recent disruption to tradition. They also emphasise the importance of agency so that we as supervisors, teachers and examiners must critically and collegially engage in the future of the doctorate.

Drawing from Karl Marx's early works on alienations, Alistair McCullough, Chapter 2, argues that the doctorate risks becoming alienated from its core values by regarding doctoral research as 'work' and doctoral researchers as 'knowledge-workers'. He questions the global trend focussing on individual doctoral researchers as workers trained in entrepreneurship and a whole range of generic work-related skills for the good of the society as well as for the employment in or outside the academia. That is, in McCullough's view, a focus on a future individual career rather than on the creative and new research contributing to knowledge in the field, what many regard as the essence of doctoral research. The well-intentioned recommendation for a 9–5 job for doctoral researchers, focusses on the importance of doctoral researchers' wellbeing and need of a balanced work-life, however, according to McCullough, it also influences how the doctorate is viewed. He refers to the power of metaphors where 'work/job' implies set work hours and agendas, which in the case of doctoral education or research means efficiency, 'just in time' thesis completion and career planning. In addition, he highlights how the globalised trend to regulate, systematise and evaluate doctoral education has intensified and added to the notion of doctoral research as work in a more neo-liberal sense. McCullough urges the reader to consider the main reasons why many doctoral researchers pursue a doctoral education, i.e., intrinsic motivation involving a lust for researching and digging deep into a particular aspect in order to contribute to knowledge in that area.

In Chapter 3, Britt-Marie Apelgren, Sverker Lindblad and Gun-Britt Wärvik explore the restructuring of doctoral education through a review of Swedish national policy documents and a content analysis of twelve Swedish syllabi for a PhD in Education over a period of 50 years. Of particular interest is how governance and structure of doctoral research studies have changed and transformed the roles of supervisors and doctoral researchers. The examples taken from the Swedish context are both akin and dissimilar to changes in other regional settings. As ideas tend to travel and follow similar trends, more similarities than differences are found. The three main themes that were identified can be observed in several international contexts: 'schoolification' (regulated, structured, performance-based education), increasing interest in stress management (doctoral researchers' wellbeing and working conditions), and societal relevance in terms of professional competences for future careers (transferable generic skills). Their results show how doctoral education during past decades transformed from loose forms of academic research towards a highly regulated policy and management driven education. The authors emphasise that there is a risk that the focus for the doctoral researcher will shift from the actual research itself to working to meet all the many other requirements of the doctorate. Hence, their chapter echoes concerns raised by McCullough from his Australian context, that there is a danger that there has emerged a stronger focus on output governed by extensive regulation than on intellectual contributions and autonomy.

Bing Lu, in Chapter 4, problematises the Chinese centralised system for doctoral education through the use of interpretative analysis of national policy documents produced during a period of three decades, giving insight into a unique context not so well-known outside China. In her chapter, Bing Lu gives numerous examples of a national monitored system of doctoral qualifications, recruitment and admissions, leading to a slow pace of change, even with a national policy aiming to decentralise doctoral admission and supervisory assessment to the institutional level. The author shows how, at the institutional level, parallel systems of degree committees and assessment of doctoral applicants and supervisors are set up, eschewing an enhanced agency for actors involved in doctoral education. Thus, in a system where doctoral education is scarce and where very few doctoral researchers are admitted and few supervisors qualified, competition is high and elitists. Bing Lu reveals how the gatekeepers have moved from the national level to the institutional level. She concludes that actors involved in doctoral education should be encouraged to challenge policy barriers because policies are implemented and enacted at the local level.

In Chapter 5, the final chapter in this part, Pam Denicolo, Dawn Duke and Julie Reeves discuss the fundamental issue of doctoral final examinations and their match (or mismatch) with the aim and purpose of contemporary doctoral programmes. The authors critically question if the traditional doctoral examinations, normally a final written thesis and some form of *viva voce* examination, are sufficient and adequate for examining the new requirements introduced as a consequence of the Bologna Agreement (1999). The national and local implementation, or rather enactment, of the Bologna Agreement (the so-called Bologna process) brought extensive changes to higher education, which for the doctorate meant a unification in terms of learning outcomes, credits, and not the least a focus on the development of generic and professional skills.

Drawing on their huge international experiences of doctoral education, assessment, and examination, Denicolo, Duke and Reeves conclude that now is the time to seize the day (*carpe diem*) to collaboratively and collegially work to develop common general criteria for assessing the written thesis, as well as for the more elusive general professional skills. The authors propose the following challenging questions as a start and invite our readers to be part of exploring these by writing to the authors: (1) Can we develop broad, measurable objectives that nevertheless accommodate diversity for skills that must be developed regardless of context?, (2) What necessary and sufficient doctoral quality criteria could we communicate globally to candidates, supervisors and examiners to guide their practice?, and (3) How could such elaborated criteria be adequately conveyed to the general public, including prospective employers, to aid recognition of both universal and individual specific professional qualities derived from doctoral study?

The chapters in the first part of this volume have explored the more systemic and conceptual matters of the doctorate in a globalised world. In the next part, Part 2, the focus is on the essential supporters in doctoral education and process, the supervisors and research developers.

2 Overview of Part 2: Challenges and Opportunities for the Staff Supporting Doctoral Researchers

Given the prominence of supervisors (advisors) in the life of doctoral researchers and their role in guiding them to successful completion, four of the five chapters in this section of the book address the changes and potential, often thwarted, of this supportive role. The fifth and final chapter, though, reminds us that there are other contributors to that support, focussing especially on staff charged with the development of the wider skills required of a successful holder of a doctorate. Those people became part of the research support team more than twenty years ago and endured, with supervisors and their charges, the rapid and pervasive change to the doctoral process that took place in those years.

In Chapter 6, Pam Denicolo, Julie Reeves and Dawn Duke refer to that multitude of developments as they demonstrate how super-complex academic work has become. One paradox that pervades their argument is that because their research areas increasingly demand boundary-crossing, multi-disciplinary and multi-national effort they involve collegiality, collaboration and networking, while simultaneously competitive pressure has increased between institutions for funding, for example, and between individuals for esteem recognition for promotion.

Another paradox presented is that their multiple roles (teacher, researcher, administrator, manager, mentor, etc. for undergraduate and postgraduate students) are subject to a reductionist approach, being differentially supported and separately evaluated, whereas a more holist approach, recognising when sub-roles could be symbiotic and when others are conflict-generating, might be more professionally and personally enhancing. The authors suggest ways in which improvements to Continuing Professional Development (CPD) of supervisors could help them cope and flourish more effectively within their shape-shifting, super-hero roles. In turn, if there were greater consistency within and between institutions in the provision of CPD, this would contribute to academics' ability to support their established and new colleagues including their doctoral supervisees whom they could then induct into an authentic community of scholars.

The authors of the next chapter, Chapter 7, continue the theme of raising the quality of supervision, and thereby the doctoral products through the medium of professional development. Isabel Huet, Diogo Casanova and Fabiane Garcia also posit that such development opportunities mitigate against numerous problems experienced by both new supervisors and their supervisees. They seek to support those contentions, building on their own international experience in the field, by systematically reviewing the literature written in either English or Portuguese, on continuous supervisor development practices as they are implemented in different countries. They identify and define three forms of learning undergone as professional development: formal, informal, and situated.

Having provided detail of their search methods, they note a wide range of commitment to such development from 'desired but not available' through to 'well-supported' in some universities, the latter being mainly sited in countries with a strong culture of theorising supervision as professional pedagogic activity within a system that favours accountability. This reinforces the call for the professionalisation of supervision found in the previous chapter. Extensive examples are provided and examined from a range of countries that favour either 'on the job' learning or some form, no matter how limited, of formalised training. Taking Brazil as a case in point, they acknowledge the tension between supervisors offering their students a sense of belonging to a community while simultaneously valuing their autonomy as researchers. They suggest that this can, in turn, lead to resistance to cultural change through more formalised training, a topic that the authors intend to research further.

Matthew Sillence's Chapter 8 is also based on research using a literature resource, this time UK national and institutional policy and practice documents and reports. These are subjected to critical discourse analysis to examine both the information content and rhetorical devices used about the doctoral process and the researcher, especially in relation to supervisor development.

He notes that such documents are frequently couched in managerialist language propounding a personal responsibility perspective whereas, in contrast, the education research literature promotes a more ecological, person-valuing approach. This contrast between management policies and humane practices emerges in different ways throughout the book. Sillence provides considerable detail of both his methodology and findings which will enable readers to look afresh at documents in their own domain for comparison. His discussion includes a review of the implications of his findings for supervisor CPD, advocating a range of pedagogic strategies within a person-centred approach to empower all participants in developing their practice over time.

Building on her extensive experience of developing the quality of doctoral education and her own doctoral research into the viva voce as conducted in the UK, Gillian Houston in Chapter 9 focusses on a specific supervisory role, that of preparing researchers for that final oral examination. She begins by reflecting on the dual role, of supporter and critical friend, of the successful supervisor who attends to the changing balance of those roles as the research, and researcher, progresses towards completion. Again, we are reminded of the chameleon-like nature of multi-role academic practice. She then identifies specific topics for consideration drawing on case studies from her research, in which candidates and examiners, who are also supervisors themselves, express their perception of integral issues such as readiness to submit, preparedness to defend the thesis and the forms and values of mock vivas as preparation for the real event. From the experiences of her research participants, Houston not only draws conclusions about the complex role of supervisors but also provides advice for doctoral researchers as prospective candidates. This guidance would also serve to alert newer supervisors and examiners to important, but seldom articulated, aspects of their roles.

The final chapter, Chapter 10, in this part is provided by Julie Reeves who, while acknowledging the complexity of the supervisor's role, reminds us that the development of researchers is a shared enterprise and has become increasingly so in recent years. Many specialists contribute to this endeavour, not the least being those with titles such as 'Researcher Developer' as designated in the UK. First, she reflects on the evolution of the researcher development role from a first response to the need for novice researchers to acquire broader professional skills. She acknowledges that the researcher developer role had endured more than twenty years of fluctuating financial support before the advent of the pandemic. She charts the development of its purpose and its acceptance as a key contribution to the doctoral process, providing examples of how its remit was fulfilled in specific circumstances and is now spreading internationally as an expectation of doctoral support.

Nevertheless, she identifies studies that demonstrate that developing professional skills does not obviate psychological stress and mental health problems, nor does requiring researchers to undertake 'resilience training' or supervisors to take mental health first aid courses. A salient point is made that the researcher developers, like supervisors and doctoral researchers, are expected to be agentic in voluntarily identifying their own development needs and then finding sources to service them instead of it being an obligation to the professions embedded in institutional structures and resourced by them.

Reeves uses teaching skills as an exemplar of a key skill required of many staff in academia, such as librarians, careers advisors and other 'third space' professionals as well as researcher developers and researchers themselves. These are key skills for which training is seldom provided or officially requiring update by institutions. All these professionals must be motivated and have access to the right networks both to sustain and advance their careers and to maintain professional credibility.

Seeking to highlight the positive aspects as well as the vulnerabilities of these roles, Reeves concludes by observing that the pandemic encouraged experimentation with and development of new ways of working with researchers and, saliently, with other developers and supervisors. As a spin off from the pandemic, the notion emerges once more of a collaborative community working in a transdisciplinary, intra and inter-institutional way, using electronic and face to face communication. This model has gained further traction since it presents opportunities for improving the work experience and well-being of a range of higher education colleagues. Wellbeing is the key topic of Part 3, this time in relation to the main participants in the doctoral process, the researchers themselves.

3 Part 3: Challenges and Opportunities for Doctoral Researchers' Wellbeing

The third part of this volume bring to the fore the important issue of the well-being of doctoral researchers. The authors problematise the concept of 'well-being' as well as give extensive empirical examples of doctoral researchers' voices on the matter. The sometimes rollercoaster experiences of doctoral research and education are explored and discussed, as well as constructive ideas for what can (and sometimes should) be done to change and transform both conceptual factors and individual experiences. Considering that the doctoral researchers are the future of our academies, the issue of a good and decent doctoral education is fundamental.

In the first chapter in this part, Chapter 11, Martin Gough invites us to join him into a philosophical exploration of the concept of 'Wellbeing' in higher education contexts, pointing out a paradox at the heart of the concept leading to contending understanding. Gough's prior aim with his chapter is to investigate how wellbeing and mental health issues are conceptually understood in higher education, because it has been found that a high proportion of the doctoral researchers give testimony of experiencing health problems such as stress. He disputes that the terms wellbeing and mental health are used interchangeably. By giving concrete examples of scenarios from a workshop for university staff, Gough discusses in what way those scenarios give evidence of wellbeing. He asks the possibly provoking question "Following through the expectations of the Wellbeing Agenda, should, for instance, supervisory practice, as individual action but also as an institutional support framework, now become mainly about ensuring the continued wellbeing of doctoral researchers?" A question to which he himself answers paradoxically both 'yes' and 'no'.

Gough then leads the reader further into the more philosophical parts of his chapter where the reader is introduced to two different philosophical stances of wellbeing: (1) the Utilitarian concept of well-being including psychological and medical health issues, and (2) the Aristotelian perspective on wellbeing as flourishing which focuses on the opportunities of fulfilling oneself intellectually. This is then problematised through what is coined 'The Wellbeing Agenda' found within an emotional epistemology, which in its worst-case scenario can lead to discouragement of 'intellectual boldness' in students. This, Gough argues, will in turn oppose the core of doctoral research where the individual doctoral researcher has a responsibility to make an original contribution to knowledge. The chapter concludes that supervision must indeed also include pastoral care ensuring the wellbeing of doctoral researchers, for his/her to enable intellectual flourishing within the context of developing the academic discipline, but this should not, he contends, be prioritised over academic endeavours.

Manuela Schmidt and Erika Hansson, in Chapter 12, take their point of departure from headlines in Nature's editorials concerning the theme of increasing predominance of mental health problems and lack of wellbeing among doctoral researchers globally. They, just like Gough in his chapter (Chapter 11), emphasise that wellbeing is a complex and multidimensional concept, including social, cultural, physical, spiritual, and psychological dimensions and emotions (positive/affirmative and negative/destructive). In their literature review and SWOT analysis (strength, weakness, threat, opportunities), they conclude that there is more 'ill-being' than 'well-being' found. This in turn leads to attrition and non-completion rates of doctoral researchers, and to negative connotations, such as doctoral research as "survival, torture, peril, struggle, love-hate (hurt) relationships, fights and conflicts, burden, a battlefield and war" (Gough, Chapter 11).

They then widen the problem to being part of the new norm of academia in which both staff and students are feeling mentally ill, stressed, exhausted and depressed. Around 50% of the reviewed articles includes stories of ill-being. Schmidt and Hansson found that articles about well-being of doctoral researchers seem to arise around 2000 and beyond, steadily growing in numbers (see similar results in Apelgren, Lindblad and Wärvik, Chapter 3). In this chapter they discuss what kind of mental health problems and conditions are caused by or related to doctoral education, and what can be done by academia to create a healthy and creative environment for doctoral researchers and the organisation alike. As doctoral researchers recurrently state the importance of belongingness and its impact on their well-being, academia, according to the authors, should start with improving that state. Referring to the research of Denicolo, Reeves and Duke (2018), they end by suggesting a shift from a negative perspective to a more proactive or a positive approach, which they introduce through a list of recommendations.

In Chapter 13, Shane Dowle introduces the conceptual tools of 'liminality' (in between stages) and 'reflexivity' in order to better identify, understand and illuminate for doctoral researchers their own progress and transformative steps. He points out that others involved in doctoral education can help along the way through the doctoral experience, but it is only the doctoral researcher him/herself who is the agent who can act and drive the process forward. Progress is not always a smooth and easy highway forward, rather a bumpy country lane with unsettling moments and sometimes even intimidating events leading up to new ideas and breakthroughs, all important for idea evolution. Liminality and reflexivity, according to Dowle, are concepts to be regarded as positive and empowering tools. He talks about 'enticing space', the in-between stage of a knowledge creation process and new understandings, which drives the doctoral project forward. For Dowle, reflexivity is one essential means of helping the doctoral researcher to get through liminal moments. In his chapter he provides the reader and doctoral researchers with constructive and helpful suggestions for creating reflexive time and scaffolding reflexive practices. Dowle concludes that "there are no safe paths through the doctorate", but there are ways of manoeuvring through the doctoral process towards completion and, importantly, doing this with agency.

In the last chapter of this part, Marie-Louise Österlind offers readers insights into the personal and lived experience of the vicissitudes of being a doctoral researcher, taking the example from the Swedish context. She uses the intriguing metaphor of 'heavenly hell' and aims, like Sillence, at exploring the complex situation for doctoral researchers' in relation to their working conditions, which can often result in work-related illness and attrition. Importantly, as Österlind reminds us, high dropout rates, delay in progress, and unhappiness among doctoral researchers are equally common problems in doctoral education globally. Echoes of this have been heard in previous chapters from different national contexts.

In her chapter, Österlind presents statistics from Swedish national surveys and points out that for many Swedish doctoral researchers, doctoral education is usually experienced as 'Heaven': being employed to conduct research for 4–5 years, feeling experiences of freedom, independence, creativity and good career trajectories. However, for others or at times, their doctoral education at times is better described as 'Hell': very high demands and stress levels, unclear or contradictory goals and expectations, lack of acceptance, acknowledgement and support. For most doctoral researchers, the ups and downs are present in tandem and at different stages of their education. Österlind proposes a radical change of academic culture, with a constructive and encouraging research community that is inclusive and cooperative: a research community far from the competitive and managerial logic of productivity and performance. She concludes with a personal reflection which highlights how essential both a supporting collegial context and a good doctoral researcher-supervisor relationship are for a high-quality doctoral education as well as for productive outcomes.

Our book *Doctoral Education as If People Matter: Critical Issues for the Future* features international authors of research *in*, *of* and *with* doctoral research. Most importantly this is a book with a focus on the people who matter therein: the doctoral researcher, the supervisor/advisor and the doctoral supporters/research developers. We hope that our book will provide you, the reader, with enlightened ideas about and recognisable examples of both the opportunities and the challenges of doctoral education. We intend this to raise the prospect that all of us together might continue to improve and develop current and future doctoral education in a critical, constructive and collaborative way.

PART 1

Challenges and Opportunities for the Key Participants in Doctoral Education

CHAPTER 2

Alienation and the Problem of Work in Doctoral Education

Alistair McCulloch

Abstract

In recent decades, Karl Marx has had something of a bad rap. The fall of the Soviet empire in 1990 coupled with a self-confident neo-liberal international economic system delivering seemingly unlimited benefits to the victors of the Cold War seemed capable of bringing an end to both ideology and history. More recently some of the tarnish has come off this new economic system and its associated philosophies and Marx has received a degree of reinstatement in the halls of academe through the work of scholars such as Eagleton (2011) and Wright (2010). Much of this work has focused on the macro-level socio-economic system and contributes to the ongoing development of what can be termed a scholarship of the future intended to steer the planet and its various intertwined economies in a more sustainable direction. The initial rejection of Marx and its newfound focus, however, has allowed us to ignore one of the philosopher's most enduring areas of work, and to my mind, one of his most significant contributions to the social sciences, that concerning the importance of work to human beings, and our 'true' nature, and the implications of the way in which work is positioned for how it is experienced. This chapter draws on this element of Marx's work arguing that current tendencies in both higher education generally, and more specifically doctoral education and the doctorate, risk the very creativity upon which the doctorate's defining characteristic of 'an original contribution to knowledge' is based. It begins with a few comments on contemporary doctoral education.

Keywords

alienation – creativity – motivation – performativity – work

 | DOI:10.1163/9789004529304_002

1 Work, Jobs and Skills – Changes to the Doctorate

The socio-economic positioning of the doctorate has shifted significantly over the last half century or so. From a situation where it was regarded simply as the 'highest education' (Rudd, 1975), it has now been increasingly integrated into national economic and strategic innovation policies and accordingly becomes 'of increasing concern to national governments as the notion of the knowledge economy finds purchase globally and impacts on … (those) policies' (McCulloch, 2018, p. 86). Universities as institutions have become more important to governments globally, and their activities have become more aligned with the world of work. In the realm of doctoral education, the confluence of these three tendencies has been described in the following way:

> High expectations have been placed on well-trained researchers to contribute as knowledge-workers and innovators to the further development of the knowledge society, whether as intrapreneurs changing and modernizing established enterprises or as entrepreneurs, creating new jobs themselves. Universities have been given the public mandate to train these knowledge-workers efficiently … Conversely, universities also need doctoral candidates as essential producers of knowledge in order to keep pace with international academic competition which, despite assertions to the contrary, is still strongly defined by quantitative output … The focus is now on the individuals themselves rather than the dissertation, namely that these young academics, trained through research and equipped with a whole range of skills, need to be able to embark on careers either inside or outside academia. (Zinner & Kovačević, 2021, p. 133)

The third of these three developments brings with it an increasing policy emphasis on transferable skills development, skills "relating to communication, problem-solving, team-working and networking, and business and management know-how. These give them (i.e., the research trainees) workplace competencies that are relevant for a broad job market, although the skills they need may vary in different sectors" (Organisation for Economic Co-operation and Development, 2012, p. 9). This draws upon and also feeds back into policy processes at governmental and institutional levels to promote further focus on work-related skills training. In the UK, this is illustrated through the progression from the UK Government's 2001 establishment of the Roberts Review as part of its productivity and innovation strategy, leading to the payment of what became known as 'Roberts Money' to support career-relevant training, money which would be "conditional on ensuring that postdoctoral researchers had career development plans and access to appropriate training opportunities" (Organisation for Economic Co-operation and Development, 2012, p. 39), through the subsequent establishment of, first, UKGRAD to "support the professional and career development of postgraduate researchers" and, then, VITAE with a remit expanded to include the professional and career development of academic staff and already qualified researchers. (Details of these and related developments can be found at VITAE, 2021.)

In the UK, the skills associated with research development are situated on the VITAE website (VITAE, 2010). They are contained in the 'personal effectiveness' domain of the Researcher Development Statement which contains the "personal qualities, career and self-management skills required to take ownership for and engage in professional development', itself part of the 'knowledge, behaviours and attributes of effective and highly skilled researchers appropriate for a wide range of careers". (It is worth noting that 'personal effectiveness' is positioned securely in the realm of work rather than in the realm of social life more generally.) Interestingly, while engagement with the activities designed to promote the development of this 'knowledge, behaviours and attributes' may be required to progress through the doctoral process, there is no mention in the definitive Qualification Characteristics Statement for doctoral degrees of this development being examined prior to the award of the doctorate (QAA, 2020). It is thus not seen as a fundamental part of doctorateness (see Chapter 5 on Assessment of the Doctorate).

Associated with these policy-related developments and the increasing association of doctoral education with explicit career training, there has been an increasing tendency to position the process of doing a doctorate as a 'job'. The following advice from a blog written by the Researcher Development Manager for doctoral researchers in Exeter University's Doctoral College is illustrative. "Treat your research degree like a job. Do 9–5 hours (or an 8-hour day at times that work for you) and protect your evenings and weekends as much as you can. You and your research will be better for it" (Doctoral College, n.d.). In a similar vein, an Australia blogger, archaeologist Mick Morrison (n.d.) advises: "Treat it like a job! … treat your PhD like a job. It's a 3-year contract where you are expected to do 40 hours per week. The social life of a doctoral researcher is important … but it's only part of the reason you are here. You are here to learn, think, engage, contribute and write".

This is not to say that this type of advice is ill-intentioned or wrong. Often this concern to structure the doctorate more rigidly by treating it as a job or as work is well-motivated by a desire to protect candidates' mental health and wellbeing. This concern is exemplified in the following extracts from the *Dr of What* blogsite which points out that, while the doctorate is often referred to in terms of being 'a job' or 'going to work', doctoral researchers "are much less likely to actually treat it like one ... work[ing] 50–60 hours a week (without over time benefits), work[ing] weekends, work[ing] through lunch breaks, and not tak[ing] time off over the holiday periods". The blog continues:

> However, I think we need to all try to incorporate the important aspects of a job into our PhD experience. Including, the idea of TOIL (time off in lieu). Meaning that if we have a really productive week we can have a guilt free weekend off or even an hour sleep in on a Monday ... try to leave your work at work, which is definitely a harder task for doctoral researchers because we live and breathe our thesis ... try to integrate lunch break! ... The break refreshes you, and you're entitled to it. (PhD Survival Guide, 2020)

In these examples, 'work' and 'job' are being used as metaphors and it is important to remember that metaphors have power. They structure the way we view ourselves, what we do, and how we fit into the world. It is no coincidence that the seminal book on the topic was called *Metaphors we live by* (Lakoff & Johnson, 2008). We both live by and through metaphors and can see the power of another Australian exhortation to doctoral candidates to "Treat your PhD like a job". Huysmans (n.d.) continues, "Yes, you finish with a qualification. Yes, you're called a student. BUT the reality is you are actually a worker. You are an apprentice researcher, so treat your PhD as a job. That means turning up on time and completing a full-days' work. Just because it could be flexible does not mean you need to treat it that way". The meaning is clear when he concludes that: "Finally, routines set you up for future employment, where being at work 9–5 Monday to Friday (or similar) is deemed essential, not optional".

Much of what is contained in the previous few paragraphs is good practical advice for doctoral candidates in an era when there are increasing demands being placed on the doctorate, fewer traditional academic opportunities available for doctoral graduates, and an increasing level of performativity in academia more generally. However, it is important to note that it is all couched in terms of the doctorate being like a job or like work, meaning the discourse of doctoral education is dominated by a particular metaphorical narrative and, as was noted earlier, metaphors are powerful. To give an extreme example of this power, Wall shows how metaphors operated in, first, causing, and then, helping to maintain the momentum of the Rwandan genocide with Hutus being encouraged through radio broadcasts to regard the Tutsi minority as 'cockroaches' and 'snakes' (Wall, 1997).

So, increasingly the doctorate is being positioned as work by those advising doctoral candidates at the same time as the doctorate as training for a job or career in the knowledge economy is being promoted and pursued by governments around the globe. (Both advisers and governments are in powerful and authoritative positions vis-a-vis doctoral researchers.) This shift of focus in what was once seen primarily as a form of postgraduate education, as an educational option to be pursued once the undergraduate degree or the taught Masters was completed, has almost been finalised. Alongside this, public oversight of doctoral education has increasingly been removed from the purview of ministries of education. It is regarded rather as research training, as part of a government's innovation and related economic development agenda. Institutionally, it is divorced from other parts of higher education institutions involved in 'teaching' or 'education', and this is reflected in national funding models and their related research assessment regimes. It is also reflected in the quality regimes that have developed, with an increased emphasis on efficiency, timely completion and preparation for future careers, especially those out with the academy. This positioning and reinforcement of the association of the doctorate alongside work, working, and career development results in an instrumental rather than an intrinsic focus, and thereby less focus on the research itself.

The last three decades have seen changes to the doctorate in terms of numbers of candidates pursuing the qualification, types of doctoral qualification and mode of presentation, forms of assessment, structure and additional training elements, and the development of multiple quality frameworks at both national and international levels of government (Whittington & Barnes, 2021). The doctoral quality profession has become well-established. In an earlier publication, my co-authors and I characterised the situation as follows:

> What could be referred to a mere twenty years ago as 'a cottage industry' (UK Council for Graduate Education, 1996) is now better characterized as a highly regulated production-line involving an increasing diversity of programs both in terms of mode of study and means of presentation of research (Park, 2005), and also diversity of students as a result of internationalization and widening participation strategies (McCulloch & Thomas, 2013). (McCulloch et al., 2017, p. 86)

As part of these developments, doctoral education has become: subject to a much higher level of regulation; more systematised; and, the object of quality regimes operating at institutional, national and cross-national levels both inside and out with government. Examples of the regulatory and guidance elements of these quality regimes can be seen in the work of Quality Assurance Agencies in the UK and the EU, the Australian Council of Graduate Research, and the UK Council for Graduate Education and their work has resulted in an institutional focus on quality in doctoral provision, quality which is most frequently assured through adherence to policies and procedures. The focus of these regimes has largely been to increase the emphasis on efficiency, timely completion and preparation for future careers. The implication of these changes is that the focus of the doctoral qualification is no longer solely on the creative dimension of the research. Rather it is on the development of a trained researcher who possesses not only research-relevant skills but also broader skills and attributes of character and personality that can be utilised by an employer in the world of work.

Alongside this, we see increasing evidence that universities are becoming increasingly 'neo-liberal' and sites of performativity. A recent special edition of *Management Learning* has explored these with a focus on their impact on the early career researchers and academics upon whom both universities and governments rely on to deliver their respective agendas. In their introductory essay to the special edition, Jones et al. (2020) point to the "fragility, precarity and even brutality" which have recently been wrought on and within higher education. Drawing on Ball (2003) they flesh out three ideas, the first, *quantification* which refers "to the whole of performance metrics, data and numbers that, through technical abstraction and so-called 'objective' and 'neutral' measurements, turns employees into comparable, classifiable and governable subjects". The second is the *ideal of perfect control* over a system which involves the replacement of 'more collegial forms of university administration' by authoritarian styles and practices. Following Lyotard (1984) they suggest that, while this central control is supposed to improve performance it actually does the opposite, stifling performance. Time saved through efficiency is "off-set by increases in the effort and time that need to be devoted to accounting for task work, erecting monitoring systems, collecting performance data and managing impressions and expectations" (p. 367). The third is the concept of *fabrication*, which refers to "versions of an organisation (or person) which does not exist … (entities) produced purposefully in order 'to be accountable'" (p. 367). As part of this, creativity is exhibited in:

> influencing ranking systems, (and) accreditation processes, which in their turn are used for further branding and marketing to a point where core research, teaching and social mission, and values are compromised and even displaced. Such a mad dash for visible deliverables, inevitably diminishes the rigour and long-term impact of research and teaching work. This in turn promotes a gaming mentality, where staff and students prioritise metrics over substance – where journal ranking or grades are more important than learning. (p. 368)

Additional to the challenges from neo-liberalism and performativity, the increasing economic importance of intellectual property (claimed variously by stakeholders, institutions and publishers) also impacts on the doctoral researcher's relationship to their work (doctoral candidates frequently retain only copyright on their thesis).

Developing an original contribution to knowledge does not simply involve work in the sense of an individual selling their labour to an employer to produce a product. It is fundamentally a creative act, an act in which the creator has a relationship to the product (the thesis) and the activity (the creating) which is different from that involved in the simple act of working for someone else. As Frick (2012, p. 113) states: "Doctoral study can be understood as inherently a creative endeavour". She goes on to add that "the function of the doctorate as developing generic abilities (such as creativity) is placed often in opposition to the achievement of discipline-specific, knowledge-based outcomes. Such notions discredit creativity as an asset to doctoral quality and relevance in the sciences" (p. 113). The changing nature of both higher education and the doctorate has implications for the relationship of the person pursuing the qualification both to the qualification itself and also to the process of achieving it and it has implications for the creative act. There are tensions involved in this new doctoral relationship, tensions which are surfaced as the balance between 'creative act' and 'work' changes and there are implications for the doctorate, whose defining characteristic – the gold standard – is the 'original contribution to knowledge', the touchstone of doctorateness. Taken as a whole, these developments raise issues about control of the process of the doctorate's production and also ownership of the product – the knowledge contained within the thesis and any accompanying artefacts.

2 Alienation, Marx and Doctoral Education

In this section, I introduce Marx's writings on work and alienation beginning by noting that Mann (2001) has already examined some of these issues in the context of undergraduate education and concluded that alienation and creativity are negatively related. She argues that where motivation and control are in the hands of others, the student becomes "estranged (from) … their own creative and autonomous self" as they acquiesce "to the demands and prescriptions" of others (p. 13). She notes that this is related to the alienation faced by those in higher education who are affected by increasing performativity, particularly where the "assessed work that a student produces can be seen as part of a system of exchange … undertaken for a selfish motive. The 'object', that is, what is produced … no longer belongs to the student, but, because it is part of a system of exchange, the student belongs to it" (p. 13). If this is the situation at the level of undergraduate education, it applies more strongly to the doctorate where the focus of education is on the production of new knowledge rather than a simple demonstration of an understanding of existing knowledge.

While Marx's later works are characterised by a focus on economic and social structure and on conflict between capital and labour, his early work was dominated by an analysis of the idea of alienation and its impacts on the individual worker in a capitalist society. For Marx, humans are essentially what they make or create and work is a fundamental part of what it means to be a human. In working we put something of ourselves into the product and external and institutional environments affect our relationship to both product and process and also have an impact on the creativity, the fundamental quality on which the doctorate depends. To quote Sidorkin, "… the products we create also recreate us. Productive activity is what connects humans to their existence as members of humankind, to their species-being … We literally create ourselves through the process of production" (2004, p. 252). Kai Erikson, in his 1985 Presidential Address to the American Sociological Association fleshed this out as follows:

> Human beings reach out, gather the materials of nature, and fashion them into objects of one kind or another … The true character of humankind is reflected in the objects we produce as a result of that process – a campfire, an axe, a cathedral, a sonnet. Work of that kind [of both physical and intellectual natures] is necessary for humans to fulfil their true nature … the energy and skill invested in the object is the very stuff of the person who created it.

A capitalist world, however, has disturbed 'that natural arrangement' in three ways:

> The first is the institution of private property. Both the means by which the objects are produced and objects themselves are owned by somebody else … with the result that the worker is drawn apart from the work itself … The second is the development of a more and more complex division of labor. … The third is the process by which human labor becomes a commodity like all other commodities. Workers in a capitalist economy do not ordinarily manufacture things for their own consumption, nor, presumably, do they do so for the love of it. They manufacture things for money, for cold tender. Their experience and ability – their very selves,

> in fact – are sold at market prices in much the same way as a side of beef or a sack of potatoes, and in that sense they become commodities themselves. They are objects, things of a measured worth, without any greater value than the denomination of the coin used to purchase them. (Erikson, 1986, pp. 1–2)

Alienation then should be understood as a tripartite form of separation: separation from product, from process, and from self and as something that is focused on the creative space inhabited by human beings as they manufacture both their physical and their socio-cultural environments. It occurs when they are separated or estranged from the product of their labour and from the full creative activity of which their labour is part. They can also become alienated/separated/estranged from their fellow workers since, in a capitalist system, as "commodities for sale, people are always in competition with one another and that understandably helps reduce whatever feelings of comradeship and communality might otherwise emerge". Finally, they are alienated from their true essence, their species-being and, also, from themselves (Erikson, 1986, p. 2; for other discussions of Marx and alienation, see Musto, 2010; Sayers, 2005; Schmitt, 1996; Shantz et al., 2015).

3 Conclusion

This chapter should not be read as a call for a return to a mythic past in which doctoral researchers pursued research from pure motives with no thought for what would follow. Doctoral candidates have always wondered and talked about 'what's next?'. They have discussed with each other and supervisors what awaits them once they graduate. What it is intended to do is raise some concerns about the current situation in which the doctorate is positioned as largely about preparation for a job or career, a positioning which reinforces and is itself reinforce by a discourse which situates the research degree process as itself being work or a job. The PhD is currently pursued largely in environments characterised by high degrees of performativity, high levels of competition within departments for resources, and outside those departments for relatively scarce academic positions upon graduation. There is an increased focus on efficiency in the doctoral process, notably in terms of timely completion which can lead to an emphasis on 'safe' rather than necessarily creative or edgy projects. (It is interesting to note that as recently as 2016 Eva Brodin could say that the "current literature specifically examining doctoral students' critical and creative thinking is scarce" [p. 973].) More actors are involved in the doctorate resulting in a shift of control of both process and activity away from the doctoral researcher and towards others. Part of this results from the increased degree of regulation now surrounding the doctorate. Some is due to increasing degrees of industry involvement in doctoral projects (the Australian government, for example, now requires universities to provide data on the extent of their doctoral candidates' industrial engagement). In some universities there are expectations across all disciplines that supervisors will have co-authorship with their doctoral researchers on publications coming out of their theses. For supervisors, pursuing this co-authorship is a rational response to an increasingly performative work environment. For candidates, taken together, these developments reduce their ownership and control of both process and product and shift the emphasis from intrinsic motivations and towards the extrinsic or instrumental.

To conclude, I'd like to recall the reasons doctoral researchers embark on their doctoral studies in the first place, that is, their motivation for entering the 'highest education'. Surprisingly, this is a relatively under-explored aspect of doctoral education. In an earlier work, some colleagues and I examined the then extant literature and drew on self-determination theory and social cognitive career theory to develop a framework for the analysis of motivation to enter a doctorate. We concluded that five categories of motivation for doctoral study could be determined. These are autonomy, relatedness, competence and self-efficacy, outcome expectations, and goals – only two of which (outcome expectations and goals) related to work and careers and then only partially given these categories can also relate more generally to broader life plans. Other categories concerned sense of control, a sense of being 'valued and cared for', and self-belief and self-confidence. Earlier studies by an Australian team led by Cally Guerin came to a similar conclusion. Work and career were not major motivating factors, simply one factor amongst many. Thus,

> [a] study in the broad science, technology, engineering and mathematics (STEM) area that utilized a mixed methods approach concluded that the most common reasons for beginning research degrees are: 'I wanted to do my own research', 'I am driven by a desire to invent/create/discover new things', and 'I wanted to find out more about the topic I am studying' (Guerin & Ranasinghe, 2010). A second study … involving a factor analysis of responses from current doctoral students across all disciplines identified five main factors impacting on decision-making: encouragement from family and friends to take up doctoral studies; intrinsic interest in the field of study and identification as the kind of person who can contribute to knowledge in the discipline; inspiration by lecturers, who

> sometimes actively encouraged students to continue their studies; positive undergraduate experiences of authentic research; and a desire for career advancement (Guerin et al., 2015a). (McCulloch et al., 2017, p. 88)

Doctoral researchers commence their studies motivated by a sense of enquiry, and one or more of a desire to contribute, a desire to contribute to the development of new knowledge in a particular field, a desire to continue their learning and a desire to remain in a setting in which they feel comfortable and accepted. For many, the encouragement to apply for a doctorate came from "what the doctorate was not, for example, non-academic employment which was viewed as routine and potentially (or actually) boring. Students also positioned doctoral study as 'not taught'" (McCulloch et al., 2017, p. 102). Marx reminds us that, as they produce or create their theses and/or artefacts, doctoral candidates put part of themselves into what they produce. As doctoral educators we must be careful not to allow the changes occurring in both higher education and the doctorate to damage the relationship of doctoral researchers to the qualification, the process of achieving it, and the creative activity that contributes significantly to the original contribution of knowledge that is the defining characteristic of the doctorate. Focusing too much on employability and invoking a discourse whereby the doctorate is positioned as 'work' carries with it a significant danger of increased alienation from product, process and self.

References

Ball, S. J. (2003). The teacher's soul and the terrors of performativity. *Journal of Education Policy, 18*(2), 215–228. https://doi.org/10.1080/0268093022000043065

Brodin, E. M. (2016). Critical and creative thinking nexus: Learning experiences of doctoral students. *Studies in Higher Education, 41*(6), 971–989. https://doi.org/10.1080/03075079.2014.943656

Doctoral College. (n.d.). *Working well | The doctoral college blog*. Retrieved May 3, 2022, from http://blogs.exeter.ac.uk/doctoralcollege/2018/10/15/working-well/

Eagleton, T. (2011). *Why Marx was right*. Yale University Press.

Erikson, K. (1986). On work and lienation. *American Sociological Review, 51*(1), 1. https://doi.org/10.2307/2095474

Guerin, C., & Ranasinghe, D. (2010). Why I wanted more: Inspirational experiences of the teaching–research nexus for engineering undergraduates. *Journal of University Teaching and Learning Practice, 7*(2), 117–139. https://doi.org/10.53761/1.7.2.8

Guerin, C., Jayatilaka, A., & Ranasinghe, D. (2014). Why start a higher degree by research? An exploratory factor analysis of motivations to undertake doctoral

studies. *Higher Education Research & Development, 34*(1), 89–104. https://doi.org/10.1080/07294360.2014.934663
Huysmans, R. (n.d.). *How to be a good PhD student.* Retrieved May 3, 2022, from https://www.drrichardhuysmans.com/how-to-be-a-good-phd-student/
Jones, D. R., Visser, M., Stokes, P., Örtenblad, A., Deem, R., Rodgers, P., & Tarba, S. Y. (2020). The performative university: 'Targets', 'Terror' and 'Taking Back Freedom' in Academia. *Management Learning, 51*(4), 363–377. https://doi.org/10.1177/1350507620927554
Lakoff, G., & Johnson, M. (1980). *Metaphors we live by.* University Of Chicago Press.
Lee, A., & Bongaardt, R. (2021). *The future of doctoral research: Challenges and opportunities.* Routledge.
Mann, S. J. (2001). Alternative perspectives on the student experience: Alienation and engagement. *Studies in Higher Education, 26*(1), 7–19. https://doi.org/10.1080/03075070020030689
McCulloch, A. (2018). The disciplinary status of doctoral education. *Higher Education Review, 50*(2), 86–104.
McCulloch, A., Guerin, C., Jayatilaka, A., Calder, P., & Ranasinghe, D. (2017). Choosing to study for a PhD: A framework for examining decisions to become a research student. *Higher Education Review, 49*(2), 85–106.
McCulloch, A., & Thomas, L. (2013). Widening participation to doctoral education and research degrees: A research agenda for an emerging policy issue. *Higher Education Research & Development, 32*(2), 214–227. https://doi.org/10.1080/07294360.2012.662630
Morrison, M. (n.d.). *Minimising the misery and pain: Tips for completing a doctoral thesis.* Retrieved May 3, 2022, from http://mickmorrison.com/2012/03/30/minimising-the-misery-and-pain-tips-for-completing-a-doctoral-thesis/
Musto, M. (2010). Revisiting Marx's concept of alienation. *Socialism and Democracy, 24*(3), 79–101. https://doi.org/10.1080/08854300.2010.544075
Organisation for Economic Co-operation and Development (OECD). (2012). *Transferable skills training for researchers: Supporting career development and research.* OECD Publishing.
Park, C. (2005). New variant PhD: The changing nature of the doctorate in the UK. *Journal of Higher Education Policy and Management, 27*(2), 189–207. https://doi.org/10.1080/13600800500120068
PhD Survival Guide. (2020, July 13). *How to treat your PhD like a job.* Dr.ofwhat? https://drofwhat.com/phd-survival-guide-how-to-treat-your-phd-like-a-job/?fbclid=IwAR3DbabkRbD2T8GPcmLv6yEZZfYyhY7RRQmKJ2K34G6FTOmHuYbNZIaeWUA
QAA. (2020). *Characteristics statement doctoral degree.* https://www.qaa.ac.uk/docs/qaa/quality-code/doctoral-degree-characteristics-statement-2020.pdf?sfvrsn=a3c5ca81_14

Rudd, E., (1975). *The highest education: A study of graduate education in Britain.* Routledge.

Sayers, S. (2005). Why work? Marx and human nature. *Science & Society, 69*(4), 606–616.

Schmitt, R. (1996). Marx's concept of alienation. *Topoi, 15*(2), 163–176. https://doi.org/10.1007/bf00135387

Shantz, A., Alfes, K., Bailey, C., & Soane, E. (2015). Drivers and outcomes of work alienation: Reviving a concept. *Journal of Management Inquiry, 24*(4), 382–393.

Sidorkin, A. M. (2004). In the event of learning: Alienation and participative thinking in education. *Educational Theory, 54*(3), 251–262. https://doi.org/10.1111/j.0013-2004.2004.00018.x

UK Council for Graduate Education. (1996). *Quality and standards of postgraduate research degrees.* UKCGE.

VITAE. (2010). *Vitae Researcher Development Statement (RDS) 2010.* https://www.vitae.ac.uk/vitae-publications/rdf-related/researcher-development-statement-rds-vitae.pdf

VITAE. (2021). *A brief history of researcher development in the UK.* https://www.vitae.ac.uk/policy/a-brief-history-of-researcher-development-in-the-uk

Wall, M. A. (1997). The Rwanda crisis. *Gazette (Leiden, Netherlands), 59*(2), 121–134. https://doi.org/10.1177/0016549297059002003

Whittington, K., & Barnes, S. (2021). The changing face of doctoral education. In A. Lee & R. Bongaardt (Eds.), *The future of doctoral research: Challenges and opportunities* (pp. 5–17). Routlege.

Wright, E. O. (2010). *Envisioning real utopias* (Vol. 98). Verso.

Zinner, L., & Kovačević, M. (2021). Professionalising doctoral education. In A. Lee & R. Bongaardt (Eds.), *The future of doctoral research: Challenges and opportunities* (pp. 132–144). Routlege.

CHAPTER 3

Restructuring Doctoral Education in Sweden

Britt-Marie Apelgren, Sverker Lindblad and Gun-Britt Wärvik

Abstract

This chapter reviews and presents doctoral education in Sweden in a national and longitudinal comparative perspective. By exploring and analysing national policy documents as well as twelve institutional General Syllabi for Doctor of Philosophy from the discipline of Education (1971–2021), we present a historical analysis of changes, during the past 50 years, from an independent doctoral apprentice to an employed doctoral researcher. We identified three themes in this development: schoolification, increasing interest in stress management, and relevance in terms of professional competences. It was concluded that Swedish doctoral education is increasingly regulated at the cost of doctoral researchers' individual autonomy.

Key words

doctoral education – massification of higher education – restructuring – well-being – modernisation

1 Introduction

The purpose of this chapter is to analyse changes in the Swedish system of doctoral education during the past fifty years. We do this by scrutinising and comparing national policy documents concerning doctoral education. In particular, we are interested in exploring how the governance and structure of doctoral research has changed the roles of both the supervisor and the doctoral researcher. We have identified three themes of development and transformation of the doctorate in Swedish higher education during the past 50 years: (1) 'schoolification', (2) amplified focus on working conditions of doctoral students, and (3) increased emphasis on professional relevance outside the academy. It is also our ambition to relate the Swedish case to the immense 'travelling of ideas' (Czarniawska & Joerges, 1996) and trends in higher education, not least in doctoral education (Nerad, 2020a, 2020b; Yudkevich, Altbach, & de Wit, 2020).

 | DOI:10.1163/9789004529304_003

Doctoral education in various countries exhibits both similarities and differences (Cardoso, Tavares, Sin, & Carvahlo, 2020; Yudkevich, Altbach & de Wit, 2020). In one way, the Swedish system is similar to other international systems in that students work under supervisor(s) and are assessed on the quality of their thesis and their oral defence of this thesis (HEA 1992:1434; HEO 1993:100). In other ways, however, the Swedish doctorate is quite distinct and to some extent different. The research reform in 1998 (Swedish Code of Statutes, 1998) required that the time to complete a doctorate should not exceed four years of full-time study, and that financial support for the student had to be prearranged before admission by the department.

Given this, doctoral positions are now advertised and handled like other academic positions at universities. In accordance with the Swedish Higher Education Act (HEA 1992:1434) and the Higher Education Ordinance (HEO 1993:100), doctoral candidates in Swedish higher education are employed by appointed university departments, which are responsible for funding their doctoral researchers throughout their period of study. This entails that the Head of Department is responsible for ensuring that doctoral researchers have good working environments, including work areas, personal computers and access to other equipment necessary for their studies – and the Head of Department is also responsible for the doctoral researcher's wellbeing. To achieve this, each department appoints a Director of Doctoral Studies who is responsible for overseeing activities in doctoral studies (see also Schmidt & Hansson, this volume; Österlind, this volume).

However, doctoral researchers' working environments and wellbeing are not only related to aspects of working conditions but also to the specific characteristics of a doctoral education as presented above. In recent years, doctoral education in Sweden has been affected by new regulations, 'schoolification' (i.e., syllabi, national and local learning outcomes and obligatory courses) and demands concerning throughput within a prescribed time. Simultaneously, the traditional master-apprenticeship tradition between supervisor and doctoral researcher is still alive as a main organising principle for the education of doctoral researchers; this entails that close interactions with colleagues is a vital part of doctoral studies and, thus, also an important part of the doctoral education and academic culture. All this has a bearing on how doctoral researchers experience, live and view their times as doctoral researchers.

In this chapter, we analyse changes in higher education in Sweden that have taken place since the 1960s and have led to the doctoral research system we have today, in which the working/studying conditions for doctoral researchers are paramount. Thus, our object of study is the doctorate and its governance where doctoral researchers, and their supervisor are agents and performers/executers of the same. We ask:

- What traces can be found of how change of status of the doctorate has affected doctoral researchers' and their supervisors' work and relationship?
- How has this change of the doctorate from (chosen) apprenticeship to (educated) 'student' come about in Swedish higher education?

One argument is that such changes can be understood as part of societal modernisation processes (e.g., Ziehe, 1999). These embrace institutional patterns as well as the work and life of the academic profession itself, for instance, connected to an ongoing loosening of jurisdiction. Jurisdiction over their own matters is traditionally a signum of the academic profession with medieval roots (Abbot, 1988). The changes increasingly detach the academic profession from the doctoral researchers and the planning of doctoral education, meaning a new kind of professional reproduction. Thus, the future of the doctoral student has become more differentiated and diverse and includes new individual future possibilities at the cost of a loss of the traditional and well-known – and without any guaranties of a certain future. Such modernisation processes can be seen as responses to what in a certain time is seen as 'necessary' to do given the spirit of times (e.g., Beck, Giddens, & Lash, 1994).

This chapter is divided into four parts. We start by taking a look at international trends and issues in doctoral education, followed by a historical overview of doctoral education and research in the Swedish context though the means of policy documents, higher education evaluations, commissions and legal acts. Here, we focus on structure and the funding of the doctoral studies. Next, we narrow down the context to doctoral research/education in the discipline of Education. Through an analysis of ten General Syllabi for the Degree of Doctor of Philosophy (PhD) in Education 1979–2021 at one Swedish major university, we explore the role of the doctoral candidate and the role of the supervisor. The chapter ends with a discussion on doctoral researchers and education in a reconstructed higher education, suggesting possible reasons for why stress and anxiety in doctoral education today, in Sweden and elsewhere, have become emergent and critical issues.

2 Trends and Issues in Doctoral Education – An International Outlook

In this section, the foci are on global issues and common aspects of doctoral education. One way of mapping current trends and emerging issues in higher education is to conduct review studies. In light of this, Kuzhabekova's bibliometric study (2021) is of utmost interest. She found that of almost 2500 articles (web of science) on postgraduate education between 1996–2020, the majority of research studies on doctoral education focus on the experiences of doctoral researchers, followed by doctoral supervision and curriculum issues. Governance and structural issues of doctoral education were not a prevalent theme in the researched articles. However, that does not mean that those issues are not researched; it simply indicates that what is visible in major journals is research on doctoral researchers' experiences of their studies and supervision.

The many above-published studies on doctoral experiences have revealed doctoral researchers' reported stress, which is generally connected to individual and supervision experiences. However, how much of this stress can be related to the supervision and doctoral researcher-supervisor relationship *per se*? Could it, in addition, be an effect of something else, such as, structural change where pressure on output, quality assurance and monetary issues are the main causes for reported stress? As suggested above, it may be that doctoral researchers' wellbeing, stress and anxiety are more in focus in the field of doctoral education, than for example structural issues, such as higher education governing and organisation of doctoral education.

One major trend around the world is the way in which the knowledge society and the huge expansion of higher education have transformed doctoral education and increased societal demands, on policymakers, research funding agencies – and the doctoral researcher body itself. This transformation has been identified on structural, institutional, and individual levels across different national contexts (Cardoso et al., 2020). Many of the changes can be described as tensions and dichotomies: highly standardised in governance at the same time as diversified in a variety of doctoral programmes. Standardisation may put pressure on actors on the institutional and individual levels, at the same time as it may promote mobility and possibilities for knowledge exchange and networking across borders. Economic incentives through funding and quality assurance are steering doctoral education in a way that was not frequent some twenty, thirty years ago. Nerad (2020a, p. 47) has pointed out that "existing academic reward structures discourage both border-crossing and high-risk research projects" and she suggests that the tensions that we now see might be tracked down to the Humboldtian model of a doctorate and the more pragmatic professional/industrial doctorate, whose ideals live side by side today. Also, Deem (2020) describes how 'massified' higher education has led to a shift away from academic collegial governance towards what can be understood as new public management (NPM) governance.

In addition, there has been a shift towards doctoral employment in some countries (i.e., the Nordic countries) steering away from self-funding and scholarships, which has led to doctoral researchers legally being public employees with salaries, legal rights, and duties. Furthermore, there are no course fees and funding by your own means are not allowed. Also, France, Germany and the Netherlands have adopted a scheme where most doctoral researchers today are regarded as employees (Calmand et al., 2020; Kehm, 2020; Yudkevich et al., 2020).

Given this, the above transformations have in turn led to changed positions and agency for doctoral researchers and supervisors alike and may well have initiated a new academic identity for doctoral researchers. Hence, it is essential to critically review and question what is at stake and to what precisely this transformation of doctoral education has led to. One problem worldwide is the tendency to expect doctoral education to respond to a wide range of issues: social, political and student expectations alike. Carvalho and Cardoso (2020, p. 372) ask the critical question: "Should doctoral education indeed meet such expectations?". From a global perspective, we can see that there is a trend to reform doctoral education, both on structural level and on local agency level, leading to transformations and probable tensions between different actors, including doctoral researchers and supervisors (Carvalho & Cardoso, 2020; Deem, 2020). The shift within doctoral education worldwide is essential to adhere to, since good, well-functioning and attractive academic doctoral education is the future of academia.

Since this chapter aims at critically analysing Swedish doctoral education through the lenses of institutional documents, we hope to be able to show the transformation from doctoral apprenticeship to doctoral education, from 'chosen' to being an employed doctoral researcher. In the next part, we invite you on a historical journey through Swedish policy documents, higher education evaluations, commissions (committee reports) and legal Acts on doctoral education, taking the point of departure from the concept of 'governance'.

3 A Historical Journey through Policy Documents Tracing the Reconstruction of the Swedish Doctorate

In a study of the formation of doctoral education in Sweden, Elmgren et al. (2016) observed increasing numbers of regulations and formal procedures as well as stakeholders. These changes have gone hand in hand with the expansion of higher education and a need for qualified teachers. In many ways, developments in Swedish doctoral education follow what Trow (1973) described as a transformation from an elite university to a mass university. Trow understood this transformation as growth and expansion of the higher education system that was manifested in all its activities. Among other things, it affected funding and administration as well as selection of students and ways of instruction.

We can trace such manifestations of a transformation towards a mass university in several public inquiries regarding research and higher education during the post-World War II (WW2) period and onwards; this also included the doctorate. Until this time, the doctorate was primarily a matter for university professors with limited regulations. In 1969, a doctoral degree was introduced and turned the informal doctorate into a formal four-year doctoral education (Government Bill 1969:31). An intention was that:

> A well-thought-out, systematically planned course of study must be set up for each individual doctoral researcher. In the new doctoral program, the element of teaching in methodology and supervision is intended to increase significantly. (Government Bill 1969:31, p. 1)

However, little was changed regarding the working conditions of the doctoral researchers; they were expected to support themselves as assistants to the professors. A doctoral thesis was mainly a concern for the doctoral researcher with little supervision. Clearly, such traditions were robust in the context of an elite university (Trow, 1973). We can also mention that the number of people who were awarded a doctorate was very limited. Even so, the post-WW2 period marked a shift regarding Swedish higher education as embedded in the emerging welfare state, not least since human capital ideas (Becker, 1963) emerged as a forceful driver of change. In addition, to policy makers, research became increasingly more relevant in modernisation efforts (Elzinga, 1982). This was also evident in the field of educational research in connection with major educational reforms during this period (Foss Lindblad & Lindblad, 2016).

The growth of the mass university implied an expansion of higher education and that included doctoral education. We note here a substantial increase in PhD examinations from less than 200 in 1960 up to more than 2,800 in 2020 (Figure 3.1). A doctoral thesis was previously regarded as a lifework. It was complemented by a licentiate thesis – around half a doctoral thesis. For instance, in 1960 there were 509 licentiate exams, five times more than the total numbers of doctoral theses. The new PhD was assumed to be more similar to a licentiate regarding amount of work. The licentiate almost disappeared in the 1970s when the new PhD was introduced.

Concerns regarding low efficiency, inadequate supervision, and poor study funding were raised in public inquiries during the 1980s (SOU 1981:30). The universities received extra funding from the state to support the employment of doctoral researchers (Government Bill 1989/90:90). However, it was up to the universities to decide how to utilise their resources and they were not required to employ all their doctoral researchers. Consequently, they could also accept

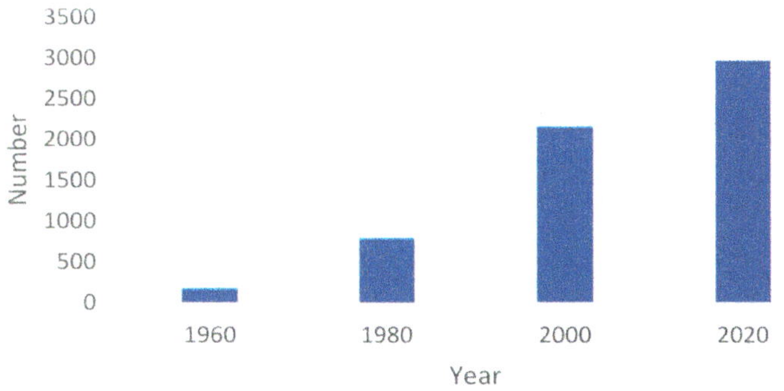

FIGURE 3.1 Total number of doctoral examinations over years in Sweden 1960–2020

more doctoral researchers than could get financial support. Some doctoral researchers received scholarships, but most were admitted without any kind of support; in some cases, it was possible to get financial support at a later stage of their education. In addition, the formal requirements for access were raised (Government Bill 1992/93:1).

Not until the end of the 1990s did the government decide that universities had to guarantee financial support for all four years of the doctoral education, either as employment or other kinds of support such as scholarships, before the university could admit a doctoral researcher. In addition, the pace of study was regulated, and each doctoral researcher was to have an individual study plan (Government Bill 1997/98:1). Over the coming years, working conditions for doctoral education were further discussed and in 2017 the scholarship was removed. From now on, everyone who was admitted was to receive employment as a doctoral researcher. This is also regulated by law.

To sum up, over a couple of decades, doctoral education was transformed from being mainly an academic affair with rather loose forms of governing towards a highly regulated education and a target for policy making and university management. Demands on societal relevance have been increasing; the production of knowledge and progression are no longer a matter between the supervisor and the doctoral researcher. Instead, doctoral researchers are seen as strategic resources for universities, faculties and departments, and with expectations of competitive advantages in the search for the talented who can contribute to high impact scores. So-called doctoral schools for externally employed doctoral researchers have developed within the framework of doctoral education regulations to meet demands of external stakeholders. These doctoral researchers are not employed by the university, but the education is the same. We can also see an increasing focus on internationalisation during the past few decades (e.g., SOU 2004:27) that also affects the everyday working life of the doctoral researchers and their research. In this context, internationalisation refers to exchange with foreign universities and to international publishing and co-publishing, index-rankings, etcetera, which are seen as signs of quality. This, we argue, is an idea of quality that is intentionally made stressful to increase productivity. It places quantification and not the knowledge contribution of the doctoral researcher at the centre, something which also McCullough (this volume), discussing Australian doctoral education, raises. These quantifications have also become embedded in the academic career ladders, meaning that doctoral researchers today often worry about future strategic career steps.

4 Swedish General Syllabi for the Degree of Doctor of Philosophy in Education (1977–2021)

Through the higher education reforms described above, we can observe how a process of reforming the Swedish doctorate has been on the agenda since the early 1980s. The main aim of the reforms has been to improve the economic conditions and social security of doctoral researchers and thus increase the efficiency of their studies (Government Bill 1989/90:90). Grants were exchanged and converted to doctoral positions. In this section, we are closing in and narrowing down the context to doctoral education in the discipline of Education. Through twelve General Syllabi for Degree of Philosophy of Doctor in Education 1979–2021 at one Swedish major university, we explore (1) the regulations and structures of the doctoral studies, and (2) the role of the doctoral candidate and the role of the supervisor.

Through a content analysis of the syllabi documents, we have tried to map the transformation of the Swedish doctorate exploring how the thematic areas of 'regulation', 'funding', and 'independence' emerge in the documents, using a scale of 1–10 (1 = low and 10 = high). By 'regulation' we indicate to what extent the syllabus is overtly regulated, for example, through obligatory courses, seminars, and supervision. 'Funding' relates to if and how the funding of the doctorate is included in the syllabus, and 'independence' adheres to the individual doctoral researcher's autonomy and independence to decide on his or her research project and studies. Figure 3.2 is intended to give a snapshot of development and change. It shows important transformations that have taken place from 1972 up till 2021. It must be said, of course, that this is what anyone would expect, as it would have been rather unexpected NOT to find any changes, when the higher education sector and the whole of society have changed dramatically during those 50 years.

In Figure 3.2, we can see how in the 1970s regulation and funding were not mentioned or given focus in the syllabi. However, the more regulated the

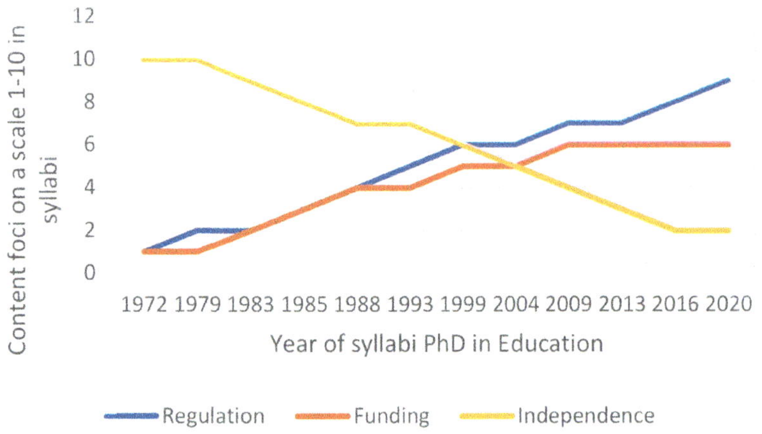

FIGURE 3.2 Development and change in Swedish doctoral education 1972–2020

doctoral education becomes, the more formal, school lookalike, the education becomes, with highly regulated rules for courses, seminars and supervision (blue line). The line for funding (orange line) is almost parallel with the line for regulation, indicating that although the doctoral researchers are employed, there are today stricter rules and regulations for their doctoral research and studies, which results in less autonomy and independence for the doctoral researchers (yellow line). Today's doctoral researchers experience a very different doctorate than we, the authors, participated in when we were doctoral researchers.

In 1972, the doctorate was quite rare and exclusive, in so far that not many had the opportunity to pursue doctoral studies and there was no funding in place (see Figure 3.1). As one of the authors remembers, as a doctoral candidate you approached the department and one possible supervisor and asked if you could start your doctoral research there. The syllabus from 1972 is short and not very detailed and the doctoral researcher had the freedom to decide most issues related to his/her research. There was little in terms of obligatory course work and the supervisor's main obligation was to review the thesis before submission. During the years, it is apparent how the doctorate gets more and more regulated, not only in the general syllabi, but also in the Higher Education Ordinance (HF 2006:1053). In a national evaluation of research in education (1997), Härnqvist describes the process of transforming grants into doctoral positions as a long-term direction starting in 1986. However, it was not until 2006 that it was stipulated in the Higher Education Ordinance as a requirement for accepting doctoral researchers. By introducing funded doctoral positions with employment, the doctoral education becomes the department's and the faculty's responsibility. In the General syllabi, for example, it is evident that the individual study plan, (introduced as early as in 1979) had become more and more regulated. In the early 1970s versions, it was the supervisor's responsibility to check the doctoral researcher's progression once a year. From 2013 onwards, individual study plans are digital plans, regularly updated by the doctoral researcher in collaboration with the supervisors. The study plan is monitored by the doctoral examiner (Director of Doctoral Studies) annually and subsequently approved by the Head of Department. It is a legal document connected to other university systems approving and allocating higher education credits to doctoral courses and obligatory seminars.

Another regulation concerns the learning objectives and goals that are stipulated in the Higher Education Ordinance and that state "for the Degree of Doctor the third-cycle (doctoral researcher) shall …" followed by two goals for *Knowledge and understanding*, six goals for *Competence and skills*, and two goals for *Judgement and approach*. This is a long way from the 1972 syllabus which specifies the goal as: "The aim of the research education is to deepen the students' subject knowledge and skills in research methodology and to develop their capacity for independent activities in pedagogical research and development work". Safety and security of regulation could well free the doctoral researcher becoming more creative. However, we argue that the tight string of learning objectives and rules and regulations may in many cases hinder autonomy, creativity and individuality – the core of an academic doctorate.

Noting the employee fully financed status of a doctorate in Sweden, one might expect the doctoral researchers' wellbeing to be thriving. However, as we previously noted and several contributions in this volume give evidence of, problems with stress and anxiety have increased since the millennium, in reports and not least in research publications in peer review journals (see also Gough, this volume; Schmidt & Hansson, this volume; Österlind, this volume). In a general super journal search on peer reviewed journal articles using the search words 'wellbeing' AND 'doctoral researcher' AND 'higher education', we found two articles from the 1970s, five articles from the 1980s, 44 from the 1990s, 225 from the 2000s, 1055 from the 2010s and 1634 from the year of 2020. As this is not a scientifically thorough review study, these numbers only indicate that the issue of doctoral researchers' wellbeing is a common theme and most certainly a real problem. It is possible to argue that stress is more prevalent in all kinds of societal sectors today and that the huge increase of stress and anxiety in doctoral education is but one testimony of the problem. However, as doctoral supervisors ourselves, we see this in our doctoral researchers' everyday work and in our supervision. According to our knowledge, we grasp and ascertain how a reconstruction of higher education, outside requirements at all levels (national, university, department) have increased and become more and more detailed, leading to a sense of burden and inadequacy in meeting all the obligations.

Although we might all remember having experienced stress for not meeting the qualifications during our doctoral studies, today's doctoral researchers in Sweden seem to experience more stress and anxiety than we did, or at least what we expressed (SFS, 2021). In addition, today's doctorates have more stipulated written goals and objectives and obligatory courses and seminars to meet. The focus seems to have shifted from the actual research to working to meet all requirements. This is visible, not least, in the current ongoing Covid-19 pandemic, which the Swedish doctoral researcher union is underlining in their report on the effect of the pandemic (SFS, 2021, p. 3):

> All levels of Swedish research have been affected. But what makes doctoral education special is that it is an education. The doctoral education is a four-year education. Delays in research and other setbacks in the education process effectively mean that, without prolongation, doctoral researchers should meet the learning goals of the education in less time than it is designed for. In a landscape, where even before the pandemic, many doctoral researchers worked overtime, the number of stress-related sick leaves was worrying, and the expectations of doctoral researchers were already rightfully high. This is simply not doable. We therefore see the issue of prolongation for doctoral researchers to be extremely important for both the individual doctoral researcher and for the whole of the Swedish research community.

The quotation above is an example of a stressed and overloaded doctorate community. The focus is on the students' education and meeting all regulations and on assuring the rights for paid prolongations; this is something which is expected from a document of the doctoral researcher union. In addition, the union brings to the fore wellbeing as an emergent issue stating that "an overwhelming majority of the groups mentioned the deterioration of mental health". It seems a sad paradox that, despite the regulated intentions in policies and legal Acts to secure and make the life for doctoral researchers more doable, stress and anxiety seem to be increasing. We, at institutional level, must address those worries, but the question remains how to instil a culture of autonomy and independency among doctoral researchers in combination with stable environments. In light of the often-stipulated reason both today as well as yesterday, for why doctoral researchers wanted to pursue a doctorate, it is devastating that we have ended up here. If the reason for engaging in doctoral research is a curiosity and urge to solve problems, to deepen one's knowledge and to explore issues, we will need to find new ways to bring about just this.

5 Concluding Remarks

In this chapter, we have reviewed the Swedish doctoral education during the past 50 years, highlighting and tracing the reconstruction and sometimes transformation of the Swedish doctorate. We asked ourselves what traces of change of status of the doctorate could be found that might affect doctoral researchers' and their supervisors' work and relationship, and how this change could be related to general changes in higher education. Research around the world gives evidence of worried and stressed doctoral researchers, as well as worried supervisors and academic leaders. We can see that doctoral researchers seem to be occupied with handling the system and fulfilling requirements, which is affecting their possibilities of emerging in their research projects. The Swedish case is no different from what has been found internationally, i.e., Deem (2020) who suggests that doctoral researchers are placed at the centre of the tensions and contradictions of higher education in transition:

> I want to suggest that the overall shape and cultures of higher education across the world, which make academic work more demanding and less enjoyable and impose instrumentalism and consumerism, rather than enhance learner/teacher relationships, may be part of the reason why more and more HE systems are reporting increased incidence of poor mental health amongst all students. The latter is especially found amongst those studying for a doctorate (Bothwell, 2017; Levecquea et al., 2017; Thomas, 2015). (p. 21)

The three themes that we have identified as transformative aspects of the doctorate in Swedish higher education during the past 50 years are (1) 'schoolification', (2) increasing interest in stress management, and (3) relevance in terms of professional competences outside the academy. The above analyses of national higher education documents and regulations as well as local general syllabi for doctoral education indicate that regulation, funding and autonomy are intertwined in complex ways, having both intended and unintended effects on the doctoral researchers and doctoral education on institutional and departmental levels. Conclusions of these analyses that can be drawn are that regulation of doctoral research and the doctoral researchers' wellbeing are increasingly being emphasised in public discourses. Hence, there is a risk that the academic intellectual contributions are less focused. This causes tensions and drives both individual doctoral researchers and institutions to navigate between different pressures from national legal acts and policies to local higher education regulations and traditions. Hence, we argue that the tight string of learning objectives and rules and regulations may, in fact, hinder autonomy, creativity and individuality – which are at the core of an academic doctorate.

References

Abbott, A. D. (1988). *The system of professions: An essay on the division of expert labor.* University of Chicago Press.

Beck, U., Giddens, A., & Lash, S. (1994). *Reflexive modernization. Politics, tradition and aestethics in the modern social order.* Polity.

Becker, G. S. (1964). *Human capital: A theoretical and empirical analysis, with special reference to education.* National Bureau of Economic Research.

Calmand, J., Chevallier, T., & Giret, J.-F. (2020). Between change and continuity: The transformation of doctoral education in France. In M. Yudkevich, P. G. Altbach, & H. de Wit (Eds.), *Trends and issues in doctoral education. A global perspective.* Sage.

Cardoso, S., Tavares, O., Sin, C., & Carvalho T. (Eds.). (2020). *Structural and institutional transformations in doctoral education: Social, political and student expectations.* Springer.

Carvalho, T., & Cardoso, S. (2020). Conclusion: Transformation in doctoral education – A comprehensive and critical approach. In S. Cardoso, O. Tavares, C. Sin, & T. Carvalho (Eds.), *Structural and institutional transformations in doctoral education: Social, political and student expectations.* Springer.

Czarniawska, B., & Joerges, B. (1996). *Translating organizational change. Travel of ideas.* De Gruyter.

Deem, R. (2020). Rethinking doctoral education: University purposes, academic cultures, mental health and the public good. In S. Cardoso, O. Tavares, C. Sin, & T. Carvalho (Eds.), *Structural and institutional transformations in doctoral education: Social, political and student expectations.* Palgrave Macmillan. https://doi.org/10.1007/978-3-030-38046-5_2

Elmgen, M., Forsberg, E., Lindberg-Sand, Å., & Sonesson, A. (2016). *The formation of doctoral education* [Report]. Joint Faculties of Humanities and Theology, Lund University.

Eltzinga, A. (1982). Forskningspolitiken och den liberala korporativismen. [Research politics and the liberal corporatism]. *Swedish Sociological Association, 19*(4), 39–63.

Foss Lindblad, R., & Lindblad, S. (2016). Higher education and research in a steady state – on changing premises and practices for educational research in Sweden. *Nordic Journal of Studies in Educational Policy, 1.* doi:10.3402/nstep.v2.32371

Gough, M. (2022). Dimensions of wellbeing in the doctoral research environment. In M.-L. Österlind, P. M. Denicolo, & B.-M. Apelgren (Eds.), *Doctoral education as if people matter: Critical issues for the future* (this volume). Brill.

Government Bill 1989/90:90. On Research.

Government Bill 1992/93: 1. The Budget Bill. Expenditure area 16.

Government Bill 1997/98:1. The Budget Bill. Expenditure area 16.

Härnqvist, K. (1997). Educational research in Sweden: Infrastructure and Orientation. In K. E. Rosengren & B. Öhngren (Eds.), *An evaluation of Swedish research in education.* Humanistisk- samhällsvetenskapliga forskningsrådet.

HEA 1992: 1434. Higher Education Act.

HEO 1993: 100. Higher Education ordinance.

HEO 2006:1053. Ordinance on Changes of the Higher Education Ordinance. (HEO 1993:100).

Kehm, B. M. (2020). The past, present and future of doctoral education in Germany. In M. Yudkevich, P. G. Altbach, & H. de Wit (Eds.), *Trends and issues in doctoral education. A global perspective.* Sage.

Kuzhabekova, A. (2021). Charting the terrain of global research on graduate education: A bibliometric approach. *Journal of Further and Higher Education.*

McCulloch, A. (2022). Alienation and the problem of work in doctoral education. In M.-L. Österlind, P. M. Denicolo, & B.-M. Apelgren (Eds.), *Doctoral education as if people matter: Critical issues for the future* (this volume). Brill.

Nerad, M. (2020a). *Doctoral education worldwide: Three decades of change.* In M. Yudkevich, P. G. Altbach, & H. de Wit (Eds.), *Trends and issues in doctoral education. A global perspective.* Sage.

Nerad, M. (2020b). Governmental innovation policies, globalisation, and change in doctoral education worldwide: Are doctoral programmes converging? Trends and tensions. In S. Cardoso O. Tavares, C. Sin, & T. Carvalho (Eds.), *Structural and institutional transformations in doctoral education, issues in higher education.* Springer.

Österlind, M.-L. (2022). This could be heaven or this could be hell. In M.-L. Österlind, P. M. Denicolo, & B.-M. Apelgren (Eds.), *Doctoral education as if people matter: Critical issues for the future* (this volume). Brill.

SFS. (2021). *Delays of doctoral education due to the corona pandemic* [Report]. Swedish National Union of Students.

SOU 1981:30. *Forskarutbildningens meritvärde: Betänkande av Utredningen om forskningens och forskarutbildningens situation i den nya högskolan [Merit rating of doctoral education. Report from the Commission on the Situation of Research and Doctoral Education in the new Higher Education*]. Ministry of Education.

SOU 2004:27. *En ny doktorsutbildning. Kraftsamling för excellens och tillväxt* [*A new doctoral education. Mobilizing for excellence and growth*]. Utbildningsdepartementet.

Schmidt, M., & Hansson, E. (2022). Sustainability of doctoral education: A well-being perspective. In M.-L. Österlind, P. M. Denicolo, & B.-M. Apelgren (Eds.), *Doctoral education as if people matter: Critical issues for the future* (this volume). Brill.

Trow, M. (1973). *Problems in the transition from elite to mass higher education.* Carnegie Commission on Higher Education.

Yudkevich, M., Altbach, P. G., & de Wit, H. (Eds.). (2020). *Trends and issues in doctoral education. A global perspective.* Sage.

Ziehe, T. (1999). Engagement and abstention. *European Education, 31*(4), 6–21.

CHAPTER 4

Challenging Policy Barriers to Doctoral Supervision

Qualifying as a Supervisor and Recruiting Students in Chinese Research Universities

Bing Lu

Abstract

Through an interpretative analysis of four national policy documents in the context of doctoral education reform over the last three decades, this chapter sets out to problematise the system of supervisor qualification and student admission in Chinese doctoral education. A further analysis of two leading Chinese research universities' major policies on doctoral education demonstrates how the individual institutions, based on their local knowledge, translate and implement national policies. The adopted interpretive policy analysis as an approach highlights the agency of both policy makers and policy audiences, showing how multiple interpretations of policy documents are made from national to institutional level. Arguably, Chinese doctoral supervisors' eligibility and authority receive far less attention seen from the reviewed documents. Centralising an interpretive approach, this chapter calls for actors at all levels involved in Chinese doctoral education actively interpreting the policies to facilitate a supportive and autonomous research environment.

Keywords

Chinese doctoral education – interpretive policy analysis – supervisor qualification – student admission

1 Introduction

In Chinese doctoral education, supervisors are widely regarded as the direct and major support for doctoral researchers in many aspects: funding applications, supervision of the doctoral project and career development (Report on China's Doctoral Education Quality, 2010). However, neither the national nor

 | DOI:10.1163/9789004529304_004

the institutional policies clearly sketch out the contours of a supervisor's role. In other words, the role of supervisor has been noticeably ambiguous and even marginalised in the context of policy. Arguably, granting autonomy to supervisors and clarifying their responsibility is significant in creating a supportive environment for doctoral researchers. This chapter sets out to challenge identified policy barriers regarding supervisor qualification and student recruitment in China. By conducting an interpretive analysis of how different levels of policymakers launch and implement policy documents, with a comprehension of the national context, this chapter also highlights how local knowledge matters in evaluating doctoral education policies in different societies.

2 The Chinese Context

For a long time, China's political centralism has meant that its tertiary education system has been guided by the 'centralist model' (Agelasto & Adamson, 1998). Since its establishment in 1980s, doctoral training in China is also implicated in this model, in that central government: (1) sets the means of admission and plans the number of doctoral students recruited annually; (2) approves new doctoral programmes for local institutions; (3) makes senior academic appointments (i.e., grants the supervisor qualification). This centralised model arguably hampers the development of doctoral education and educational decentralisation has always been a focus in reforms of doctoral education.

A series of national polices released in the last three decades have deliberately devolved the authority of the central government to lower administrative levels, from the Minister of Education (MoE) of the People's Republic of China (PRC) and the Academic Degree Committee of the State Council to local institutions. Institutions are allowed greater flexibility to explore and reform their own doctoral training. Globally, granting institutions more autonomy is also a reform agenda to imbed doctoral education to institutional structures in other regions and countries (Fortes, Kehm, & Mayekiso, 2014). China's case is distinguished in that there do not exist supranational organisations which conduct some traditional governmental tasks as independent agencies. Therefore, in China, distributing authority is only 'moving down' from the national government to the institutional level but not 'moving out' to external agencies. To conclude, policy plays a significant role in regulating and shaping doctoral education, with its relatively short history and still developing infrastructure, compared to other tertiary levels of education in China (Zhuang, 2007).

Research on policies relating to supervisor qualification and doctoral admission have received imbalanced attention. Reforms for improving admission to doctoral programmes have aroused wide discussion over issues around accountability, fairness, quality assurance, and international comparison (Xu & Qi, 2018). On the other hand, regulations for supervisor qualification have received much less attention. From a global perspective, to ensure supervision quality, some countries also have the policy that one must acquire particular qualifications to be allowed to supervise doctoral thesis (Powell & Green, 2007; Fortes, Kehm, & Mayekiso, 2014). In the story of China, when the autonomy of managing doctoral training has been transferred from central government to institutions, such autonomy has not automatically been transferred to supervisors. Seen from the policy documents, it is the institution's 'degree committee' and 'recruitment team' that now run the show in qualifying supervisors and recruiting doctoral students. These 'new authorities' maintain the standards and determine who are to be qualified as supervisors and who are to be recruited as students.

3 An Interpretive Policy Analysis: Who Is Reading?

Four major national policy documents and two universities have been selected to analyse policy barriers that may prevent wider supervision opportunities and more effective supervision practice. Here, more supervision opportunities refer to issues around education fairness, calling for doctoral supervision to be open to a wider population; effective supervision practice refers to accountability, calling for clearly defined policy guidelines on supervisors' autonomy in selecting students, and their responsibility in conducting supervision practices.

Two levels of policy analysis are involved: the national level and the institutional level. An interpretive analysis focuses on how the distinguished system of supervisor qualification and student recruitment create the environment of doctoral education and realities of supervisor in China. On the national level, the four public policy documents are analysed to understand how the national government grants autonomy to institutions and supervisors; on the institutional level, this chapter presents two leading research universities as the cases. The two universities' policies on supervisor qualification and doctoral student recruitment are analysed to show how the local institutions translate and implement national policies. All the original policies are open resources but are only available in Chinese language; all the document quotations in this chapter are translated by the author with a literary translation approach.

An interpretive approach is adopted as the analytical tool in this chapter. As Yanow (2000) notes, this approach is a 'democratic undertaking' which emphasises the potential audience for whom the documents are designed (p. 112). To be specific, an interpretive policy analysis focuses on sensemaking by recognising the agency as well as the local knowledge of the potential audience (Yano, 2007). For example, all the reviewed national policy documents have a clear target audience: the local institutions. This can be seen from the direct language such as 'local institutions should …' and through some ambiguous expressions open to interpretation such as 'setting positions according to the need of the specific department'. Over the last two decades, Chinese research universities' autonomy has been periodically increased and this is underpinned by the central government through policy documents. The central question here is: what is the educational provision that the national policies intend to develop in reforming doctoral education in China?

A review of the policy documents of the two universities under investigation adds another layer of meaning to this analysis. Guided by the national policy documents, universities implement institutional policies with respect to their own circumstances. In this double-interpretation process, the environment of doctoral education is framed and reframed from the national level to the institutional level. The central question here is: as the major stakeholder in doctoral education in China, how do universities' policy documents frame the local environment for doctoral supervisors and researchers?

This chapter identifies the supervisor as the direct support in affecting doctoral researchers' funding applications, research supervision and career development. In China, individual supervisors can use their additional human resources (other supervisors specialising in different areas) to support doctoral researchers' education through informal supervision practice, and even help to negotiate for extra funds (Bao et al., 2018). The next two sections explore how the entire doctoral training environment is constituted in selected documents on the supervisor qualification and doctoral researcher admission from the national level to the institutional level.

4 The National Story: Four Policy Documents

This chapter selects four national documents that launched major doctoral educational governance and reform (Table 4.1), referred as *Regulations, Outline, Opinions*, and *Annual Guidance* hereafter. Influenced by a planned economy and centralised administration political system, doctoral education in China has been largely based on a national plan. The MoE regulates the annual recruitment agenda, including setting the number of students recruited for individual doctoral programmes provided by institutions. Meanwhile, the

TABLE 4.1 Major national postgraduate policy documents

Publication year	Title	Released by
1995	Regulations on reforming doctoral supervisor qualification	State Council
2010	Outline of the national medium- and long-term programme for State Council education reform and development (2010–2020)	State Council
2013	Opinions on Deepening Reforms of Postgraduate Education	Minister of Education
2001–2019	Annual guidance on national doctoral admission	Minister of Education

State Council had the full authority to assess all supervisor applicants to qualify for the supervisor title until 1995. Although this centralised model ensured the quality of doctoral education through a strict selection of qualified supervisors at the initial stage, it does not favour supervisors and doctoral researchers in a long term. Within this policy context, the selection of supervisors and students is a selection among elite applicants but ignores wider social consequence. To explain this elite conception, before 2004, all willing doctoral candidates were required to first obtain the paperwork-approval from their organisation (workplace or graduate school) to be admitted to attending the admission exam (MoE, 2013), preventing individuals who are not registered in organisations that are recognised by the national government. To widen the access to doctoral education, decentralisation in educational governance has been an ongoing focus in the reviewed documents of reform.

4.1 *Doctoral Qualification*

In 1995, MoE issued the *Regulations*, first proclaiming that ADC of the State Council was no longer assessing individual doctoral supervisor applications; instead, doctorate conferred bodies (research universities and academies) would have full authority to qualify supervisors for different programmes. According to the document, the initiative of this reform is "to meet the increasing need of doctoral education and enhance the autonomy of individual doctorate conferred bodies". Moreover, this document first suggested six criteria for qualifying supervisors, including a full professor title, at least one year experience of supervising Master student or co-supervising doctoral student.

However, the document does not specify the role of supervisors in doctoral training; rather, it underscores that:

> Since 1981, the rigorous assessment and qualification of doctoral supervisors by the state council proves to be valid and important in assuring doctoral education quality and developing doctoral education system. After years of experience, involved institutions and society should have reached a consensus on some criteria of qualifying supervisors.

This rhetoric puts an emphasis on the value of the collective evaluation of supervisors. In other words, the document is framed as if it is the criteria rather than the individual supervisors' agency that can ensure the quality of the education; anyone qualified by the criteria would conduct quality supervision. In this sense, although the national government is attempting to decentralise its role in regulating doctoral education, it insists upon maintaining its tradition of approving doctoral supervisors through a process of assessment. The *Regulation* also requires that universities should organise 'institutional academic degree committees' to qualify supervisors, administered and monitored by the national government. Within this context, what the national policy recognises is not so much supervisors as an organisational committee which confers supervisor qualification. The eligibility to supervise doctoral students, in Chinese context, are legally defined by the state through supervisor qualification. In France, a higher doctorate, the 'habitation' is also required for a supervisor to supervise doctoral researcher (Taylor, 2018).

4.2 *Doctoral Admission*

Doctoral admission policies in China have experienced a shift from the old exam-based admission to the new 'application-assessment' admission system. This revolutionary change was first delineated in the *Opinions* (2013) after five years of piloting in selected universities. The new system allows other means to recruit doctoral students that differ from the old exam-based admission (though this system is still applied in many institutions today). This document does not provide detailed instructions on implementing this new system but only general guidelines. In addition, the document highlights the national goal of developing doctoral education in the next decade, which is to considerably increase the number of doctoral students recruited. The initiative of expanding the scale of doctoral education explains why the new policy encourages alternative means of recruiting doctoral students.

The role of supervisor has more visibility in the context of doctoral admission, although it is still stated rather vaguely. This can be seen from the trend reflected in the *Annual Guidance* on national doctoral recruitment. These documents published over the last two decades reveal policymakers' concerns about how supervisors should be represented in the process of doctoral admission. In general, there are policy narratives, in some years, articulating the supervisory role in relation to autonomy and responsibility in admission and doctoral training. On the other hand, more narratives stipulate that individual universities should organise their 'recruitment team' to administer doctoral recruitment according to the relevant policies implemented by MoE.

5 The Institutional Story: Two Research Universities

Peking University (PKU) and Fudan University, two prestigious research universities located in Beijing and Shanghai, were the first two pilot institutions in 2007 before the new 'application-assessment' admission system was published in the national policy in 2013. The two renowned universities in two highly developed economic zones have always been on the frontier of higher education reforms. In 2007, funded by the State Council, PKU organised the research team and conducted the national survey on China's doctoral education quality. The survey has been so far the largest scale on investigating national doctoral holders and its report *China's Doctoral Education Quality Report* (2010) has been widely quoted in studies on China's doctoral education. This section investigates how the two pioneering universities of reforms contextualise national policies to create institutional environments for doctoral researchers and supervisors.

5.1 *Doctoral Qualification*

Both universities make qualifying as a supervisor accessible to a wider range of applicants. PKU sets the policy of 'shifting from fixed qualification to flexible qualification'. Fixed qualification refers to the set of criteria suggested in the *Regulations* (1995) noted above, and the flexible qualification refers to the institution's own criteria based on its understanding of doctoral training. In a public speech in 2006, the vice dean of the postgraduate school in Peking University claimed that:

> In recent years, an increasing number of young scholars returned to China from abroad. Many of them are doctorate holders who have received rigorous doctoral training abroad. They have experienced the whole process of doctoral education and are able to supervise doctoral students. However, within the current supervisor qualification system, they are not

> entitled to recruit students. We have been actively seeking effective ways to improve this situation.

The dean's speech reflects the institution's determination to exercise its agency in challenging national policy barriers. That being said, it takes the university almost ten years to qualify the first associate professor as a supervisor in 2004 following the *Regulations* (1995). Since 2005, PKU has been conducting its own regulations in qualifying supervisors, widening the selecting range to any academic positions with obtained doctorates rather than restricted to professor applicants.

Fudan University sets the policy of 'direct qualification', emphasising the efficiency of qualifying supervisors. The policy sets two groups of people that can be directly qualified as supervisor "high-skilled talents who have been recruited in national talent programmes or undertaking national projects", and "talents in urgent need". This regulation also goes beyond the 'professor framework' indicated by the national policy. Within the institutional context, the role of doctoral supervisor is framed as 'those that have doctorates' and 'those who are talented'. However, these interpretations do not make the role of supervisor any less elite. Following the national policy, both universities have organised their own 'degree committee' and highlight that all supervisor applications should be submitted to and assessed by the institution's degree committee. To be qualified as a supervisor, the applicants have to go through a procedure of evaluation. Although the two universities demonstrate greater agency in interpreting national policy and initiating institutional policy according to their own circumstances, such agency is exercised within an understanding of local knowledge. In other words, which policy narratives are open to multiple interpretations, and which are not.

5.2 *Doctoral Admission*

As for means of admission, both universities claim in their policy documents that individual departments have full authority and responsibility in regulating their admission procedures and setting their criteria. In its 2020 doctoral recruitment guide, Peking University states that "each department can set their own standard to evaluate and select the applicants according to the disciplinary feature". Additionally, the document emphasises that "to devolve more authority to individual departments is to increase their autonomy in selecting students". At the same time, the guide clarifies the gatekeeper role of the recruitment team, that "all procedures are administered and processed by the university's recruitment team".

The recruitment team also has been a focus in Fudan University's recruitment policy. The university's 2018 doctoral recruitment guide explicates that, within the new 'application-assessment' admission system implemented by MoE, the department's recruitment team, which consists of 5 to 7 senior academics (assistant/associate professors/professors), should conduct the initial evaluation of all applications. The document explains that "the nature of the new admission system is to give supervisors more autonomy in student recruitment and education". Seen from the reviewed documents, supervisors' autonomy has been identified by both national and institutional policymakers as an issue; however, no specific documents fully attend to this matter.

Compared to the old system which aims to ensure merit selection criteria for admission through rigid exams, the new 'application-assessment' system requires a new level of accountability centring around human agency. That is, who is accountable for evaluating the submitted applications, the supervisors or the recruitment team? The second phase, assessment, is open to even more complex interpretations. According to the two universities' policy, admitted applicants must pass examinations and/or another round of interview required by the department. Who is making these decisions?

6 Discussion

The above documents establish the context of understanding doctoral education in China from a policy perspective. In this context, administering the supervisor qualification and doctoral student recruitment from national to institutional level is identified as a major barrier represented in the minimum visibility of supervisors' autonomy and responsibility. However, this is not a denial of the role of supervisor in doctoral training. Taking an interpretive approach, this chapter recognises the possibilities of multiple interpretations of policy documents. To be specific, reading policy requires not only figuring out what some expressions mean but *how* they are interpreted into practice through the process of communicating policy ideas to the intended audiences. As Yanow (2000) indicates, it is "what implementors do, rather than what the policy says in its language, [that] constitutes the truth of policy intent" (p. 8). This section explains how policymakers constitute the realities of supervisors and doctoral researchers through 'speaking' to their audiences.

6.1 *A National Provision: Ensuring Quality and Expanding Scale*

The national policies formulate a provision of doctoral education as ensuring supervision quality and expanding doctoral education scale. These initiatives are mainly seen as encouraging a larger number of approved domestic doctoral programmes, international collaborative programmes, supervisor qualification and student recruitment. To achieve these goals, the national government attempts to devolve its authority to the institution in order for them to make more independent decisions in terms of supervisor qualifications and student recruitment. This steady movement towards decentralisation makes individual institutions the new gatekeepers of supervisor qualification applicants. At the institutional level, as shown above, the two universities' establishment of their own academic degree committee is in line with what is enunciated in the national policy. These institutional committees are formed to assess applicants' academic background and decide who will become supervisors. In nature, this is a process of devolving the administrative power from central government to institutions, flowing down the hierarchy from bureaucrats at higher level to lower level.

However, doctoral training is distinguished from other tertiary education in many ways, and doctoral supervision is largely individualised and project-based (Yang, 2012). In addition, empirical studies show that supervision is highly valued by Chinese doctoral researchers (China's Doctoral Education Quality Team, 2010; Liu & Wang, 2011). Although supervisors play a central role in doctoral training, the criteria of qualifying supervisors are still rather vague and opaque. The initiative of decentralising authority to individual institutions is to expand doctoral training by increasing the number of supervisors at a faster rate. However, targeting growth without accompanying discussion of the role of supervisors and the nature of doctoral training may be detrimental. The policy documents show that the national government is formulating a national-institutional degree committee governance structure of supervisor qualification. An interpretive analysis indicates that individual institutions implement this hierarchical structure and exercise their agency only in some revisions of the criteria of qualification. Supervisors are appointed by the new local authorities replacing the prior national authority.

6.2 *Supervisor Autonomy: A Missing Link between Supervisor and Student*

At an institutional level, the policy documents frame a competitive environment for doctoral supervisors and students through localised criteria of qualification and means of admission. The relevant policy documents reflect a clear institutional policy logic: selecting the most competent supervisors and students to ensure the quality of training, and thus to improve the institution's national and even worldwide ranking. Several articles and book chapters published recently have explored the value system underlying the context of Chinese doctoral education and highlight the significance of the national context in comparing global doctoral education (Zhu et al., 2017; Zheng et al.,

2019). These studies pinpoint that the most salient recruitment criterion is the candidates' research capacity. With this underlying value, the national policy that advocates a shift from the exam-based admission to the new 'application-assessment' system makes admission an even more difficult task. To be specific, there is a tension among three elements, the permitted annual intake allocated to a programme by the central government, the institutional recruitment team's evaluation, and individual supervisors' preference.

A missing link here means that supervisors struggle to select their own students and match their research interests due to the tension mentioned above. The doctoral student in the Chinese system seems to have little influence on their own research matter, and the supervisors seem to be 'appointed' a doctoral student rather than matching. In an empirical study (Zheng et al., 2018), many interviewed supervisors requested that more autonomy should be devolved from the government in terms of student recruitment. Within the new admission system, normally the procedure is: the institution's recruitment team first evaluates all the applications and chooses potential candidates for an interview attended by several potential supervisors. The number of potential candidates is decided by the annual recruitment plan of the programme at a particular rate such as 2:1 or 3:1. Sometimes the doctoral candidates had shown a preference for certain supervisors before the application and they even exchanged a few emails; still, there is no guarantee that the candidates' applications would be accepted by the recruitment team and be given the interview opportunity. On some other occasions, supervisors are required by the department to choose students to supervise from the recruited candidates to fulfil the annual allocation given by the national government, and supervisors have to make decisions even though they do not really have an interest in any of the candidates.

On the other hand, some points in the reviewed national documents seem to be targeted at tackling academic corruption and abuse of authority in student recruitment, a phenomenon that has deeply threatened China's doctoral training and its international reputation (Yang, 2012). The ambiguous language on supervisors' autonomy reflects policymakers' concern about the public's suspicion of giving a select few individuals too much power. Such suspicion comes from an underlying value in Chinese bureaucratic culture: the importance of individual leaders is reinforced in a hierarchy; often, the person overrides the system (Agelasto & Adamson, 1998). This should explain why the role of the recruitment team has been emphasised in relevant policies repeatedly. However, making recruitment a team decision cannot ensure fair opportunities. On the contrary, this can mean desirable qualifications for admission still come down to some rigid criteria such as applicants' educational background.

One survey study shows that candidates who received their previous education in prestigious universities are more likely to be recruited to the doctoral programmes provided by prestigious universities (Wang, 2018).

That supervisors are 'appointed' a doctoral student is seen as a barrier threatening the future supervision practice. In the Mexico system, for example, where doctoral candidates are also required to take admission courses, tests and interviews, they are more likely to make their own choice based on the interviews with the research faculty (Malo & Fortes, 2008). That being said, this missing link in Chinese system is not an across-country case. Currently there exist great divisions in Chinese doctoral education, the elite versus non-elite institutions (project 985, project 211 and the double first-class university plan), economically developed versus peripheral regions, renowned/experienced versus newly appointed supervisors. A famous supervisor in an elite institution may be over-subscribed and thus have more autonomy to choose, whereas a less well-known supervisor in a less elite university may not receive an applicant for years (Zhuang, 2007). These disparities may lead to the 'elite-mass structure' that Robert Taylor (1981) predicted for Chinese higher education four decades ago, with 'the elite being the institutions which imparted crucial expertise to excellent students, the mass being the less favoured bodies teaching less important subjects to the least able entrants' (p. 18), and the inequalities being produced by the qualification and recruitment processes 'would ultimately be felt in society itself' (p. 117).

7 Conclusion

Learning from the relevant policies, this chapter identifies two common goals shared by national government and institutions, that is to expand the scale of Chinese doctoral education and ensure the education quality. However, in the reforms of decentralising the authority of qualifying supervisors and recruiting students from national to institutional level, supervisors' eligibility and authority do not receive significant attention in the reviewed documents. This chapter argues that, to facilitate an academically oriented environment for doctoral researchers, there is a need for closer examination of the new decentralised systems of admission and supervisor qualification, as they may lead to deeper inequalities rather than opening up doctoral education.

Seen from a global perspective, there is a worldwide trend of reforming doctoral education, addressing growing tensions between society and institution, institution and supervisor, supervisor and student in the context of marketisation and neoliberalism (Barnacle & Cuthbert, 2021). This chapter highlights that, in launching and implementing these reforms, different national contexts should consider their own educational and social conditions. In China, doctoral training is still a niche relatively new area, where both the central government and institutions are making an expedition into the unknown. In Thailand, another country with emerging potential in providing doctoral education, there also exists an academic committee in MoE to evaluate universities' application for offering doctoral programmes (Chittmittrapap & Luksaneeyanawin, 2007). These emerging countries both resort to central control and government regulations to ensure doctoral education quality. Many reforms, rather than targeting specific consequences, have contributed to and have been affected by the global trends. That is to say, different countries, characterised by their own reform trajectories in responding to their own needs, contribute national views to the worldwide doctoral education; meanwhile, the changing nature of PhD makes the global institutions alike defined by increasingly clear criteria, compelling individual countries to react to and compete for the global accountability.

An interpretive policy analysis assumes that all policy-relevant audiences have agencies to interpret and take actions. Following this logic, this chapter aims at raising the awareness of actors in the picture of doctoral education, encouraging them to exercise their expertise in their own domain to challenge policy barriers. In the national context of China, which is known for its long-held centralised model and bureaucratic system, all levels of administrators, professionals and scholars should not just take this system for granted but actively interpret the policies to make a change. Afterall, doctoral training has yet to become a standard practice in China (Zhu et al., 2017; Shin et al., 2018), so there is scope for stakeholders in Chinese doctoral education to foster some local features to facilitate a supportive and autonomous research environment for supervisors and doctoral researchers.

References

Agelasto, M., & Adamson, B. (1998). *Higher education in post-Mao China: An ecology of Hong Kong* (Vol. 1). Hong Kong University Press.

Alcantara, A., Malo, S., & Fortes, M. (2008). Doctoral education in Mexico. In M. Nerad & M. Heggelund (Eds.), *Toward a global PhD? Forces and forms in doctoral education worldwide* (pp. 146–168). University of Washington Press.

Bao, Y., Kehm, B. M., & Ma, Y. (2018). From product to process. The reform of doctoral education in Europe and China. *Studies in Higher Education, 43*(3), 524–541.

Barnacle, R., & Cuthbert, D. (2021). The PhD at the end of the world: Provocations for the doctorate and a future contested – Introduction. *The PhD at the End of the World, 4*, 1.

China's Doctoral Education Quality Research Team. (2010). *Report on China's doctoral education quality.* Peking University Press.

Chittmittrapap, S., & Luksaneeyanawin, S. (2007). Doctoral education in Thailand. In S. Powel & H. Green (Eds.), *The doctorate worldwide* (pp. 217–228). McGraw Hill.

Codd, J. A. (1988). The construction and deconstruction of educational policy documents. *Journal of education policy, 3*(3), 235–247.

Fortes, M., Kehm, B. M., & Mayekiso, T. (2014). Evaluation and quality management in Europe, Mexico, and South Africa. In M. Nerad & B. Evans (Eds.), *Globalization and its impacts on the quality of PhD education: Forces and forms in doctoral education worldwide* (pp. 81–109). Brill Sense.

Liu, C. Q., & Wang, L. Z. (2011). Completion rates of doctoral students: A study of Beijing Forestry University. *Heilongjiang Researches on Higher Education, 2*, 141–144.

MOE. (1995). *Regulations on reforming the assessment of doctoral supervisor qualification by academic degrees.* Committee of the State Council. https://wenku.baidu.com/view/6917ca3067ec102de2bd8954.html

MOE. (2013). *Opinions on deepening reforms of postgraduate education.* http://old.moe.gov.cn/publicfiles/business/htmlfiles/moe/A22_zcwj/201307/154118.html

Mok, K. H. (2002). Policy of decentralization and changing governance of higher education in post-Mao China. *Public Administration and Development: The International Journal of Management Research and Practice, 22*(3), 261–273.

Mok, K. H. (2003). Globalisation and higher education restructuring in Hong Kong, Taiwan and Mainland China. *Higher Education Research & Development, 22*(2), 117–129.

Powell, S., & Green, H. (2007). *The doctorate worldwide.* McGraw-Hill Education (UK).

Shin, J. C., Postiglione, G. A., & Ho, K. C. (2018). Challenges for doctoral education in East Asia: A global and comparative perspective. *Asia Pacific Education Review, 19*(2), 141–155.

Taylor, R. (1981). *China's intellectual dilemma: Politics and university enrolment, 1949–1978* (Vol. 1). University of Washington Press.

Taylor, S. (2018). *Eligibility to supervise: A study of UK institutions.* UK Council for Graduate Education.

The State Council of the People's Republic of China. (2010). *Outline of the National Medium- and Long-Term Programme for Education Reform and Development* (2010–2020). http://www.gov.cn/jrzg/2010-07/29/content_1667143.htm

Wang, H. (2018). The comparing of college background, research ability and academic passion between the doctoral students selected by the application. *Research in Educational Development, 9*(1), 43–49.

Xu, Z., & Qi, C. (2018). Hot issues and evolution of doctoral enrolment system research in China. *Heilongjiang Researches on Higher Education, 287*(3), 100–104.

Yang, R. (2012). Up and coming?: Doctoral education in China. *The Australian Universities' Review, 54*(1), 64–71.

Yanow, D. (2000). *Conducting interpretive policy analysis* (Vol. 47). Sage.

Yanow, D. (2007). Interpretation in policy analysis: On methods and practice. *Critical Policy Analysis, 1*(1), 110–122.

Zheng, G., Kivistö, J., Shen, W., & Cai, Y. (2019). Comparing doctoral education in China and Finland: An institutional logics perspective. In H. Liu, F. Dervin, & X. Du (Eds.), *Nordic-Chinese intersections within education* (pp. 197–231). Palgrave Macmillan.

Zheng, G., Shen, W., & Cai, Y. (2018). Institutional logics of Chinese doctoral education system. *Higher Education, 76*(5), 753–770.

Zhu, C., Cai, Y., Shen, W. Q., & François, K. (2017). Reforms and collaborations in Europe-China doctoral education. *European Journal of Higher Education, 7*(3), 219–226.

Zhuang, L. (2007). Doctoral education in China. In S. Powel & H. Green (Eds.), *The doctorate worldwide* (pp. 155–167). McGraw Hill.

CHAPTER 5

Doctoral Final Examinations

(Ir)Relevance to New Skills and Future Challenges

Pam Denicolo, Dawn Duke and Julie Reeves

Abstract

The contemporary rapid evolution of doctoral programmes with their emphasis shifting to the development of a skilled, versatile researcher from the production of an erudite thesis, has not been matched by parallel progression in the final examination. Those who supervise and examine doctoral candidates seem only to have custom and practice and their own limited experience to steer their decisions in a fast-changing environment. We raise challenging questions about how assessment could be adapted to maintain the benefits of doctoral diversity while providing transparent evidence to employers and the wider society of the specific valuable skills of successful doctoral candidates.

Keywords

doctoral assessment – doctoral defence – doctoral examination – doctorateness

1 Introduction – A Developing Focus of Concern

> Online learning has transformed curriculum and teaching in ways that could be mild compared with the artificial transmutations to come. Student cohorts have grown and diversified. New fields have sprouted and matured. Yet much assessment is being done today much as it was a century ago. (Coates, 2020, p. 92)

The focus of this chapter is on the final assessment of the doctorate, specifically, whether it is fit for contemporary purpose and if all doctorates are comparable, regardless of their discipline or geographical base. We intended to review both what is assessed and how, considering the lengthy period of

 | DOI:10.1163/9789004529304_005

change in both the content and structure of doctoral support and training in recent decades. However, while we were preparing this chapter, other areas of pre-doctoral education were facing challenge to content, structure and assessment, emphasising the importance of attention to purpose and curriculum in its widest sense. These developments provided us with food for thought, comparing what was a highly regulated pre-university educational assessment process with the highly generalised assessment of the pinnacle of educational achievement.

England was beginning its third Corona Virus lockdown and the government had announced, after much pressure from teachers and their unions, that the Secondary Level examinations, GCSEs (usually taken at about 16 years of age and often as precursors to 'A' levels) and A levels (usually taken at 18 years of age, often as precursors to university entrance) that are used as evidence of acquired knowledge and skills suitable for specific work or further/higher education, would not take place in the summer of 2021. Instead, they were intended to be replaced by allocation of grades by means other than examinations that were expected to be safer, fairer, and more equitable, given the unequal loss of lessons and access to virtual teaching experienced by students across the country during the turbulent year of the pandemic. Employers and university admissions professionals, who previously had relied on those widely understood and recognised examination grades as indicators of fitness for the work in their jobs and courses, potentially now faced multiple assessment procedures with varying degrees of standardisation, much as they do with doctoral degrees. They responded in various ways.

Some universities lowered their entrance grade requirements. Others refused to do so, expressing concerns that students with lower grades would not be 'ready' in terms of knowledge level to begin their courses. Employers wondered whether and with what certainty the grades acquired by these other means would be equivalent to those previously earned through examination, some reflecting further and suggesting that those previous grades had not aligned with employability criteria anyway. Teaching organisations suggested reducing the curriculum, then using teacher assessment or classroom tests to compensate for the missing examination marks. Debate ensued in both quarters about whether the traditional grades represent specific knowledge acquired or an ability level, and about whether the assessed grades would be norm or criterion referenced. Educators reminded government that, recently, the current 'end of two years of study' examinations had replaced a combination of continuous assessment plus end of course examination. They noted that missing out on specific teaching does not mean that people stop learning altogether.

Currently the UK government continues to state that national high stakes examinations are the 'fairest' for all students because of the lack of teacher bias, however, there are recent studies that question this logic, emphasising the limitation of formulaic test learning (Barrance, 2019; Coates, 2020; Woods et al., 2019). Therefore, speculation ensues about whether it might not be better/fairer, beyond the Covid era, to return to a more holistic process.

Conclusion to these debates have not yet been reached at the time of writing but the fact that this debate exists has relevance to our consideration of the assessment of the doctorate. In England the introduction of A levels in 1951 and GCSEs in 1988 was intended to provide information about students' ability in different subject disciplines, each of which is defined at each level by a curriculum, with grade names/numbers (which changed over time) used to denote levels obtained. Examination markers are experienced professionals, teachers trained in the task, who work as a community of practice preparing for each examination with its curriculum, which includes a syllabus, specific aims and objectives. Multi-step standardisation processes are used to produce marking schemes, intended to measure the achievement of those aims and objectives. Post-examination moderation exercises and external checks are undergone to ensure common levels of understanding of what is required to gain marks and what each mark signifies in order to make the marking process as reliable as possible (AlphaPlus, 2014). However, simultaneously, this method has led to an approach to teaching and learning that focuses on passing this assessment, instead of deep learning with individual growth and creativity.

This provides a basis on which to compare traditional education assessment with the examination of the doctorate, considering, inter alia, purpose, criteria, examiner preparation and curriculum issues such as syllabus, aims and objectives. It also alerts us to the issues of standardisation: whether it is relevant and possible at doctoral level, and meaningful/desirable to stakeholders.

2 Context – Pressures and Their Sources

The effects of the pandemic on the pinnacle of doctoral education have not been, as for school levels, a sudden trauma after years of stability. Rather, it has been an added challenge, albeit a huge one, to doctoral education following nearly 25 years of turbulence, as other chapters in this volume illustrate.

In brief, the Bologna Agreement (1999) and its subsequent elaborations produced a metamorphosis of higher education in the European Union, with reverberations and similar transformations occurring globally. With respect to the third cycle (doctoral) education, the 2004 Dublin Descriptors, the 2005 Salzburg Principles and the European Charter for Researchers and Code of Practice, followed in 2011 by Salzburg II and the European Commission: Principles for Innovative Doctoral Training, are examples of initiatives that shook traditions and previously unchallenged practices at the postgraduate level. These developments have been well-rehearsed and discussed in the literature (Boud & Lee, 2009; Brown, 2001; Burgess, 1997; Clarke & Lunt 2014; Denicolo, 2007, 2010; EUA, 2007; Golde & Walker, 2006; Harris, 1996; HEFCE, 2014; Jorgensen, 2014; Phillips, 1992).

The drivers of these changes included the massification/accessibility and diversification of education and the growth of credentialism. As global economies cycled through 'boom and bust' phases the content of the doctorate became increasingly tailored towards employment needs within and outside the academy. Politically, researchers have been sequentially viewed as shouldering the burden for economic recovery, suffering derision as experts during the rise of popularism, then being lauded as saviours of the world as governments 'followed the science' during the pandemic.

3 Impact of Changes

These changes largely affected the content and teaching aspects of doctoral programmes with the emphasis shifting from the production of a thesis to the development of a skilled, versatile researcher. This has not been matched by parallel progression in the final examination processes. As we have seen at preceding educational levels, assessors/evaluators/examiners have the guidance of aims, objectives and standardised criteria and moderation exercises to guide them. Those who work with doctoral candidates have little more than the high-level Dublin descriptors (the equivalent of high-level, generic aims and objectives, perhaps), vague and self-produced university regulations, custom and practice and their own limited experience to steer their assessment decisions in a fast-changing environment. We will now elaborate on those contentions and their impact potential.

There have been significant regional efforts to provide innovative programmes and opportunities for doctoral candidates to develop and enhance a wide range of research and professional skills relevant to global challenges.[1]

What is concerning is that corresponding effort has not gone into aligning the developments in accrued learning with in-programme assessment and final examination processes. However, because of concerns about completion rates, there has been tightening of assessment procedures throughout registration across the sector, mainly focussing on guiding the research project to a timely, successful completion as opposed to doctoral pedagogy (Dowle 2020; Winfield, 1987). The evaluation of the developing researcher's universal professional skills is sparse and erratic at best (Gilbert et al., 2004), varying within institutions, never mind between them.

These skills, now deemed to be important to the candidates' future employment in all sectors, are seldom and only perfunctorily addressed in the final examination with assumptions being made that their acquisition has been assessed throughout the programme. Thus, there is no specific, universal indicator of the range or level of skills acquired by a doctoral candidate. Hinchcliffe et al. (2007) noted that the UK Research Council's Joint Skills Statement made "no mention … of the level of skill to be attained – just that individuals should have them". That situation remains unchanged.

Notwithstanding that different countries have different doctoral entry requirements, amount of coursework to be undertaken in addition to research per se, and widely varying regulations pertaining to the examination, the focus of the final examination remains on the quality of a written thesis, which stands as a description of a research project and, crucially, an argument for its process and procedure (see e.g., Houston, 2019; Kumar & Stracke, 2017; Lee & Danby, 2012). While that manuscript remains of good value in demonstrating traditional research abilities associated with academic apprenticeship, it fails to be a source of accessible, transparently demonstrable evidence of acquired professionally relevant skills to key stakeholders in society beyond the academy, and indeed beyond national boundaries. However, that is precisely where most will find employment. Further, employers who require workers with the problem-solving skills traditionally expected of doctoral degree holders now need further guidance to enable them to be more selective amongst an increasing number of candidates, yet they have little means to guide them about the specific package of other research or professional skills that each one has acquired through their doctoral research.

For higher education employers, the achievement of a non-trivial contribution to knowledge and the production of work worthy of scholarly publication is an increasingly essential requirement of candidates. Nevertheless, they, like most other employers, seek more detailed information about other useful attributes while non-HE employers would benefit from greater clarity about benefits for their organisation of employing an academic doctor. The ability to defend their work in person is a transferable skill that doctoral candidates demonstrate in viva voces, but only when these forms of assessment are used. However, there has been discussion about whether a challenging viva voce: a) is still relevant in regions that have it; b) could be useful in regions that do not; c) might be adapted to demonstrate transferable skill acquisition.

Although most institutions provide courses or encourage practices that develop professional skills there is, as yet, little evidence that candidates can translate them into diverse contexts (Denicolo & Reeves, 2014). Further, there continues to be argument about the general relevance of the traditional assessment process in more recently emerging forms of doctorate such as professional and arts-based degrees that involve performance or the production of artifacts (e.g., Grushka & Holbrook, 2019; Kiley et al., 2018; Webb et al., 2013; Winter et al., 2000).

4 The Engendered Doctorateness Question

Fundamental to these debates is the concept of doctorateness (Denicolo & Park, 2013), what differentiates the holder of a doctorate from those who hold other degrees and qualifications. A doctorate itself can be described as the pinnacle in the hierarchy of academic awards, in which the bachelor level degrees denote the acquisition of a body of knowledge, master's degrees require the acquisition and application of knowledge, while doctorates additionally, and most importantly, require the creation and extension of knowledge. Therefore, a doctorate is different in kind, rather than being simply the next in an additive progression. However, judging what constitutes the achievement of doctorateness for an individual candidate is bedevilled by the fact that the concept itself is elusive and contentious (Park, 2013; Poole, 2015; Wellington, 2013) and by the lack of detailed and consistent criteria to guide both supervisors and examiners.[2]

This situation arose because each country and each independent higher education institution within them has historically formulated their own doctoral regulations, while disciplines have superimposed their own evolving idiosyncratic requirements (Kandiko & Kinchin, 2012). Originally a doctorate was a rare award required only as a qualification for academics (though even that has not been without contention – see 'the Tyrannical Machine' in William James, 1903). Nowadays, a doctorate is a requirement for many professional roles both within and beyond academe with the added complications of the proliferation of new forms of doctorate alongside the need for international recognition of qualifications.

A reflection of the mix of qualities required of a person who has or is acquiring doctorateness includes such things as intellectual excellence and confidence, independence of thinking, enthusiasm and commitment, ability to adapt to changing circumstances and opportunities, and persistence in the face of challenge. Though these could constitute potential avenues of inquiry about how they have been acquired through the doctorate in a candidate's viva voce, they are seldom required for report by examiners in institutional regulations. Instead, regulations focus on generic, high-level criteria such as described in the Dublin Descriptors (Jackson et al., 2007), which could be interpreted as the objectives, or learning outcomes, of the aims for doctoral education as presented in the Bologna Agreement. Those aims were to make qualifications more transparent and comparable so to aid the employability and mobility of all degree holders. That those aims have yet to be globally achieved for doctoral degrees takes us to the crux of the matter, that the criteria are not yet universally understood or applied.

5 Establishing Equivalence

As the doctorate became manifestly in a process of transition from the turn of the century (Jackson et al., 2007), so too did interest in the development of supervisors' and examiners' skills and expertise (e.g., Wisker & Kiley, 2012). Many of us felt that we were remarking on the emperor's new clothes, or rather the lack of them. The veil is gently being lifted on the arcane practices and nebulous criteria applied previously in attempts to defray the confusion caused by implicit understandings exacerbated by lack of communication between supervisors and examiners, as well as between institutions within and between countries. Gradually, we are realising the importance of supervisors and examiners working to the same script and of institutions making provision for a coherent series of assessments leading up to the final examination.

Most institutions now provide some training for supervisors, and many provide voluntary basic workshops on assessing and examining, albeit usually for newer recruits. A rare few institutions, for instance some in Eire, insist on attendance at a relevant workshop to gain a licence to practise as a supervisor or as an examiner, internal or external.

That academics themselves are concerned is attested to by the number voluntarily attending workshops, courses and conferences to debate with peers how these important roles can be improved (cf. the workshops provided in the UK by the Society for Research into Higher Education [SRHE], the UK Council for Graduate Education [UKCGE], and Vitae, as well as the biennial Stellenbosch Supervision Conference, the regular Australian 'Quality in Postgraduate Research' conferences and the European Universities Association Council for Doctoral Education [EUA-CDE] meetings and conferences). Responses to presentations at these venues convinced your chapter authors that there was a need for clear and concise guidance for academics on the processes of doctoral assessment but also alerted us to perturbation pervading the sector.

As a prelude to producing books for researchers, supervisors, and assessor/examiners (see the Sage Success in Research Series), we surveyed and interviewed academics from a wide range of disciplines and from widely dispersed countries about their current practices. As well as describing the rubrics, some supervisors expressed that they are sometimes under pressure to uphold institutional statistics, and thus focus more on timely submission than on ensuring that the thesis has been crafted to the requisite quality, leaving examiners to suggest corrections or amendments to bring it up to standard for completion. Examiners then complain that they are tacitly assessing supervision but overtly penalising the candidates. Some are also concerned that their own understanding of the criteria may be idiosyncratic or out of date. The latter concerns are brought into sharp relief when academics are asked to examine multi- or cross disciplinary theses or theses in other countries because of the lack of agreed and consistent procedures and explicit criteria beyond those summarised in the Dublin Descriptors (Holbrook et al., 2008; Houston, 2021; Nerad & Heggelund, 2015).

6 Standards, Not Standardisation

We have borrowed the title of this section from Webb et al. (2013) who discussed the examination of creative arts doctorates. Given the uniqueness and increasing diversity of doctorates, it is important that we aim now to find imaginative ways to ensure equivalence of doctoral degrees. It is also critical that the criteria in use are both practically translatable to diverse contexts and to different stakeholders, especially to employers outside academia. Of course, such aims will be difficult to achieve.

Traditionally, the issue of equivalence has been addressed by including an external academic expert in examination panels. This inclusion appears to be consistent globally although other regulations about the constitution of the panel, in particular the role of the supervisor/s, differs. At one extreme, some institutions consider the final examination the last step of the move into independence by the candidate, with the supervisor/s excluded from influencing that autonomy, either positively or negatively. For others, notably in the USA, the supervisory team makes a significant contribution to the examining process, while yet others adopt stances in between.

Equally diverse are the regulations about examiners' qualifications for the role, all requiring demonstrable topic and/or methodological expertise, but few requiring some form of training for the role. In general, external examiners are intended to ensure comparability of standard across the relevant discipline/s while internal examiners are expected additionally to ensure compliance with the regulations of the institution. However, both they and the candidates are challenged by the lack of agreed criteria that denote achievement of generalised objectives (Denicolo et al., 2020; Tinkler & Jackson, 2004; Trafford & Leshem, 2008.) Nevertheless, the unsatisfactory situation is that despite examiners having diverse experience and training for the role, outcome decisions about the roughly four years of study/research cannot be challenged other than on procedural grounds.

7 Moving forward on the Crest of a Wave/Tsunami

It is not surprising that academics and other commentators find it astonishing that, despite the otherwise radical changes to the structure and function of the doctorate, little attention had been paid to ensuring that the final assessment keeps pace with changes, especially those related to purpose. There may be resistance to further change, or anxiety about challenge to implicit professional expertise, or concerns that it would be impossible to gain agreement across and between disciplines, institutions, and countries. Even if scholars agree a procedure and criteria, the variance and strictness of national regulations will also present challenges. Then there may be fears that the doctorate would become too automated, too circumscribed, perhaps losing its distinctiveness if it were subject to tighter regulation and standardisation.

Of course, these are genuine concerns but confronting such challenges is what researchers do. Naturally, examining our own professional practice is a significant challenge, but one better conducted collaboratively within the sector than imposed upon us by external bureaucrats and/or politicians. Increasingly, there is international co-operation between researchers from most disciplines in monitoring and then providing creative means to counter climate change, alongside other global challenges such as the development of vaccines for Covid-19. Researchers are, in unprecedented ways, sharing, collaborating, reviewing and supporting each other's efforts. They are engaging in online collegial discussions and debates worldwide and are learning new skills to both supervise and examine at a distance.

In a recent Society for Research into Higher Education (SRHE) webinar involving speakers from ten countries, from both hemispheres, addressing a global audience, contributors noted that the pandemic has provided a unique opportunity for reform, for solving transnational and transboundary problems. Never was there a better time to respond to the imprecation 'carpe diem'. We are now inhabiting a very different world to the one that produced the traditions associated with the doctorate, and we have different purposes, tools, and skills with which we could remedy the cracks appearing in the doctoral process. For instance, we suggest that such international debating opportunities would be ideally suited for working on lists of criteria expected by examiners in different disciplines and countries, and how they expect them to be evidenced, to distil out common and disparate criteria and their relevance to national or disciplinary contexts. This might be the beginning of a new zeitgeist as we explore the following challenging questions[3]:

- Can we develop broad, measurable objectives that accommodate diversity for the skills that must be developed regardless of context?
- What necessary and sufficient doctoral quality criteria could we communicate globally to candidates, supervisors, and examiners to guide their practice?
- How could such elaborated criteria be adequately conveyed to the general public, including prospective employers, to aid recognition of both the universal and individual specific professional qualities derived from doctoral study?

Notes

1 For example, see Gilbert et al. (2004) for an international review; Vitae (2010) for a UK example; and for an Australian example see https://www.canberra.edu.au/research/graduate-research/researcher-development/researcher-development-skillsframework/RDSFSkillAreas.pdf

2 This led, incidentally, to the provision of a synopsis of suggested criteria collated from our own research and practice in our books of guidance for supervisors and examiners: Denicolo, Duke and Reeves (2020) and Denicolo, Reeves and Duke (2020). We include that synopsis at the end of this chapter in case it is of use to others.

3 Answers by email to the chapter authors, please! We will acknowledge your contributions.

References

AlphaPlus. (2014). *Standardisation methods, mark schemes, and their impact on marking reliability*. Ofqual/14/5380. Retrieved January 14, 2021, from https://www.gov.uk/government/publications/standardisation-methods-mark-schemes-marking-reliability

Boud, D., & Lee, A. (2009). *Changing practices of doctoral education.* Routledge.

Bologna Declaration. (1999). Retrieved January 19, 2021, from https://www.eurashe.eu/library/bologna_1999_bologna-declaration-pdf/

Brown, D. K. (2001). The social sources of educational credentialism: Status cultures, labor markets, and organizations. *Sociology of Education* (Extra issue: Current of Thought: Sociology of Education at the Dawn of the 21st Century), *74*, 19–34.

Burgess, R. (1997). The changing context of postgraduate education in the United Kingdom. In R. Burgess (Ed.), *Beyond the first degree: Graduate education, lifelong learning and careers.* The Society for Research into Higher Education and Open University Press.

Clarke, G., & Lunt, I. (2014). *International comparisons in postgraduate education: Quality, access and employment outcomes.* HEFCE.

Coates, H. (2020) Reforming assessment. In *Higher education design.* Palgrave Macmillan. https://doi.org/10.1007/978-981-15-9216-4_7.

Crossouard, B. (2008). Developing alternative models of doctoral supervision with online formative assessment. *Studies in Continuing Education, 30*(1), 51–67.

Denicolo P. M. (2007). The metamorphosis of doctoral education in the UK and Europe: Perspectives from a teacher as learner. In J. Butcher & L. McDonald (Eds.), *Making a difference: Challenges for teachers, teaching and teacher education* (pp. 235–250). Sense Publishers.

Denicolo, P. M. (2010). Bologna ten years on. In *Academic exchange No. 9 The postgraduate student experience.* The Higher Education Academy.

Denicolo, P. M. (Ed.). (2013). *Success in research: Achieving impact.* Sage.

Denicolo, P. M., Duke, D., & Reeves, J. (2020). *Success in research: Delivering inspiring doctoral assessment.* Sage.

Denicolo, P. M., & Park, C. (2013). Doctorateness – an elusive concept? In M. Kompf & P. M. Denicolo (Eds.), *Critical issues in higher education.* Sense Publishers.

Denicolo, P. M., & Reeves, J. (2014). *Success in research: Developing transferable skills.* Sage.

Denicolo, P. M., Reeves, J., & Duke, D. (2020). *Success in research: Supervising to inspire doctoral researchers.* Sage.

Dowle, S. (2020). *Retheorising doctoral completions: Exploring the role of critical events, structure and agency* [Unpublished thesis]. Royal Holloway University of London.

Dublin Descriptors. (2004). Retrieved January 19, 2021, from https://www.aqu.cat/doc/doc_24496811_1.pdf

European Charter for Researchers and Code of Practice. (2005). Retrieved January 19, 2021, from https://euraxess.ec.europa.eu/jobs/charter-code-researchers

European Commission Principles for Doctoral Training. (2011). Retrieved January 19, 2021, from https://euraxess.ec.europa.eu/sites/default/files/policy_library/principles_for_innovative_doctoral_training.pdf

European Universities Association (EUA). (2007). *Doctoral programmes in Europe's universities: Achievements and challenges.* EUA.

Gilbert, R., Balatti, J., Turner, P., & Whitehouse, H. (2004). The generic skills debate in research higher degree. *Higher Education Research & Development, 23*(3), 375–388.

Golde, C., & Walker, G. (Eds). (2006). *Envisioning the future of doctoral education.* Jossey-Bass.

Grushka, K. M., & Holbrook, A. (2019). Examining the case for artful participatory inquiry in the visual art education doctorate. In A. Sinner, R. L. Irwin, & J. Adams (Eds.), *Provoking the field* (pp. 43–62). Intellect.

Harris, M. (1996). *Review of postgraduate education.* Higher Education Funding Council for England.

Higher Education Funding Council for England (HEFCE). (2014). *International comparisons in postgraduate education: Quality, access and employment outcomes.* HEFCE.

Hinchcliffe, R., Bromley, T., & Hutchinson, S. (Eds.). (2007). *Skills training in research degree programmes: Politics and practice.* Open University Press.

Holbrook, A., Bourke, S., Lovat, T., & Fairbairn, H. (2008). Consistency and inconsistency in PhD thesis examination. *Australian Journal of Education, 52*(1), 36–48.

Houston, G. (2019). *A study of the PhD examination: process, attributes and outcomes* [Unpublished thesis]. Oxford University. Retrieved January 14, 2021, from https://ora.ox.ac.uk/objects/uuid:07291f0e-e80b-4b06-a6af-b3ac8b90a00e

Houston, G. (2021). Doctoral examiners' judgements: Do examiners agree on doctoral attributes and how important are professional and personal characteristics? In A. Lee & R. Bongaardt (Eds.), *The future of doctoral research: Challenges and opportunities.* Routledge.

Jackson, C., Tinkler, P., & Denicolo, P. M. (Eds.). (2007). *A guide for internal and external doctoral examiners.* Society for Research into Higher Education.

James, W. (1903, March). The PhD octopus. *Harvard Monthly.*

Johnson, T., & Hirt, J. B. (2014). Universities, dependency and the market: Innovative lessons from Kenya. *Compare: A Journal of Comparative and International Education, 44*(2), 230–251.

Jorgensen, T. (2014). Global trends in doctoral education and the European perspective. *Journal of the European Higher Education Area, 1*, 17–34.

Kandiko, C. B., & Kinchin, I. M. (2012). What is a doctorate? A concept-mapped analysis of process versus product in the supervision of lab-based PhDs. *Educational Research, 54*(1), 3–16. https://doi.org/10.1080/00131881.2012.658196

Kiley, M., Holbrook, A., Lovat, T., Fairbairn, H., Starfield, S., & Paltridge, B. (2018). An oral component in PhD examination in Australia: Issues and considerations. *Australian Universities Review, 60*(1), 25–34.

Kumar, V., & Stracke, E. (2017) Reframing doctoral examination as teaching. *Innovations in Education and Teaching International, 55*(2), 219–227. http://dx.doi.org/10.1080/14703297.2017.1285715

Lee, A., & Danby, S. (Eds.). (2012). *Reshaping doctoral education: International approaches and pedagogies.* Routledge.

Nerad, M., & Heggelund, M. (Eds.). (2015). *Toward a global PhD? Forces and forms in doctoral education worldwide.* University of Washington Press with the Center for Innovation and Research in Graduate Education.

Park, C. (2007). *Redefining the doctorate.* The Higher Education Academy.

Phillips, E. (1992). The PhD – Assessing quality at different stages of development. In O. Zuber-Skerritt (Ed.), *Starting research – Supervision and training.* Tertiary Education Institute, University of Queensland.

Poole, B. (2015). The rather elusive concept of 'doctorateness': A reaction to Wellington. *Studies in Higher Education, 40*(9), 1507–1522.

Quality Assurance Agency. (2015). *Characteristics statement: Doctoral degree.* Retrieved January 14, 2021, from https://www.qaa.ac.uk/docs/qaa/quality-code/doctoral-degree-characteristics-statement-2020.pdf?sfvrsn=a3c5ca81_14#:~:text=European%20partner%20providers.-,1.3%20Purposes%20of%20the%20doctorate,thought%2C%20based%20on%20independent%20study

Saltzburg Principles I. (2005). Retrieved January 19, 2021, from https://eua.eu/downloads/publications/salzburg%20recommendations%202005.pdf

Saltzburg Principles II. (2010). Retrieved January 19, 2021, from https://eua.eu/resources/publications/615:salzburg-ii-%E2%80%93-recommendations.html

Society for Research into Higher Education (SRHE). (2015, June). *Examiners' dilemmas and resolutions workshop.* SRHE.

Tinkler, P., & Jackson, C. (2004). *The doctoral examination process: A handbook for students, examiners and supervisors.* SRHE and Open University Press.

Trafford, V., & Leshem, S. (2008). *Steppingstones to achieving your doctorate: Focusing on your viva from the start.* Open University Press – McGraw-Hill Education.

Vitae. (2010). *Researcher development framework.* Retrieved January 23, 2021, from https://www.vitae.ac.uk/researchers-professional-development/about-the-vitae-researcher-development-framework

Webb, J., Brien, B., & Burr, S. (2013) "Standards, not standardisation": examining the creative arts doctorate in Australia. In J. Holmes (Ed.), *The CALTN papers: The refereed proceedings of the Creative Arts Learning and Teaching Network symposium* (pp. 36–60).

Wellington, J. (2013). Searching for 'doctorateness'. *Studies in Higher Education, 38*(10), 1490–1503. https://doi.org/10.1080/03075079.2011.634901

Winfield, G. (1987). *The social science PhD: The ESRC inquiry on submission rates.* ESRC.

Winter, R., Griffiths, M., & Green, K. (2000). The academic qualities of practice: What are the criteria for a practice-based PhD? *Studies in Higher Education, 25*(1), 25–37.

Wisker, G., & Kiley, M. (2012). Professional learning: Lessons for supervision from doctoral examining. *International Journal for Academic Development, 19*(2), 125–138.

Appendix: Summary of Criteria Used by Many Examiners for Assessing the Written Thesis

This appendix originally appeared in Denicolo, P., Duke, D. & Reeves, J. (2020). *Success in research: Delivering inspiring doctoral assessment.* Sage. Reprinted here with permission from the publisher (© Pam Denicolo, Dawn Duke & Julie Reeves).

OVERALL, a Thesis Should Have

- a careful, clear presentation that has the reader's reading and understanding needs in mind;
- if necessary, or helpful, a glossary of terms and/or of acronyms preceding main text and succeeding Contents list;
- the contribution to knowledge expected and achieved be made explicit;
- chapters that are coherent in themselves and which contribute to an integrated whole which follows a consistent argument.

SECTIONAL ATTRIBUTES Sought

Abstract

- clearly describes main aspects of the thesis (purpose, theoretical and methodological base and general outputs and outcomes) within the word limit.

Introduction

- rationale for undertaking study clearly explicated.
- the appropriateness of the researcher conducting this study made clear. (Science Note: this is less applicable to the sciences where the positivist framework requires a design that supports researcher neutrality.)
- a brief overview of thesis provided, demonstrating the 'story line' chapter by chapter.

Review of Relevant Literature

(Science Note: often the introduction and literature review chapters are integrated as one.) (English Literature Note: often the entire thesis is in essence a critique of

literature, and so detailed and sophisticated argumentation relating to the literature will be evident in the majority of chapters.)
- succinct, penetrating, challenging, critical, analytical approach.
- demonstration of thorough knowledge of field.
- primary rather than secondary sources used.
- recent references except where older seminal work is acknowledged.
- quotations (NB page numbers required) used to illustrate or exemplify rather than substitute for own words in argument.
- organised to show a developing argument for the hypotheses/research questions.

Statement of Research Problems or Plan for Development of a Creative Piece

- clear and succinct hypotheses or questions or basic plan derived from/revealed by the literature review.
- should have a novel theoretical or methodological or creative slant and/or bring together previously unrelated fields and/or a new area of application.
- well-articulated rationale for 'worthwhileness' of research.

Approach and Methods of Enquiry Adopted (Theoretical Argument-Methodology Rather Than 'Methods')

- rationale for general approach closely argued giving reasoned case for rejecting other possible approaches.
- justification of research design presented, taking account of potential advantages and limitations.
- research techniques argued as theoretically and practically relevant to research problem; reasons given for rejection of possible alternatives; rationale provided for amendments to standard tests and procedures or for detailed design of innovative techniques.
- rationale provided for the selection of the analysis procedures, choice of statistical tests, etc.

Data Collection (Description of Actual Process Where Appropriate)

- clearly set out and easy to follow, possibly including a flowchart, Gantt chart or similar device.

- relevant details included (how access was achieved, number of subjects/respondents, relevant profiles, timing of interventions, duration of interventions, etc.) or (what materials and equipment were used, what procedures were followed, etc.)
- ethical issues – what permissions were obtained, what guarantees were given, how ethical issues have been acknowledged and dealt with
- difficulties encountered and how they were dealt with so that the research was not compromised.

Arts Note: If a piece is being created (performance, a book, an artwork) or an extended argument based on the literature, for instance, being prepared then data collection, analysis and presentation may not apply. They would be replaced by the artwork or argument with a description of how they emerged.

Analysis of Data (Where Appropriate)

- mode of analysis theoretically justified.
- any assumptions stated and justified.
- congruent with research questions/hypotheses and approach adopted.
- details of procedure clearly presented.

Science Note: Sometimes statistical expertise is utilised to analyse scientific data. This does not mean you do not have to understand your data and what the analysis entails. Make sure you work with any expert, so that you can answer any questions about the analysis of your data.

Presentation of Data (Where Appropriate)

- clearly structured.
- data 'trail' evident.
- details of why, who, what, when and where provided.
- tables, figures, diagrams to summarise data clearly numbered and titled and referred to in the text.

Science Note: Graphs, tables and figures are extremely important in a science thesis. These should be clear, well labelled, and self-explanatory with just the legend. Examiners spend a good deal of time looking at figures; ensure there are no mistakes.

Discussion of Outcomes or Conclusions of Argument

- main points summarised and evaluated in interpretations made of raw data.
- links made to literature previously presented, e.g., what previous research/theory has been supported, substantiated, challenged, amended, rejected, etc.
- reflections on the research process – limitations addressed and consequent implications for results.
- suggestions for repeat or further research based on this research.
- implications of results for theory and for practice.
- clear articulation of contribution/s to knowledge.

References

- all references in the text are included in an appropriate style.
- no references are included that do not appear in the text – but a separate, short bibliography of influential texts is sometimes (in some institutions/disciplines) acceptable.

Appendices

- all appendices are clearly numbered in the order of appearance in the main text.

PART 2

Challenges and Opportunities for the Staff Supporting Doctoral Researchers

CHAPTER 6

Re-framing Supervisor Development for Internationalisation and Professionalisation

Pam Denicolo, Julie Reeves and Dawn Duke

Abstract

In 2000 Barnett discussed the transformation of university scholarship and research in a world he described as 'supercomplex' (Barnett, 2000). It is more so now. Even doctoral research problems increasingly require collaborative multi-disciplinary support so that theoretical and practical outcomes can be made relevant, impactful, and accessible to diverse audiences. Although universities should provide doctoral supervisory training to enable supervisors to excel in this current and any new context, we posit here ways in which supervisors could take greater agency in both achieving CPD and in gaining help from other colleagues with specific areas of expertise so that doctoral research becomes truly a team effort.

Keywords

'supercomplex' – collaboration – intersection – networks – agency – communities of research

1 Introduction

The multiple impacts on the structure and purpose of the doctorate which has metamorphosed over the preceding 20+ years have been rehearsed in other chapters in this book. That those demands and challenges have repercussions for supervisors has preoccupied over many years those of us concerned with and about supervisor support and development. For instance, as part of a team (Tarragona Think Tank, TTT) associated with the EUA-CDE (European Universities Association – Council for Doctoral Education) and committed to developing ideas and research related to the professionalisation of doctoral supervision (Reguero et al., 2017), this chapter's authors have widened the remit of the original chapter on supervision planned for this book as we all

 | DOI:10.1163/9789004529304_006

gained in experience from the challenges to doctoral supervision caused by the pandemic.

When Barnett (2000) described the transformation of university scholarship and research in a world as 'supercomplex', he could not have imagined the escalation in complexity of the academic world today. Amongst the upheaval of our day to day personal and working lives caused by this worldwide pandemic, we also see the power of supercomplex research in impacting and improving lives. The development of vaccines for Covid-19 within a year is a striking example of what can be done when researchers from across boundaries of nation, sector, and discipline work together with focused determination to make an impact. Many such complex research problems increasingly require multi-disciplinary perspectives, global cooperation, and multi-national funding, with both theoretical and practical outcomes made relevant, impactful, transparent, and accessible to diverse audiences. For instance, similarly, and simultaneously, we are faced with a need for multi-disciplinary research on the plethora of issues related to climate change and other global challenges.

The researchers engaged with this work are very often also supervisors of doctorates. Indeed, within any institution the doctoral researchers themselves, individually and en masse, make huge contributions to this knowledge-generating activity. See, for example, Lariviere's (2011) research that found that PhD students contributed to about a third of the publication output in his Canadian province, with collaboration with peers and advisors being an important component. This demonstrates that doctoral researchers cannot perform this important function without considerable support as they change from knowledge imbibers to knowledge producers (Halse & Mowbray, 2011).

2 Preparation for a Critical Role – The Current Situation

Supervisors are expected to keep up with the pace of change within both their own research practice and the developing demands of the doctorate. The latter requires them to transmogrify frequently between tutor/colleague, guide/assessor, supporter/challenger throughout each individual doctoral candidature. The pervading rhetoric now challenges the master/apprentice model of the doctorate for being inadequate to the contemporary needs of candidates in some key respects, whilst the practice of supervisor development remains stagnant in all but a few dispersed situations (for example, the training programmes offered by Australian universities (Cally et al., 2017; Kiley, 2010). Many universities have compulsory, usually short and intensive, workshops for new supervisors while some try to provide additional workshops on specific topics such as doctoral examining. A small number of institutions provide longer programmes, see for instance Aarhuss University which has a programme consisting of four seminar days and requiring 40 hours of individual work.[1]

Whilst these programmes are impactful and beneficial (McCulloch & Loeser, 2016), they are often not accredited or regulated (Taylor, Kiley, & Holley, 2021), and many tend to focus on administrative and regulatory matters, with some addressing interactive issues such as supervisory style. Very few programmes or courses support the supervisory skills of collaborating with industrial or practice-based supervisors, or with end users of research. It has long been recognised (Denicolo, 2016, 2018; Denicolo & Pope, 1999) that supervisors are crucial to researcher development while inter-institutional and inter-sector collaboration has increasingly become important in all forms of research (Duke & Denicolo, 2016; Jorgensen, 2014).

This is significant because external bodies and organisation, demanding collaborative approaches to tackle global challenges, are becoming increasingly entwined with doctoral education. Even at a minimal level, candidates might be expected to consider the impact and wider benefits of their research, and to engage with the public and end users outside academe. This is certainly the case in the UK, where some consideration of the impact of research or a placement in the research context are required by many/most funders. For example, the EPSRC's *Doctoral Training Partnerships* and *Doctor Prize* aim to increase the impact of doctoral research and BBSRC funding includes a *Professional Internship for PhD Students* (PIPS).

External engagement is gaining prominence not simply because the topics of such study are diversifying but also because the backgrounds and purposes/ambitions of the researchers are broadening, with the demands made of them and their expectations expanding correspondingly. A doctorate may not yet be an official requirement for entry to all professions, as it is for academic and academic-support work, but it certainly is considered useful for progression in many fields. For example, senior corporate roles in German companies are often occupied by executives holding doctorates, and this is set to be a growing trend across Europe as successful doctoral researchers graduate into a wider employment field than the traditional one of academia.

It continues to be the case that most of the supervisory skills of academics are acquired 'on the job', being random combinations of emulation or rejection of their own early research experience as doctoral researchers and post docs, observation of colleagues, and trial and error experiments, with little time or space for reflection, practice sharing or skill development. Just as knowing your subject well does not automatically make you a good teacher of it, so being an experienced researcher does not imply that you will be automatically a good research supervisor.

From a doctoral candidate's perspective, this is not reassuring, especially given the huge investment, financial-emotional-intellectual-social-temporal, required to complete a doctorate successfully. A 'survivorship bias' prevails in supervision, as one doctoral candidate has noted in discussion with one of the authors. Neither is it comforting for those supervisors dedicating time, energy, and professional reputation to the task. Doctoral study is a perilous business in many ways so that reducing the risk to all concerned (to candidates, supervisors, and to the institutional reputation) should be a priority for institutions. There is an expectation that this can simply be achieved through ensuring a minimum quality of support and training for competent supervision by professionals who are experts in their specific research field. However, determining what should comprise that minimum quality of support and training is not a simple matter.

Other chapters in this part of the book demonstrate that there is an increasing literature about supervision and a growing demand for Continuing Professional Development (CPD). We, the authors, have been caught up ourselves in responding to that need, by delivering tailored supervisor training to increasing demands from supervisors for training and development opportunities within their institutions or through the auspices of professional bodies and learned societies. One specific frequent, urgent request, reflecting the nature of academic life in 2020–21, is for guidance and support focussed on how to supervise and/or to examine remotely during a pandemic. However, these are piecemeal responses to frustrating and/or emergency situations from very busy professionals.

What has become increasingly clear to us is that the higher education system has become too reductionist in its consideration of its key professionals' jobs, considering each activity separately. It must be a very rare academic whose job only consists of being a doctoral supervisor, even though that role has increased in profile from its original 'master to an apprentice' job description. That traditional master-apprenticeship structure of supervision within institutions relied very heavily on an autonomous and largely 'private' relationship between supervisor and supervisee. The 'on the job' training passed between successive generations has also ensured discriminatory practice and systemic bias prevailed (Arday, 2020), as there were few independent or institutional points of intervention or opportunities to challenge performance, attitude, knowledge or behaviour. Even revising the rhetoric to one of mentorship or stewardship does not challenge the 'on the job' learning institutions rely on, discussed above, nor does it deconstruct any of the inherent limitations in the system, such as the pressure (perceived or real) on individuals to take on a growing range of tasks.

Narrowly focusing on only one role within the multiple aspects of an academic job neglects the inevitable interactions and intersections with other roles and responsibilities. Separating and compartmentalising roles and the attending professional development they require, as institutions have historically done, is not only inhumane and burdensome for individuals, but may no longer be as relevant as it once was given the extent of change in doctoral education. Some of these sub-role interactions have negative impacts while others are co-facilitatory, as we explore in the next section.

3 Supervision as Part of an Interacting and Intersectional System of Roles and Responsibilities

Taking a more holist perspective, we recognise that no supervisor is an island. Despite what new doctoral researchers might hope, their supervisors' work lives are not solely focussed on their researchers' projects and well-being. A considerable portion of the normal academic work role is undergraduate and postgraduate teaching, including assessment and course organisation, which is subject to internal and external evaluation processes that require considerable documentation. Recent history has seen rapid moves towards massification/democratisation of participation at the Bachelor degree level and subsequently throughout the award-bearing courses (Giannakis & Bullivant, 2016), which increase the teaching and research support roles of all academics. Contemporaneously, universities have been pressured into ensuring that all graduates are more employment ready, requiring those who provide their teaching and support to incorporate the learning of transferable or universal skills into their courses and to liaise with employers to negotiate work experience opportunities. The net result is an increased administrative load that is impinging on teaching in the first instance while both, then, impact on research time.

Alongside those developments, governments encouraged greater awareness among researchers of the impact of their research, which necessarily and inevitably required closer collaboration with other sectors and the public. In turn, whilst the imperative to demonstrate a track record of publications and research funding remains for academic posts, it means that ever more time must be dedicated to both publishing and writing research proposals. This litany does not constitute a complaint about academic work being multi-faceted, because that is what makes it an interesting career. Indeed, it has been long argued that teaching and research must inform each other in order that both be successful. Indeed, one of us has argued since the mid-90s that teaching and research must form a triangular, symbiotic relationship with learning as developments are required in each (Denicolo, 1997). However, it is important to recognise that even proficient jugglers can be overwhelmed when the balls become bigger and more numerous.

Using the juggler analogy highlights another facet of academic life – autonomy. While academics, like most professionals, to some extent enjoy some leeway in the combination of additional activities they add to their basic teaching roles, their individual continued employment and promotion is dependent on their dispersed audiences: students, peers, managers, funders and external reviewers, each with their own agendas and requirements. Intersecting with these audiences and navigating a career pathway, especially one that is largely but not wholly determined by generating new research projects, is rather more entrepreneurial and collaborative today than perhaps it was at the turn of the century. This has been amply illustrated in the last year as researchers sought to contain the pandemic, find ways to ameliorate its physical, psychological and social effects and reduce infection rates by collaborating across disciplines, institutions, sectors and international boundaries to create medical solutions and equipment, support services, behavioural interventions and vaccines. It seems that professional values are upheld and international/intersectoral collaboration are taking place 'on the ground' but global solutions and the development of permanent supportive structures are lagging. The latter will be difficult and slow to influence and change. The former activities are more amenable to promote and strengthen in the shorter term, making use of the variety of communication conduits with which we are all becoming all too familiar.

4 Professionalisation and Internationalisation at Grass-Roots Levels

Standing by professional decisions to undertake only work activities that can be done competently within given timeframes demands considerable strength if undertaken alone. It does take courage to admit to oneself, never mind to colleagues, that the combined workload is too burdensome. For academics to go further to acknowledge that they are not a super-supervisors, heroes who can take on all challenges on their own, is taxing especially if such expectations pervade the culture of their institutions which historically defended their academic autonomy. However, simply waiting to wear out or give up in the face of the odds are not good options either.

It is time to cast off these academic superhero cloaks, relinquish some autonomy and embrace collegiality. In fact, it is way beyond time since Elton and Pope made a strong case for the value of greater collegiality in supervision in 1989. They argued that it could be fostered through a constructive interplay between organisational, personal and inter-personal factors (Elton & Pope, 1989). It is indeed sad that we are still having to advocate for such collegiality despite the increase in numbers of third space professionals in academe with complementary expertise and skills that are especially valuable for doctoral researcher support.

The requirements for a greater range of skill development in doctoral researchers, rather than being an additional burden on supervisors, can indeed be an opportunity for collaborative support through working with people from a range of different perspectives and backgrounds that can enrich the educational experience of doctoral researchers. These professionals include but are not limited to researcher developers (for universal/transferable skills), academic staff developers (for teaching and writing skills), librarians (for open data/science, information management and bibliometric skills), and statisticians, public and external engagement, well-being and specialist careers consultants and advisers (for their eponymous skills). Growing collaborations in researcher support with experts in other disciplines or related professions is another way of providing a broader skills base and experience for researchers.

Of course, this does entail supervisors expending effort in becoming familiar with whom and what is available both on and off campus, utilising the networking skills they developed for their own research. We recognise that networks grow over time, but they also grow exponentially as each contact introduces others. Moreover, building networks is a skill that supervisors could instil in their researchers while sharing their networks with them. Indeed, as the researchers' experience develops, within and beyond the doctorate, they may share their networks with supervisors. Critically, what needs to be embraced is the willingness to work to one's own advantage and that of the doctoral researchers with a range of professionals with complementary expertise.

One prime example of productive sharing, both with colleague supervisors and researchers, is an understanding of the criteria used to judge doctorateness (see also Chapter 5). In workshops for supervisors, it has been demonstrated that most embark on this role with little explicit information about what those criteria are in detail and how candidates from a range of backgrounds and starting points could achieve them. Further, if the needs of internationalisation are to be met as well as those of the professionalisation of supervision, there needs to be collaboration between universities globally on quality standards for doctoral support to which supervisors contribute. This is a huge and radical undertaking but one that could be activated by first establishing general standards across universities within each country. Indeed, the levels of cooperation demonstrated during the pandemic lead a potential way for such an undertaking.

Common metrics such as completion rates and 'happiness sheet' evaluations of supervision, while providing some information, offer little to supervisors wishing to professionalise their practice. Rather, in line with other comparable professions with CPD requirements for practice such as psychologists, pharmacists, lawyers, and medical professionals, they have need of guidance on and opportunities to update regularly on such things as: the currency of their discipline knowledge and that of related disciplines; the relevance of their discipline to society (impact value); new advancements in research methodology; the latest criteria used by examiners; and the recent/relevant developments in doctoral education, as well as the contemporary expectations of inclusive supervisory practice.

Current frameworks, such as those in the UK provided by the Academic Professional Apprenticeship Level 7[2] and the mapping of supervisory skills to the Professional Standards Framework in education (see Taylor, 2016) adapt doctoral supervision to a pre-existing and exogenous standard, rather than to one based on continuously changing contemporary reality and estimated future requirements. Whilst these frameworks are helpful and address core development needs of supervisors, we suggest an expansion in scope and scale is needed to truly support both supervisors and doctoral researchers to thrive in the supercomplex research world of today.

5 Nurturing Collaboration Rather Than Competition

To support our doctoral researchers as well as academic supervisors it is necessary to create communities of collaboration as opposed to competition. We need to address toxic cultures that discourage seeking outside views and undervalue a wide range of experience and expertise. Building diverse communities of practice and engaging in CPD with colleagues requires a degree of trust to expose oneself as 'not completely confident' and as 'not omniscient'. Further, there are times when supervisors may need not only to shed their hero capes but to adopt cloaks of invisibility to give themselves liminal space in which to reflect on their practice (Maistry, 2017).

It is important that institutions, departments, and disciplines enable academics to draw on their creative spirit, providing a culture that values collaboration, reflective practice and professional development. On one's own it is difficult to halt the time-consuming fire-fighting that accompanies the managing of multiple roles. However, support from communities of research can aid the adoption of such a professional activity, even if this is not institutionally forthcoming. Note the deliberate use of the phrase 'communities of research' here, rather than the more usual 'communities of professional practice', to encompass the wider range of professions within our community who contribute to research.

Establishing such communities may require resistance to the pressure imposed by those who seek to engender competition not just between countries but between universities and between colleagues. In such instances, university colleagues find themselves in dilemmic situations. The imposition of evaluation exercises focussed on teaching and on research which in turn lead to unequal disbursement of funding is only one of the tools brought to bear to accomplish competition between institutions and individuals. Yet, at the same time, and in contrast, evidence of working with others at a national and international level is an important metric for career progression while researcher mobility is encouraged for personal and disciplinary skill and knowledge enhancement.

This tension between co-operation and competition in the field of research was played out publicly in recent times. The rapid development of vaccines during the Covid pandemic was dependent on collaboration between researchers from different fields and from diverse countries – a human success story. On the other hand, rivalry between governments over procurement was less than edifying. It is the role of researchers of all kinds, including supervisors and those whom they mentor, to maintain integrity in such trying circumstances as we describe here and to strive to build and maintain a supportive, collaborative community which will foster researcher development as well as creative, innovative research.

The demands being made of academic staff in general, and those supervising doctoral researchers in particular, are unlikely to diminish. The context for research continues to change, crossing more and more of the traditional boundaries for discipline, sector, and nationality to tackle ever more urgent worldwide challenges. Similarly, the expectations and needs of researchers are changing with each generation. Supervisors' career prospects have altered considerably since they aspired to a doctorate; the demand to share the benefits of research more widely with other sectors and the public is expanding and is a key motivator for many researchers at all career stages.

Increasingly, it is not possible for the single supervisor or even a small team to meet these demands with the level of expertise required, or to keep up with best practice in each of the component areas. By collaboratively working across our institutions, sectors, and countries we can help each other individually improve our support of doctoral researchers and enhance our combined research outputs. Teamwork produces more than the sum of individual contributions (Mesmer-Magnus & DeChurch, 2009) as motivation and enjoyment of task increases. More importantly, it stimulates the creativity needed to deal with the multi-faceted problems inherent in Barnett's (2000) supercomplex world (Hackman, 2011).

Working as a team, collaborative group, or as a larger community of research, supervisors and third space professionals can embrace similarities while respecting differences. This is only a step-up from how they work with diverse doctoral researchers over a professional lifetime, but it is an essential one in order to prosper in the current and future research contexts. The next challenge will be to tackle the change in institutional cultures required, but supervisors are not without the ingenuity and fortitude to accomplish that. They have already demonstrated those aptitudes in quickly adapting to remote doctoral supervision and examining while transforming other aspects of academic roles to deal with the pandemic crisis. Many if not most of us have recognised that we are more resourceful, flexible and adaptable than we had previously thought.

Notes

1 https://bss.au.dk/en/centre-for-teaching-and-learning/courses/masters-and-phd-supervision-for-associate-professors-and-professors/ (accessed 21 March 2021).

2 https://www.instituteforapprenticeships.org/apprenticeship-standards/academic-professional-v1-0 (accessed 21 March 2021).

References

Arday, J. (2020) Fighting the tide: Understanding the difficulties facing Black, Asian and Minority Ethnic (BAME) doctoral students' pursuing a career in Academia. *Educational Philosophy and Theory*. doi:10.1080/00131857.2020.1777640

Barnett, R. (2000). University knowledge in an age of supercomplexity. *Higher Education, 40*(4), 409–422.

Denicolo, P. M. (1997). Teaching, learning and research: Analogous, symbiotic or independent? *Forum, 39*(2), 60–65.

Denicolo, P. M. (2016). International developments in the purpose and process of the doctorate: Consequences for supervision, examining and the employment of graduates. In M. Fourie-Malherbe, R. Albertyn, C. Aitchison, & E. Bitzer (Eds.), *Postgraduate supervision: Future foci for the knowledge society* (pp. 15–32). SUN MeDIA.

Denicolo, P. M. (2018). Preparing postgraduate researchers for life beyond the degree. In R. Erwee et al. (Eds.), *Postgraduate education in higher education*. University Development and Administration. https://doi.org/10.1007/978-981-10-0468-1_24-1

Denicolo, P., & Pope, M. (1999). Alternative perspectives on research supervision and responsibilities. In O. Zuber-Skerritt (Ed.), *Supervising postgraduates from non-English speaking backgrounds*. Open University Press.

Duke, D. C., & Denicolo, P. M. (2016, June). *The whole is greater than the sum of its parts: Employer-doctoral researcher engagement facilitated by cross-institutional collaboration* [Paper]. The EUA-CDE conference, Tarragona.

Elton, L., & Pope, M. (1989). Research supervision: The value of collegiality. *Cambridge Journal of Education, 19*(3), 267–276.

European University Association. (2016). *Doctoral education-taking Salzburg forward: Implementation and new challenges*. EUA-CDE.

European University Association Council for Doctoral Education. (2018, June). Annual meeting, Excellence through diversity: Doctoral education in a globalised world, Ljubjana.

Giannakis, M., & Bullivant, N. (2016). The massification of higher education in the UK: Aspects of service quality. *Journal of Further and Higher education, 40*(5), 630–648.

Guerin, C., Walker, R., Aitchison, C., Laming, M. M., Padmanabhan, M. C., & James, B. (2017). Doctoral supervisor development in Australian universities: Preparing research supervisors to teach writing. *Journal of Academic Language & Learning, 11*(1), A88–A103.

Hackman, J. R. (2011). *Collaborative intelligence: Using teams to solve hard problems*. Berrett-Koehler.

Halse, C., & Mowbray, S. (2011). The impact of the doctorate [Editorial]. *Studies in Higher Education, 36*(5), 513–525. doi:10.1080/03075079.2011.594590

Jorgensen, T. (2014). Global trends in doctoral education and the European perspective. *Journal of the European Higher Education Area, 1*, 17–34.

Kiley, M. (2011). Developments in research supervisor training: Causes and responses. *Studies in Higher Education, 36*(5), 585–599.

Lariviere, V. (2011). On the shoulders of students? The contribution of PhD students to theadvancement of knowledge. *Scientometrics, 90*(2). https://doi.org/10.1007/s11192-011-0495-6

Maistry, S. M. (2017). Betwixt and between: Liminality and dissonance in developing threshold competences for research supervision in South Africa. *South African Journal of Higher Education, 31*(1). https://doi.org/10.20853/31-1-841

McCulloch, A., & Loeser, C. (2016). Does research degree supervisor training work? The impact of a professional development induction workshop on supervision practice. *Higher Education Research & Development, 35*(5), 968–982. https://doi.org/10.1080/07294360.2016.1139547

Mesmer-Magnus, J. R., & DeChurch, L. A. (2009). Information sharing and team performance: A meta-analysis. *Journal of Applied Psychology, 94*(2), 535–546.

Reguero, M. C. J.-J., García, M. E., & Valverde, M. (2017). *Good practices in doctoral supervision: Reflections from the Tarragona think tank.* Universitat Rovira i Virgili.

Society for Research into Higher Education. (2018, December). Annual conference, Celtic Manor. https://srhe.ac.uk/events/past-events/

Taylor, S. (2016). UK Professional Standards Framework (UKPSF) dimensions of the framework for doctoral supervisors. *Higher Education Academy.* Online. https://www.teaching-matters-blog.ed.ac.uk/

Taylor, S., Kiley, M., & Holley, K. A. (Eds.). (2021). *The making of doctoral supervisors: International case studies of practice.* Routledge/Taylor and Francis.

CHAPTER 7

The Professional Development of Doctoral Supervisors through an International Lens

Isabel Huet, Diogo Casanova and Fabiane Garcia

Abstract

This chapter aims to explore the different nuances that exist in the professional development of doctoral supervisors worldwide by reflecting on the data collected through a literature review. The discussion is also informed by the personal experiences of the authors as international doctoral supervisors and upon experiences drawn from delivering training for doctoral supervisors in the UK and Portugal. The authors introduce the concept and relevance of professional development in higher education, present the methodology of the study and explore what has been written in the literature about the professional development of doctoral supervisors. Lastly, the authors discuss the case of Brazil in more detail and present the next steps of this research.

This conceptual chapter, which emerges from the literature review and autobiographical writing, sheds light on the future of professional development by reinforcing a conversational enquiry approach where learning occurs in the workplace and in communities of practice and where learning emerges as instrumental, dialogic, and self-reflective.

Keywords

professional development – professional learning – informal and formal learning – communities of practice – doctoral supervision

1 Introduction

The professional development of doctoral supervisors has been an area of growing interest because of the impact it may have on raising the quality of doctoral supervision. This quality impacts the doctoral student progression, timely completions, and attrition rates (Ives & Rowley, 2005; Van der Westhuizen & De Wet, 2002) and on the quality of the student experience (Taylor, 2018).

 | DOI:10.1163/9789004529304_007

Several studies have also indicated that the initial professional development of supervisors helps to enhance the experience of new supervisors, contributing to understanding the participants' behaviour and professional practice (McCulloch & Loeser, 2016), and to mitigate problems often associated with loneliness, insecurity, lack of rights, distress and incompetence (Emilsson & Johnsson, 2007) or the challenges imposed by international, part-time and distance doctoral candidates (Bitzer et al., 2013). Acknowledging this relevance, the authors of this chapter aimed to understand how the professional development of doctoral supervisors occurs and is valued in different parts of the world, and it was initiated by the authors' assumption that professional development, as an institutional culture that is taken for granted in some countries, may not necessarily be the same in others. For example, in the UK Quality Assurance Agency (QAA) code of practice professional development for new internal supervisors is highlighted as mandatory (Taylor, 2018) and continuous professional development (CPD) for academic staff is indeed a current and well-established practice in some UK institutions. Nevertheless, this culture of professional development for academic staff, and doctoral supervisors, specifically, is not so well established in southern European or South American countries, such as Brazil.

Moving away from this assumption that was based on the professional experience of the authors, this study presents the findings of a literature review that highlight the cultural differences of how the professional development of doctoral supervisors takes place and learning is perceived in different parts of the world, and it presents a set of recommendations based on the literature and the professional experience of the authors, for the online professional development of doctoral supervisors in the Amazonas state in Brazil.

The concept of professional development is used in this chapter as the commitment to learn in the workplace that individuals pursue to enhance their professional practice. Learning can occur either in formal, informal, or situated learning contexts (Bitzer & Matimbo, 2017; Carnevale & Goldstein, 1983; Evans, 2018; Lave & Wenger, 1991; Marsick, 1988). According to Evans (2018), informal and situated learning occurs when participants engage in the workplace with "forms of professional learning and development that are not explicitly labelled or signposted as such" (p. 6). Situated learning also occurs through social interactions where individuals engage in professional dialogues with each other to take informed decisions (van der Sluis & Huet, 2021). These professional dialogues are often promoted in communities of practice where newcomers need time to adjust and to move towards "full participation in the social-cultural practices of the community" (Lave & Wenger, 1991, p. 29).

Formal learning, on the other hand, is more explicit and usually takes place through formal training where individuals learn in more restricted groups and follow a pre-established programme.

In other words, the purpose of professional development is to instigate significant learning that can be translated into the development of an individual's skills, knowledge, and expertise that are essential for performing the job well. Learning needs to be meaningful and related to specific professional and disciplinary contexts with a focus on scholarship and (self-) reflection, which requires engagement with the relevant literature, as well as with communities of practice (Lave & Wenger, 1991; Mezirow, 1985; Sawyer, 2002; Schön, 1983).

2 Methodology

The findings presented and discussed in this chapter emerged from a systematic literature review of the manuscripts published in English and Portuguese between January 2000 and October 2020, available on EBSCO, SCOPUS, SciELO, CAPES – database of journals, thesis, and dissertations from the Brazilian Coordinating Agency for Improvement in HE Personnel, and the Portuguese Scientific Open Repository (RCAPP). This literature review is the continuation of the study conducted by the same authors in 2019 (Huet & Casanova, 2022).

The search parameters for the Portuguese literature review were translated to best address the meaning of the keywords used in the English study (Table 7.1). The idiosyncrasies of the language were addressed which led to a higher number of keywords in Portuguese. The authors also acknowledge the challenge to conduct a systematic literature review in two languages, admitting that the grey literature or even literature written in other languages may have been missed from this study. For example, no manuscripts were found related to the topic in France, Germany, Italy, Greece, or Spain among other countries. Does this mean that the professional development of supervisors is not an object of investigation or interest? Could this be related to the search parameters used in the study or to a language barrier? In summary, this literature review should be read as a first attempt to provide a holistic understanding of the topic bearing in mind these limitations.

In total, 150 manuscripts in English and 32 in Portuguese were selected for review. The authors were looking for conceptual or empirical studies published in English and Portuguese. Due to the limited scope of these studies in the Portuguese language, the search in Portuguese was expanded to published theses, dissertations, or reports (grey literature) that explored or investigated any

TABLE 7.1 Search parameters – literature review

English and Portuguese		
'phd supervisor' OR 'postgraduate supervisor' OR 'doctoral supervisor' OR 'advisor'	AND	training OR development OR 'professional development'
'orientador de doutoramento' OR 'orientador de pesquisa' OR 'supervisor de doutoramento' OR 'professor universitário' OR 'orientador de pós-graduação' OR 'orientador de doutorado'		'formação' OR 'desenvolvimento' OR 'formação pedagógica' OR 'desenvolvimento pedagógico' OR 'pedagogia'
'supervisor' OR 'advisor'	AND	'doctoral education' AND 'training' OR 'professional development' OR 'professional learning'
'orientador' OR 'orientador de doutorado' OR 'pesquisador'		'educação doutoral' OR 'formação' OR 'desenvolvimento profissional' OR 'pedagogia'

aspect related to the professional development or learning of doctoral supervisors. Manuscripts that did not explore this topic or those exploring doctoral education or supervision more broadly were removed from the analysis. These exclusion criteria resulted in the selection and analysis of 27 manuscripts written in English and 3 in Portuguese.

The analysis conducted of the manuscripts followed a deductive and inductive thematic analysis (Braun & Clarke, 2019) where the authors coded the data to find patterns of meaning and responded to three research questions: how does professional development take place in different institutions around the world? How is this shaped by national and institutional cultures? What is the impact on the professional development of supervisors? In this chapter, the authors systematised the main themes that emerged from this analysis: (i) professional development as an institutional and national culture; (ii) formal professional development; (iii) informal or situated professional development; and (iv) impact on practice.

The manuscripts selected for analysis were produced in Australasia (12), followed by the United Kingdom (9) with one co-author from Canada, and another one with co-authors from Australia, South Africa (2), Denmark (2), Sweden (1), Uganda (1) and Brazil (3).

3 Data Findings and Discussion

3.1 *Professional Development as a National and Institutional Culture*

The development of supervisors is still minimal in some countries (Amundsen & McAlpine, 2009; Baibich, 2016; Huet & Casanova, 2022; Lee, 2018) moving, from desired and not available (Amundsen & McAlpine, 2009; Rukundo, 2020), to well supported in some universities (Brew & Peseta, 2004; Kiley, 2011; McCulloch & Loeser, 2016; Taylor, 2018). Nevertheless, there is a growing awareness that supervision is a professional activity that needs to be developed over time based on the role/work of supervisors and the approaches to supervision (Halse & Malfroy, 2010; Lee, 2018; Taylor, 2018).

Most of the papers that explored the professional development of postgraduate research supervisors were produced in Australasia and the United Kingdom. This data reveals an institutional culture around the professional development of supervisors in these regions, as reported in the paper by Kiley (2011) and Taylor (2018). Professional development of supervisors and research on the topic is stronger in countries where there is a strength of theorising doctoral supervision as professional work or activity (Emilsson & Johnsson, 2007; Halse & Malfroy, 2010) and where the investment in the professional development of supervisors is strongly related to an increasing culture of accountability and quality assurance in doctoral education (Halse, 2011; Kiley, 2011), as it is the case of Australasia, the UK, and Denmark.

In the study conducted by Taylor (2018) he identified that of the 142 institutions in the UK, 56 had mandatory CPD but only 39% of the 142 required supervisors to refresh their knowledge and skills at regular intervals. Mentorships of new supervisors were required in 34 institutions. The author concludes that there is still a gap between the national guidelines and recommendations for the need to engage supervisors in CPD initiatives – which is expressed in the QAA code of practice, and what is happening in reality. As the author noted, the mandatory CPD initiatives "seem impressive in principle, but is perhaps less so in reality" (Taylor, 2018, p. 17). He highlights that, initial programmes only took a day or less which is not enough to cover the complex and demanding job of supervisors, the diversity of the student population, or the nature of the doctorates.

Findings from an international study conducted by Lee (2018) reveal that the majority of supervisors in her study did not have to undergo training to advise doctoral candidates (71% in the US and 59% in the UK).

In Denmark, professional development for academics has been an established practice since 1993 and alongside other Scandinavian countries, the professional development of supervisors has become standard practice (Raffing et al., 2017; Vehviläinen & Löfström, 2016; Wichmann-Hansen et al., 2020).

The professional development of doctoral supervisors in Uganda is still in the early stages of development (Rukundo, 2020) and in Brazil, it has not been explored or has not deserved enough attention from the academic community (Baibich, 2016; Massi & Giordan, 2017). Currently, doctoral supervisors in Brazil face major challenges in terms of managing supervisory workloads, competing for research funding, and international research collaborations which are driven to academic career and performance as determined by the country research evaluation model (Bianchetti & Quartiero, 2010; Ramos & Velho, 2013). In other words, the institutional culture in place is driven by research outputs, leaving aside the discussion around the pedagogy of the doctorate or the professional development of supervisors. Supervisors are expected to learn on-the-job – learning is perceived as situated and informal, and there is the assumption that doctoral supervisors, who are experts in their disciplines, are good supervisors by default (Baibich, 2016; Massi & Giordan, 2017). This institutional culture is therefore strongly related to the national policy for research and science, which emphasises the scientific development of academics with PhDs (Ramos & Velho, 2013).

The search made in Portuguese did not find any manuscript published by Portuguese academics. This result may be related to the fact that in Portugal, the professional development of academics, in general, is also in the early stages of development with very limited institutional investment in the professional development of doctoral supervisors or recognition from peers (Huet, 2012; Baptista et al., 2011). Doctoral supervisors admit that there is a deficit of professional conversations about the pedagogy of the doctorate, which in part is due to the lack of a culture of reflection on university pedagogy (Baptista et al., 2011; Baptista, 2013; Baptista & Huet, 2012). Professional learning of supervisors is also expected to occur on-the-job with inexperienced supervisors working in collaboration with more experienced ones. Nevertheless, this learning often replicates the practices of the more experienced ones, for good or bad with limited reflection in and on action.

3.2 *Formal Professional Development*

One of the first accredited professional development programmes for postgraduate supervisors in the UK dates back to 1998 and was a response to students' low satisfaction in terms of lacking supervisory development and any correspondent accreditation (Cryer & Mertens, 2003). Since then, institutions have been investing in the training of new supervisors with a strong focus on instrumental learning – task-oriented problem solving, with a focus on technical learning where reflection is usually that of single cause-effect as in single-loop learning (Marsick et al., 2015). The content of this training focuses primarily on the university regulations and the code of practice. There are also some references to pedagogy, diversity, students' support, and progression and completion (Taylor, 2018). In Australia, there has been an expansion of formal programmes aligned to instrumental learning, where the objective is to equip supervisors with an 'administrative framing' for doctoral supervision (McCormack, 2009). Furthermore, McCormack and Pamphilon (2004) argue that only a few programmes explicitly rely on a reflective practice model. They argue that supervisors' development needs to be more holistic and centred on the individual's conceptions and approaches to being a supervisor as well as discussing the importance of reflecting on the process of becoming critical professionals. Learning should be perceived as more dialogic and reflective in nature, rather than purely instrumental. The same approach is also defended by Brew and Peseta (2004) who encourage learning through reflection and feedback.

According to Halse (2011) formal programmes which are associated with instrumental and administrative aspects of the doctorate, often lead to a 'transmission model of learning', which views propositional knowledge as superior to experiential knowledge. This model of professional development is rooted in behaviourist models of practice where the development exists to meet the needs of an organisation with performance outcomes that need to be observable, quantifiable, and criterion-referenced (Marsick, 1988).

In this literature review, seven models or frameworks of formal professional development were found. Emilsson and Johnsson (2007) present a model of formal professional development where supervisors learn through dialogue and self-reflection. The learning process starts with the supervisor's 'perceived problem' which is then focused on the 'personal explanatory theories', including the experienced reason to the problematic situation, as imaginable solutions. These 'personal explanatory theories' are then mapped against 'theories in social science', through reflexive thinking, leading to new knowledge or new personal theories. It suggests how important is to situate the personal experiences within the literature and a more holistic understanding of students' learning and motivation. Nevertheless, Guerin, Kerr, and Green (2014) advocate that, programmes for supervisors cannot rely merely on their own experiences: "while supervisor development programmes should facilitate self-reflection on supervisors' idiosyncratic experiences of being supervised, this must be critiqued concerning contemporary challenges" (p. 116). Also, Pearson and Brew (2002) present a framework for an approach to supervisor development, based on the assumption that to discuss supervisor development it is important to understand what supervisors do and why, in particular in terms of their conceptions of research. Supervisors must extend their understanding of the nature of research and supervisory practice to deal with variations in these learning and career goals of different students and differing institutional, disciplinary, and professional contexts. There is a need for supervisors to reflect on their practice and critically engage with educational research. The conceptions of research will therefore shape their supervisory practices. For the authors, the important outcome from any professional development programme is "the development of adaptable, flexible supervisory practice based on an awareness of the broader issues associated with the induction of research students, not only into the academic community but into a world" (Pearson & Brew, 2002, p. 148).

Henderson (2017) questions how supervisors are invited to think about and represent supervision in more formal learning environments such as courses or through the readings of handbooks on supervision or the questions that researchers pose about supervision. This autobiographic study reveals the importance of development opportunities to broaden the invitations to reflect on the role of doctoral supervision, create narrative representations of supervision, and open spaces for dialogue. Learning is therefore dialogic and self-reflective in nature.

Huet and Casanova (2020) present a model of professional development for those who supervise online and distance students. According to these authors, distance or online doctoral supervision bring different challenges to the supervisory process. The authors argue that the best way to understand some of these challenges is to engage with other supervisors in online communities of practice which can occur in parallel, or sequentially, with more formal training opportunities such as workshops, seminars, accredited courses, or through a college of mentors.

Anderson et al. (2018) designed an institutional framework that has a strong focus on the pedagogy of research supervision that aims to prepare supervisors to view supervision as a form of teaching – as a 'unique pedagogy'. The authors came up with three guiding theoretically focused principles: welcoming research community; the pedagogy of supervision; and researcher development.

Brew and Peseta (2004) present the University of Sydney Postgraduate Supervision Development Programme, which is presented back then as an innovative, flexible programme delivered online and supported by face-to-face workshops and resources. This was one of the first online programmes found in this literature review, alongside the programme presented by Wisker et al. (2003).

3.3 *Informal or Situated Professional Development*

According to Amundsen and McAlpine (2009), Halse (2011), and Turner (2015), learning occurs as part of everyday working life. This type of learning is often referred to in the literature as experiential or situated (Lave & Wenger, 1991; Sawyer, 2002). These papers report that whilst formal training can include reflection and critical reflection, it may be easier to examine these phenomena where they occur more naturally, that is, through informal learning in the workplace, with this leading to reflection in and on action. The results of an empirical study conducted by Amundsen and McAlpine (2009) reveal that supervisors learn their role from and through experience and that learning occurs consistently and is often unsolicited, emerging from personal experiences, such as their own experiences as doctoral students or their own experiences as supervisors. Also, learning occurs through observation of more senior colleagues, in doctoral *Vivas*, committees, team meetings, and through informal conversations with co-supervisors or other colleagues.

Additionally, Spiller, Byrnes, and Bruce-Ferguson (2013) state that learning occurs through informal conversations in a community of practice, which is a useful approach to ensure that further discussions and more informed reflections take place. McCormack and Pamphilon (2004) explore one dimension in the development of supervisors: the power of story-dialogue group work as a catalyser for greater depth of understanding of the postgraduate experience and the supervisory relationship. They argue that the story-dialogue approach encourages participants to examine the metaphors and myths that construct the experience of postgraduate research without simply being a confessional experience. Critically reflecting within a supportive structured process, such as the one offered by the story-dialogue approach, provides individuals with the space for building their narratives that will inform and enhance the knowledge about, and quality of, postgraduate supervision. In this case, dialogue and self-reflection are interrelated: the dialogue between supervisors leads to a process of self-reflection involving an act of looking at the past from the present with an eye to the future. McCormack (2009) also argues that storytelling approaches, such as telling, receiving, reading, writing, and re-writing stories can create an environment for doctoral supervisors to negotiate the chaotic pedagogy of becoming and being a doctoral supervisor.

With a very similar approach, Turner (2015) believes that the experience of sharing supervisors' Journey Plots, depicting the high and low points of their supervisory experience with their students, helps supervisors to identify what they have learned and what might be useful for shaping other supervisory experiences.

3.4 *Impact of the CPD*

Evaluation of the impact of professional development programmes is still scarce (McCulloch & Loeser, 2016) despite the growing accountability culture of measuring the quality of academic work in institutions. McCulloch and Loeser (2016) unpack the concepts of 'impact' and 'evaluation' and assess the medium and longer-term impact of a doctoral supervisory induction programme in an Australian University. They suggest that the programme leads to the acquisition of supervisors' understanding and knowledge and they report that, for the majority of attendees, the programme had an impact on supervisory practices.

A study conducted in Denmark (Wichmann-Hansen et al., 2020) points towards a positive impact of the long-term professional development of more experienced supervisors. The authors conclude that supervisors' initial resistance and passivity towards their participation in the programme decreased as they progressed throughout the year and admitting that, in the end, they learned significantly more than expected. Overall, this long-term and mandatory professional development programme had a positive impact on supervisors' competence development and learning, the institutional supervision culture, and it indicated a possible, though indirect, effect on doctoral students' satisfaction with their supervisors.

Some other studies presented a positive impact of formal programmes for the professional learning of supervisors (Brew & Peseta, 2004; Emilsson & Johnsson, 2007; Halse, 2011; McCulloch & Loeser, 2016; Raffing et al., 2017). As Anderson et al. (2018) indicate, this learning helps supervisors to develop their skills and knowledge of supervision, as well as enabling them to become increasingly aware of their students' needs, interests, and abilities. Brew and Peseta (2004) believe that overall, the formal programme for postgraduate research supervisors promoted and enhanced the quality of postgraduate education in the University of Sydney. There was evidence that the programme developed the supervisory skills of supervisors, improved their ability to manage the supervisory process, and ensured that supervisors know the university's policies for postgraduate study (Brew & Peseta, 2004).

An evaluation study conducted by Kandlbinder (2005) demonstrates that it is the supervisors' reflection about their supervision practice that has the greatest impact on what they do with their students. Self-reflection is therefore the most important learning form to promote change in practice.

Despite this positive impact on professional learning, there has also been some opposition or resistance to the professional development for supervisors (Halse, 2011; Spiller et al., 2013). For instance, Halse (2011) refers to a growing body of literature that points to the continuing resistance of supervisors to undertake formal professional development, particularly among senior supervisors. This resistance is related to the omission of pedagogy in existing professional development programmes, which are often focused on instrumental and administrative aspects of the doctorate, areas that are seen by senior supervisors as unattractive. This focus is often a result of a culture of increased accountability and quality assurance in doctoral education in different countries around the world (Halse, 2011; Kiley, 2011). Roumell and Bolliger (2017), for example, found that supervisors were not satisfied with the institutional support they received, even though most believed their institutions value the quality of the supervision of doctoral students. In summary, professional development needs to be carefully thought through to address the needs and motivations of supervisors, allowing them to cope with the changing nature of the doctorate, diverse student population, and modes of delivery.

4 Conclusion and Further Studies for the Brazilian Context

The professional development of doctoral supervisors occurs in different forms and is shaped by the different national and institutional cultures and policies as also explored in Chapter 6 of this book (Denicolo, Reeves, & Duke, 2022). Learning and continuous professional development, although considered important for the enhancement of doctoral supervision, is not always clearly assumed, or established in many institutions where the professionalisation of higher education is not widely adopted or where there is still a strong focus on research productivity for the recognition or academic progression of academics as it is the case in Brazil or Portugal. While in some countries the formal development of supervisors exists and is an important dimension for the professional development of staff, other countries do not offer the same developmental opportunities for their academic staff. The professional development of doctoral supervisors is rare, exists in isolated initiatives, or is still inexistent in many universities worldwide (Huet & Casanova, 2022; Massi & Giordan, 2017; Rukundo, 2020).

Professional development activities need to be meaningful and related to specific professional and disciplinary contexts with a focus on scholarship and (self-)reflection, which requires a vigorous engagement with the relevant literature, as well as with communities of practice where supervisors can discuss their experiences with peers (Halse & Malfroy, 2010; Lave & Wenger, 1991; Mezirow, 1985; Sawyer, 2002; Schön, 1983). Also, the recognition and support of senior management and the necessary cultural transformation are essential to promote long-term engagement and therefore, contributing to a 'true' change of the professional development culture in the institution.

In Brazil, professional learning of doctoral supervisors is not a common topic of discussion. From the analysis of the literature review and also from the experience of the authors in this field, the authors believe that professional learning is targeted only to teaching and learning, in other words, for those who teach at undergraduate or postgraduate programmes (Behrens & Junges, 2016; da Silva Silva & Klüber, 2012; Meyer et al., 2018; Nóbrega, 2018; Rivas et al., 2009). Doctoral supervision is not considered a form of teaching in these countries. There is an assumption among the academic community that doctoral supervisors know how to become good doctoral supervisors, independently of their experience as supervisors (Baibich, 2016). Doctoral supervisors live in an academic culture where their scientific knowledge and academic recognition are expressed in their research outcomes and internationalisation (Ramos & Velho, 2013). This is still the key factor to become a doctoral supervisor. The professional development of doctoral supervisors is therefore strongly supported in their development as researchers.

Supervisors are the 'gatekeepers of science', guiding the students through the maze of the doctorate and facilitating their academic enculturation and emancipation (Lee, 2018). In other words, doctoral supervisors are expected to offer their students a sense of belonging to the discipline and the academic culture and to enable the candidates to become autonomous researchers. Bearing in mind this academic culture, formal professional development may be seen as something not needed or, as already reported in other studies (Halse, 2011; Manathunga, 2005; Spiller et al., 2013), supervisors may resist participating since they may consider 'others' to be invading their pedagogical space or academic domain; or it is needed but not considered to be a priority since the number of research outputs that need to be produced takes most of their time (Oscar & Bastos, 2011).

In order to change this academic culture in Brazil, the authors, as part of a broader project funded by the UK Academies and CONFAP-CNPq & FAPEAM, will investigate the needs of doctoral supervisors in the Amazonas state with a focus on professional learning. This needs analysis will then form the basis for the development of a theoretical framework for promoting the professional learning of doctoral supervisors in Brazil.

The next step is to run a pilot study to develop a form of professional learning with a group of postgraduate research supervisors in the Amazon region followed by a longitudinal study where the authors will monitor the changes in practice and the capacity of supervisors to reflect in and on action.

Acknowledgements

The authors would like to thank the UK-Academies and CONFAP-CONFAP-CNPq & FAPEAM for funding this research.

References

Amundsen, C., & McAlpine, L. (2009). 'Learning supervision': Trial by fire. *Innovations in Education & Teaching International, 46*(3). https://doi.org/10.1080/14703290903068805

Anderson, M., Mitchell, B., Northcote, M., Williams, A., & Petrie, K. (2018). The construction of a postgraduate student and supervisor support framework: Using stakeholder voices to promote effective postgraduate teaching and learning practice. *Journal of University Teaching and Learning Practice, 15*(2). https://doi.org/10.53761/1.15.2.6

Baibich, T. M. (2016). Orientação de doutorado: uma relação tão delicada. *ANPED*, 1–16.

Baptista, A. V., Huet, I., & Jenkins, A. (2011). Quality of doctoral supervision: supervisors' conceptions of learning, supervision and students' profiles. In N. Jackson, L. Frick, C. Nygaard, & N. Courtney (Eds.), *Postgraduate education: Form and function* (pp. 43–58). Libri Publishing.

Baptista, A. (2013). *Qualidade do Processo de Supervisão da Investigação Doutoral* [Tese de Doutoramento]. Universidade de Aveiro, Aveiro.

Baptista, A. V., & Huet, I. (2012). Postgraduate research supervision quality: Rethinking the value of doctoral supervision to design an integrative framework. *International Journal of Learning, 18*(5), 175–194.

Behrens, M. A., & Junges, K. dos S. (2016). Uma formação pedagógica inovadora como caminho para a construção de saberes docentes no Ensino Superior. *Educar Em Revista, 56*, 211–229.

Bianchetti, L., & Quartiero, E. M. (2010). Researchers under pressure: A comparative study of new forms of producing, advising and transmitting knowledge in Brazil and the European Union. *European Educational Research Journal, 9*(4), 498–509. https://doi.org/10.2304/eerj.2010.9.4.498

Bitzer, E. M., Trafford, V. N., & Leshem, S. (2013). "Love it when you speak foreign": A trans-national perspective on the professional development of doctoral supervisors in South Africa. *South African Journal of Higher Education, 27*(4), 781–796. https://hdl.handle.net/10520/EJC150427

Bitzer, E., & Matimbo, F. (2017). Cultivating African academic capital – Intersectional narratives of an African graduate and his PhD study supervisor. *Innovations in Education & Teaching International, 54*(6), 539–549. https://doi.org/10.1080/14703297.2017.1304825

Braun, V., & Clarke, V. (2019). Reflecting on reflexive thematic analysis. *Qualitative Research in Sport, Exercise and Health, 11*(4), 589–597. https://doi.org/10.1080/2159676X.2019.1628806

Brew, A., & Peseta, T. (2004). Changing postgraduate supervision practice: A programme to encourage learning through reflection and feedback. *Innovations in Education and Teaching International, 41*(1), 5–22. https://doi.org/10.1080/1470329032000172685

Carnevale, A. P., & Goldstein, H. (1983). *Employee training: Its changing role and an analysis of new data*. American Society for Training and Development.

Cryer, P., & Mertens, P. (2003). The PhD examination: Support and training for supervisors and examiners. *Quality Assurance in Education, 11*(2), 92–99. https://doi.org/10.1108/09684880310471515

da Silva Silva, V., & Klüber, T. E. (2012). Formação e docência no ensino superior: uma meta-análise de artigos publicados em revistas brasileiras de educação [Formation and teaching in higher education: A meta-analysis of articles published in revistas brasileiras de educação]. *Acta Scientiarum. Education, 34*(1), 87–97. https://www.redalyc.org/pdf/3033/303325322006.pdf

Emilsson, U. M., & Johnsson, E. (2007). Supervision of supervisors: On developing supervision in postgraduate education. *Higher Education Research & Development, 26*(2), 163–179. https://doi.org/10.1080/07294360701310797

Evans, L. (2018). Implicit and informal professional development: What it 'looks like', how it occurs, and why we need to research it. *Professional Development in Education, 5257*, 1–14. https://doi.org/10.1080/19415257.2018.1441172

Guerin, C., Kerr, H., & Green, I. (2014). Supervision pedagogies: Narratives from the field. *Teaching in Higher Education*. https://doi.org/10.1080/13562517.2014.957271

Halse, C. (2011). "Becoming a supervisor": The impact of doctoral supervision on supervisors' learning. *Studies in Higher Education, 36*(5), 557–570. https://doi.org/10.1080/03075079.2011.594593

Halse, C., & Malfroy, J. (2010). Retheorizing doctoral supervision as professional work. *Studies in Higher Education, 35*(1), 79–92. https://doi.org/10.1080/03075070902906798

Huet, I. (2012). Academic development as a strategy to enhance teaching quality in research intensive universities: The Portuguese context. *Higher Education Research Network Journal, 5*, 9–18.

Huet, I., & Casanova, D. (2020). Exploring the professional development of online and distance doctoral supervisors. *Innovations in Education and Teaching International*, 1–11. https://doi.org/10.1080/14703297.2020.1742764

Huet, I., & Casanova, D. (2022). Exploring the professional development of doctoral supervisors through workplace learning: A literature review. *Higher Education Research & Development, 41*(3), 774–788. https://doi.org/10.1080/07294360.2021.1877629

Ives, G., & Rowley, G. (2005). Supervisor selection or allocation and continuity of supervision: Ph.D. students' progress and outcomes. *Studies in Higher Education*. https://doi.org/10.1080/03075070500249161

Kandlbinder, P. (2005). Postgraduate supervisor development through ICT. In *Quality issues in ICT-based higher education*. https://doi.org/10.4324/9780203416198

Kiley, M. (2011). Developments in research supervisor training: Causes and responses. *Studies in Higher Education, 36*(5), 585–599. https://doi.org/10.1080/03075079.2011.594595

Lave, J., & Wenger, E. (1991). *Situated learning: Legitimate peripheral participation*. Cambridge university press.

Lee, A. (2018). How can we develop supervisors for the modern doctorate? *Studies in Higher Education, 43*(5), 878–890. https://doi.org/10.1080/03075079.2018.1438116

Manathunga, C. (2005). Early warning signs in postgraduate research education: A different approach to ensuring timely completions. *Teaching in Higher Education, 10*(2), 219–233. https://doi.org/10.1080/1356251042000337963

Marsick, V. J. (1988). Learning in the workplace: The case for reflectivity and critical reflectivity. *Adult Education Quarterly, 38*(4), 187–198. https://doi.org/10.1177%2F0001848188038004001

Marsick, V. J., Watkins, K., & Watkins, K. (2015). *Informal and incidental learning in the workplace (Routledge revivals)*. Routledge. https://doi.org/10.4324/9781315715926

Massi, L., & Giordan, M. (2017). Formação do orientador de pesquisas acadêmicas: um estudo bibliográfico nacional e internacional. *Revista Brasileira de Pós-Graduação, 14*.

McCormack, C. (2009). Stories return personal narrative ways of knowing to the professional development of doctoral supervisors. *Studies in Continuing Education, 31*(2), 141–156. https://doi.org/10.1080/01580370902927485

McCormack, C., & Pamphilon, B. (2004). More than a confessional: Postmodern groupwork to support postgraduate supervisors' professional development. *Innovations in Education and Teaching International, 41*(1), 23–37. https://doi.org/10.1080/1470329032000172694

McCulloch, A., & Loeser, C. (2016). Does research degree supervisor training work? The impact of a professional development induction workshop on supervision practice. *Higher Education Research and Development, 35*(5), 968–982. https://doi.org/10.1080/07294360.2016.1139547

Meyer, P., Vosgerau, D. S. anna R., & Borges, C. (2018). Colaboração entre pares em programas de desenvolvimento profissional docente. *Praxis Educativa, 13*(2), 312–329. https://doi.org/10.5212/PraxEduc.v.13i2.0004

Mezirow, J. (1985). A critical theory of self-directed learning. *New Directions for Adult and Continuing Education, 25*, 17–30. https://doi.org/10.1002/ace.36719852504

Nóbrega, M. H. da. (2018). Orientandos e Orientadores no Século XXI: desafios da pós-graduação. *Educação & Realidade, 43*(3), 1055–1076. https://doi.org/10.1590/2175-623674407

Oscar, S. C. de, & Bastos, J. C. (2011). "Estado da Arte" da profissão docente: I Colóquio Internacional sobre o ensino superior(2008). *IV EDIPE-Encontro Estadual de Didática e Prática de Ensino, 2008*, 16.

Pearson, M., & Brew, A. (2002). Research Training and Supervision Development. *Studies in Higher Education, 27*(2), 135–150. https://doi.org/10.1080/03075070220119986c

Raffing, R., Jensen, T. B., & Tønnesen, H. (2017). Self-reported needs for improving the supervision competence of PhD supervisors from the medical sciences in Denmark. *BMC Medical Education, 17*(1). https://doi.org/10.1186/s12909-017-1023-z

Ramos, M. Y., & Velho, L. (2013). Formação de doutores no Brasil: o esgotamento do modelo vigente frente aos desafios colocados pela emergência do sistema global de ciência. *Avaliação: Revista Da Avaliação Da Educação Superior* (*Campinas*), *18*(1), 219–246. https://doi.org/10.1590/s1414-40772013000100012

Rivas, N. P. P., Mello, K., Marques, C. A., & Leal, M. A. I. (2009). A formaçao pedagógica do docente para a educaçao superior: algumas aproximaçoes. *Cuadernos de Educación*, 313–324.

Roumell, E. A. L., & Bolliger, D. U. (2017). Experiences of faculty with doctoral student supervision in programs delivered via distance. *Journal of Continuing Higher Education, 65*(2), 82–93. https://doi.org/10.1080/07377363.2017.1320179

Rukundo, A. (2020). A comparative analysis of a pathway model and manuals to assess efficiency of pedagogical training in doctoral supervision in Uganda. *Innovations in Education and Teaching International, 57*(1), 29–37. https://doi.org/10.1080/14703297.2019.1657033

Sawyer, R. D. (2002). Situating teacher development: The view from two teachers' perspectives. *International Journal of Educational Research, 37*(8), 733–753.

Schön, D. (1983). *The reflective practitioner: How professionals think in action.* Basic Books.

Spiller, D., Byrnes, G., & Bruce-Ferguson, P. (2013). Enhancing postgraduate supervision through a process of conversational inquiry. *Higher Education Research and Development, 32*(5), 833–845. https://doi.org/10.1080/07294360.2013.776519

Taylor, S. (2018). *Eligibility to supervise: A study of UK institutions.* UKCGE.

Turner, G. (2015). Learning to supervise: Four journeys. *Innovations in Education and Teaching International, 52*(1), 86–98. https://doi.org/10.1080/14703297.2014.981840

Van der Sluis, H., & Huet, I. (2021). Providing opportunities for professional learning: A sketch of professional development in the UK. In I. Huet, T. Pessoa, & F. Murta (Eds.), *Excellence in teaching and learning in higher education: Institutional policies, research and practices in Europe.* Coimbra University Press.

Van der Westhuizen, P., & De Wet, J. (2002). The training needs of supervisors of postgraduate students in the social sciences and humanities. *South African Journal of Higher Education, 16*(3), 185–195. https://doi.org/10.4314/sajhe.v16i3.25231

Vehviläinen, S., & Löfström, E. (2016). 'I wish I had a crystal ball': Discourses and potentials for developing academic supervising. *Studies in Higher Education, 41*(3), 508–524. https://doi.org/10.1080/03075079.2014.942272

Wichmann-Hansen, G., Godskesen, M., & Kiley, M. (2020). Successful development programs for experienced doctoral supervisors – What does it take? *International Journal for Academic Development*, 25(2), 176–188. https://doi.org/10.1080/1360144X.2019.1663352

Wisker, G., Waller, S., Richter, U., Robinson, G., Trafford, V., Wicks, K., & Warnes, M. (2003). On nurturing hedgehogs : Developments online for distance and offshore supervision. In *Learning for an unknown future: 26th Annual HERDSA Conference.*

CHAPTER 8

Towards a Person-Centred Discourse in Doctoral Supervisor Development

Matthew Sillence

Abstract

This chapter employs critical discourse analysis to examine the language of national and institutional policy and practice documents. These texts inform the design of doctoral supervisor continuing professional development at one UK university and appear to reflect a bias favouring regulatory processes over people. Although rhetoric emphasises systems and functional interactions between supervisors and doctoral researchers, this study identifies themes that frequently relate to personhood. It proposes a model of supervisor development that engages with disciplinary knowledge, the workplace and institution through person-centred pedagogy.

Keywords

supervisors – discourse – pedagogy

1 Introduction

In the United Kingdom, supervisor development is influenced by both national and institutional policy and practice documentation, with most professional development programmes focusing on regulatory and pedagogical matters rather than doctoral researcher support and development (Taylor, 2021, p. 186), reflecting observations from the literature review by Huet, Casanova and Garcia in the previous chapter. The increasing scholarship around supervisor continuing professional development (CPD) emerges in tandem with concerns about the working conditions of doctoral researchers before and during the Covid-19 pandemic (Metcalfe, Wilson, & Levecque, 2018; Office for Students, 2020), which is explored by Reeves in Chapter 10.

 | DOI:10.1163/9789004529304_008

2 Research Aims

The premise of this chapter is that texts play a key role in CPD. They can be examined not simply for factual information, but for rhetoric, reflecting the views of McCulloch in Chapter 2 and Lu in Chapter 4 that the language used to describe higher education policies and practices affect how individuals experience the university. Adopting criteria from critical discourse analysis (hereafter, CDA), it aims to:

- Demonstrate how the language of national and institutional policy documents and reports construct ideas of the doctoral process and the researcher;
- Demonstrate how the language of materials for supervisor CPD within the Faculty of Arts and Humanities constructs the doctoral process and researcher;
- Identify the pedagogical affordances and constraints of these ideas of doctoral education;
- Propose a realignment of policy, procedure and pedagogy in supervisor CPD to address these constraints.

3 Managerialism in Doctoral Education

A focus on regulation in higher education has been associated with the wider ideological and organisational trends of 'New Management' and 'New Public Management' (Deem, Hillyard, & Reed, 2007). Ronald Barnett has also identified the growing complexity of administrative procedures within the UK university (2011, p. 46), which is leading to the kind of 'super-complexity' that Denicolo, Reeves and Duke note in Chapter 6 (Denicolo, Reeves, & Duke, 2022). Within a doctoral context, 'managerialism' encourages researchers to organise their personal and professional lives to obviate problems (Kelly, 2017, pp. 49–51). This discourse interprets events, such as the non-completion of a thesis, as a form of 'mis-management' (Owler, 2010). From an institutional perspective, the doctorate itself can appear distinctly and inherently entropic.

4 Modelling Doctoral Education

Doctoral education, however, is not a system of self-managing individuals. Elliott et al. (2020), building on Barnett (2016, pp. 135–136), have drawn attention to a complex ecosystem of academic, emotional, social and psychological support. The 'Doctoral Learning Ecology Model' (hereafter, DLEM) outlines

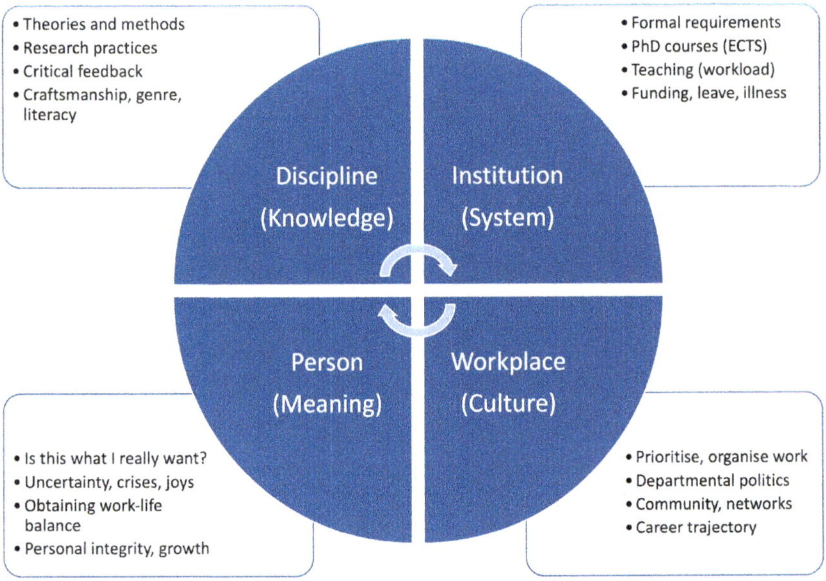

FIGURE 8.1 Doctoral Learning Ecology Model (© Elliot, Bengtsen, Guccione, & Kobayashi, 2020; reproduced with permission of the authors)

four domains: discipline, institution, workplace, and person. Together these form a holistic, and potentially more realistic, view of doctoral education as it is experienced by doctoral researchers.

5 Doctoral Pedagogy

Over the last two decades, educationalists have explored ways of facilitating doctoral learning. For example, supervisors may employ active listening techniques, which involve attending to the words and behaviour of the student, seeking clarification and adopting a non-judgemental attitude (Bengtsen, 2016; Godskesen & Wichmann-Hansen, 2013). Psychologist and educationalist, Carl Rogers, outlined the benefit of active listening for both learning and wellbeing (Rogers, 1980, pp. 116, 155). Even when disciplinary knowledge is discussed, an individual may feel valued, or 'prized' by being heard (Bengtsen, 2016, pp. 115–121; Rogers, 1980, pp. 151, 271–272).

Doctoral researchers can also develop 'academic literacies'. This involves examining what counts as knowledge, the identity and position of the researcher. It may also address uncomfortable 'truths', namely the power relations involved in research activity, or the reason for different approaches in different fields (Bastalich et al., 2014; Magyar & Robinson-Pant, 2011).

There is also a value of modelling academic behaviours and thought processes explicitly through 'cognitive apprenticeship'. This approach makes tacit knowledge explicit, and helps doctoral researchers manage this quantitatively and qualitatively (Austin, 2009; Collins & Kapur, 2006; Posselt, 2018). Affective and cognitive experiences can be channelled through reflective writing to enhance doctoral researchers' annual progress reviews (Brew & Peseta, 2004; Cahusac de Caux et al., 2017; Manathunga et al., 2010), whilst at the same time supporting supervisors.[1]

Each of these aspects of doctoral learning stress student support and development and are essentially person-centred. Researcher developers have advocated person-centred models for doctoral students (Elliott et al., 2020, pp. 45–59), but it appears that discourse in supervisor CPD in UK universities has yet to follow the same path.

6 Methodology

6.1 *Dataset*

Between 2010 and 2012, in the Faculty of Arts and Humanities at the University of East Anglia, supervisors were briefed on key institutional policies and procedures, including monthly reporting mechanisms, annual progress reviews, probationary requirements and interruptions to study. From 2013, the Faculty created fictional scenarios to exemplify problems that can emerge during a doctorate (Eley & Jennings, 2005).

The dataset comprised 30 documents, produced by 5 different organisations: the Quality Assurance Agency for Higher Education (QAA), Research Councils UK (RCUK, now UK Research and Innovation), the University of East Anglia (UEA), the UK Council for Graduate Education (UKCGE), and Vitae. The form of each document varied, and included those in PDF, Microsoft Word and PowerPoint. All national policy documents considered in this study are in the public domain, accessible as current documents, or archived through the Web Archive. The training materials are not publicly available and were produced by the researcher as scripts for screencasts, worksheets and guidance documents. The research protocol was reviewed and approved in 2020 by the Faculty Research Ethics Sub-Committee.

As this study is concerned with the analysis of language, each document format required conversion to raw text and was imported into qualitative data analysis software (NVivo).[2] Due to the relatively small number of documents, conversion errors (such as character encoding, leading or trailing white space, or split words) were amended manually.

6.2 *Word Frequency Analysis*

Word frequency analysis was performed in NVivo for the 1,000 most frequent words in the source texts. This performed a count of each word and generated a weighted percentage based on all words in each document. Stop words were applied by default, with some manually added that were common but not necessarily meaningful in this context, such as 'education' or 'research'.

The second stage involved thematic coding of words with a count of ≧ 100 (0.18–3.63% weighted values). Words with a count of < 100 were also coded and, where appropriate, merged (as in the case of synonyms) or created as sub-codes. The code book was revised fourteen times and reviewed by another colleague, who categorised these independently to form higher-level themes.

6.3 *Critical Discourse Analysis*

The purpose of CDA is the identification of rhetorical features in texts to demonstrate (1) how social issues are constructed/reflected; (2) how institutional power relations are negotiated and performed; and (3) how certain ideologies are produced and reinforced. Paltridge and Hyland's (Paltridge, 2012, pp. 186–203) CDA framework is a systematic search for features that signal the genre of a text, namely the framing of a particular domain and relevance for a particular audience. It explores the connotations of key words and phrases to establish related topics and higher-level themes.

CDA highlights how certain topics are addressed more frequently and prominently (foregrounding), and others less so (backgrounding). It considers the ways in which these topics are introduced across each genre, and how individuals who act or are subject to action (agents and patients) are addressed and discussed. CDA is also concerned with linguistic elements, such as modal verbs, that convey not simply action but intention, such as 'should' or 'must'. Certain words can be indicators of formality and certainty, such as 'obligation' or 'possibility'. Phrases that signify increased specificity or definition such as roles, groups or categories.

The following section introduces the findings from the dataset for each rhetorical feature: genre, connotation, foregrounding, backgrounding, topicalisation, agent-patient relations, levels of formality, degrees of certainty, levels of technicality. The final part of this chapter provides a discussion of these findings in relation to the four research aims outlined in the introduction.

7 Findings

7.1 *Genre*

Genres of texts are crucial to CDA and can be determined by both domain and audience. Document domain can be either explicit, such as the word 'policy'

TABLE 8.1 Documents mapped to genre sub-domains, and examples of readers

	National	Institutional
Policy	Quality assurance (6) *Managers* *Directors*	Research degree policies (13) *Supervisors* *Managers* *Directors* *Students*
Practice	Supervisor CPD (2) *Supervisors* *Managers* *Directors*	Code of practice (1) *Supervisors* *Students*
		Supervisor CPD (8) *Supervisors*

in the title of the document, or implicit, conveyed elsewhere in the body of the document. The documents in this study fall into two domains: policy and practice. The context of use also allows these domains to be sub-divided into national and institutional levels. An example of the types of documents assembled for this study have been mapped to the matrix in Table 8.1, with the number of documents in parentheses.

Documents are produced by national regulatory bodies and the university, but they are designed for different readers, shown here in italics. Institutional supervisor CPD, for example, is very specifically aimed at academic staff within that institution, but supervisor CPD at a national level may be read by supervisors, managers or directors of departments or Graduate Schools or Colleges. Whereas some readers may move between sub-domains, postgraduate researchers – who are not employees of the university in the UK – may be more concerned with certain sub-domains and not others.

7.2 *Connotation*

The possible meanings of words are interpreted based on context and coded accordingly. For example, 'experience' may be discussed in relation to level of academic development rather than as a broader existential category. Table 8.2 lists the higher-level codes created in NVivo. These have been separated into key themes and rhetorical features from CDA.

The coding distribution across the 30 texts varies. 'Activities' covers all 30 documents, as do references to 'degree courses' (30), followed by 'labour' (28) and more abstract themes, namely 'ontological' (28), 'processual', 'relational'

TABLE 8.2 Themes and rhetorical features of the CDA framework

Code	CDA features
Activities	Agent-patient relations
Collaborative	Degrees of certainty
Course	Levels of formality
Epistemological	Levels of technicality
Experiential	
Interpersonal	
Labour	
Metrics	
Obstacles	
Ontological	
Processual	
Psychological	
Relational	
Subjectivity	

(27), 'collaborative', 'epistemological', 'experiential' (26). The codes that cover fewer texts (≦ 25) comprise 'pedagogical' (25), 'metrics' (22), 'interpersonal' (21), 'obstacles' (20), 'subjectivity' (16) and 'psychology' (14).

Word frequency analysis is the method used to determine whether or not certain themes are foregrounded or backgrounded. The reordering of the themes by total number of references reveal a split between those above 500 and those below 400.

7.3 *Foregrounding*

The most frequent codes (> 500) are categorised as foregrounded themes. The most frequent are 'collaborative' (717), 'pedagogical' (653), 'course' (617), 'activities' (556), 'experiential' (537), 'labour' (524), and 'processual' (514). Although each of these themes encompasses a variety of sub-codes, they all appear to focus on the educational system.

7.4 *Backgrounding*

The themes that appear less frequently (see Figures 8.2 and 8.3) in the dataset (<400) are 'relational' (395), 'ontological' (381), 'obstacles' (309), 'interpersonal'

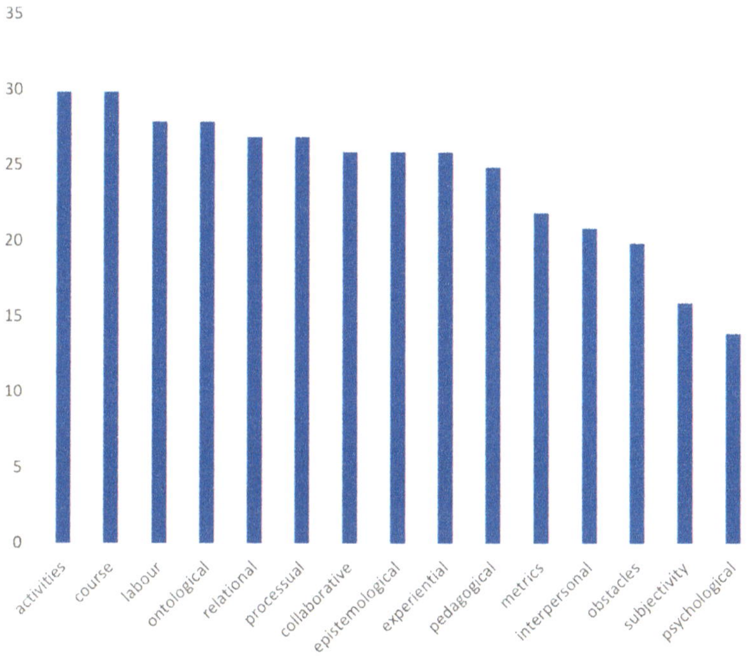

FIGURE 8.2 Number of documents per theme in the dataset

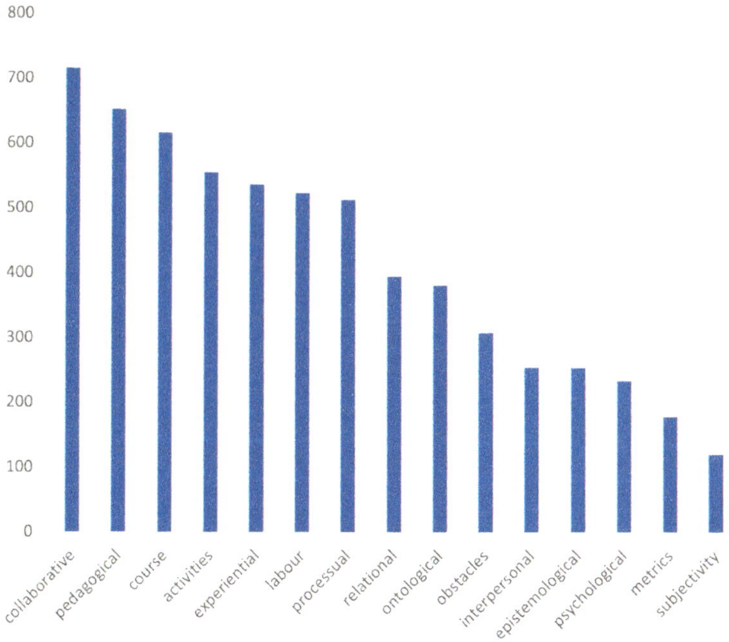

FIGURE 8.3 Number of references per theme in the dataset

(255), 'epistemological' (254), 'psychological' (234), 'metrics' (179), and 'subjectivity' (121). Unlike the foregrounded themes, these are primarily existential, concerned more with lived experience. There are two significant features of the backgrounded themes. The first is that of all of the 'relational' sub-codes that connote communication, the most significant omission is 'listening'. Secondly, under the theme 'obstacles' the sub-code 'problem' is mentioned only 36 times, with the more generic term 'issues' appearing much more frequently (116), followed by 'concerns' (38), 'difficulty' (30), 'stress' (28) and 'conflict' (23). This is much lower relative to other themes than anticipated.

7.5 *Topicalisation*

The thematic overview above provides a picture of word frequency across the dataset. It does not, however, demonstrate how topics are addressed in different genres. This section demonstrates the percentage of references for foregrounded themes according to the genre matrix above: national policy, institutional policy, national practice and institutional practice.

Table 8.3 reveals a number of significant points. Firstly, 'collaborative' sub-codes that address how individuals work together are more prominent at a national level than within institutional documents. 'Pedagogical' sub-codes also feature more prominently at national policy level than in other sub-domains. There is also a marked distinction between national and institutional levels for three themes: 'experiential', 'labour' and 'processual'. This suggests that national policy and practice texts address the educational system to a greater degree than do institutional texts.

TABLE 8.3 Foregrounded themes coverage in genre sub-domains

	National policy	National practice	Institutional Policy	Institutional Practice
Collaborative	7.3%	9.3%	3.3%	1.76%
Pedagogical	6.03%	3.18%	2.61%	3.65%
Course	1.52%	3.9%	4.09%	2.88%
Activities	3.13%	4.38%	3.4%	0.78%
Experiential	3.53%	3.13%	1.18%	1.71%
Labour	2.51%	2.82%	0.98%	0.59%
Processual	3.56%	2.23%	0.63%	0.88%

TABLE 8.4 Coverage of agents/patients across the genre sub-domains

	National policy	National practice	Institutional policy	Institutional practice
Student	17.2%	7.4%	4.61%	11.64%
Institution	0.84%	0.91%	2.42%	0.75%
Supervisor	3.73%	13.15%	1.99%	5.53%
Postgraduate researchers	2.78%	0.43%	0%	0%
Candidate	0.53%	8.61%	5.21%	1.39%

TABLE 8.5 Matrix query of references for doctoral researchers, supervisors and the institution

	Supervisor	Institution
Student	108	34
Candidate	27	9
Postgraduate researchers	41	33

7.6 *Agent-Patient Relations*

The subjects of the policy and practice texts are namely those who act (agents) and receive, respond or are subject to actions (patients). Both feature prominently in the texts across the genres, averaging 23.95% of all references coded. The terms which feature most prominently are 'students' (757), 'institutions' (479), and 'supervisors' (451). Related terms include 'postgraduate researchers' (309) and 'candidates' (267), which have been disaggregated from 'student' as they hold different connotations, which are treated in the discussion below. Table 8.4 summarises the percentage coverage of these references across the four genres.

The coincidence of each of these entities can also be revealed through matrix coding, with 'student'/'candidate'/'postgraduate researcher' forming one axis, and 'institution'/'supervisor' the other. Table 8.5 shows the number of intersecting references between each entity.

The highest co-occurrence is between the terms 'student' and 'supervisor', which is of particular importance for this study for the supervisor CPD. Excerpts from the dataset suggest that students and supervisors are presented in five ways:

Contact	... contact between research student and supervisor varies depending on ... (ed_21)
Relationship	If a research student-supervisor relationship is not working well ... (ed_01)
Agreement	Supervisors and research students agree between ... (ed_21)
Responsibility	Research students and supervisors are jointly responsible ... (ed_21)
Awareness and communication	... for ensuring that students and supervisors are aware of ... (ed_06)

When these figures are mapped to the genre matrix, the highest coincidence of doctoral researcher and supervisor is within national policy (94), followed by institutional practice (8), national practice (3), and institutional policy (3). The term 'candidate' does not co-occur with 'supervisor' at all within national policy texts, but does appear in national practice documents (14), followed by institutional practice (12) and only rarely in institutional policy (1). Significantly, 'postgraduate researcher' and 'supervisor' co-occurrences are completely absent in institutional policy and practice documents, and for national practice, but they feature more prominently in national policy (41).

7.7 *Levels of Formality*

Formal language averages 9.85% across the four genres of the dataset. The most frequent are terms related to 'regulation' (992), 'health' (298), 'permission' (192), 'appropriateness' (171), and 'obligation' (128) (see Table 8.6).

How each of these formal themes apply to the different agents in the dataset is summarised in Table 8.7.

The highest coincidences of themes for each agent are 'regulation'/'student' (112), 'health'/'postgraduate researchers' (90), 'regulation'/'candidate' (45),

TABLE 8.6 Levels of formality coverage in genre sub-domains

	National policy	National practice	Institutional policy	Institutional practice
Regulation	3.38%	2.82%	3.11%	2.88%
Health	2.49%	1.33%	0.2%	0.2%
Permission	1.69%	0.8%	2.56%	1.31%
Appropriateness	1.02%	0.32%	0.72%	0.18%
Obligation	0.15%	0%	0.18%	0.25%

TABLE 8.7 Matrix query of levels of formality and agent/patient

	Candidate	Institution	Postgraduate researchers	Student	Supervisor
Appropriateness	7	0	2	30	15
Health	0	28	90	32	25
Obligation	6	3	0	12	4
Permission	10	7	2	36	29
Regulation	45	12	9	112	29

'permission'/'student' (36), 'health'/'student' (32), and 'appropriateness'/'student' (30).

Regulatory language covers a range of phenomena relating to 'student' or 'candidate', including 'appeal', 'complaints', 'examination', 'probation', 'progress', 'registration', 'review', 'rules', 'submission', 'supervision' and 'suspension'.

Most references within the 'health'/'postgraduate researchers' or 'student' categories mention mental health and wellbeing and are limited to 5 out of the 30 documents in the dataset.

Permissive language relates to situations in which doctoral researchers can exercise choice or initiate a process:

> Students may choose to register for … (ed_21)

> Full-time students may undertake paid employment … (td_01)

Language addressing 'appropriateness' involving doctoral researchers casts the latter in the role of patient (receiving or subject to action), with the agent being the higher education provider, supervisors or particular processes:

> Providers ensure that each student has an appropriately skilled and knowledgeable supervisory team … (ed_01)

> Research students have appropriate opportunities for developing research, personal and professional skill … (ed_21)

7.8 *Degrees of Certainty*

The language of policy and practice not only exhibits formality, but necessarily addresses uncertainty, which has a role in decision making. The average coverage of this theme is 2.36% across the dataset. This is sub-coded into three categories: 'possibility' (255), 'unlikelihood' (11) and 'impossibility' (6). Taking 'possibility' as the foregrounded sub-code, the highest coverage can be found in institutional policy (2.97%), closely followed by national practice (2.56%) and national policy (2.31%), with institutional practice least frequent (1.1%). Language of possibility occurs across the dataset (22 documents). It concerns four phenomena:

External influence	... of circumstances or concerns that may affect their work ... (ed_01)
Sanctions	The student may be required to intercalate/withdraw ... (td_02)
Awareness	Candidates may be unfamiliar with oral examinations ... (ed_04)
Solutions	... to enhance their practice, which may include workshops and programmes ... (ed_03)

7.9 *Levels of Technicality*

Related to the formal language of the documents in the dataset, are terms that describe and define entities and processes within the higher education context. Although this averages 4.32% across the dataset, the level of precision is most pronounced in national practice (6.76%) and policy (6.57%), with institutional policy (2.77%) and practice (1.18%) respectively. A matrix query between the sub-codes of levels of technicality and the agents in the documents reveals several patterns (see Table 8.8).

The first is that language relating to responsibility ('ensuring') is weighted towards the doctoral researcher and supervisor:

> ... the supervisors and other relevant staff members ensure that research students receive sufficient support ... (ed_01)

> To ensure consistency of supervision, supervisors working in industry or professional practice are made aware of and enabled to ... (ed_21)

The same is true of terms of 'inclusion' or 'within', namely, when entities are grouped together and subject to particular processes:

> Effective induction programme, including for international students (ed_05)

TABLE 8.8 Matrix query of levels of levels of technicality and agent/patient

	Candidate	Institution	Postgraduate researchers	Student	Supervisor
Ensuring	10	6	1	24	14
Inclusion	9	6	14	60	31
Information	2	1	1	21	1
Need	3	2	10	25	17
Quality	1	0	0	7	2
Relevance	0	1	1	12	5
Role	4	2	7	6	29
Skills	1	1	0	6	4
Specificity	2	4	10	10	7

Information requirements are connected to students, and needs relate mostly to postgraduate researchers, students and supervisors. Significantly, language related to defined roles occurs more frequently for supervisors:

> How and where are the roles and responsibilities of research students and supervisors made clear and accessible? (ed_01)

> … set of roles involved in modern research supervisors. (ed_03)

Supervisors also tend to mediate the institution's responsibilities, rather than hold them in full, notably if the term 'provider' is included in this matrix query.

8 Discussion

8.1 *Constructions of the Doctoral Process and Researcher*

The language of national and institutional policy documents and reports construct the doctoral process and doctoral candidate in ways that foreground the educational system and background themes that are existential. National policy and practice texts are concerned with the workplace context, working conditions, career trajectory, and processes of the doctorate itself. The genre matrix shows that doctoral researchers and supervisors are typically presented in the third person, rather than being addressed directly in the second person or providing insights in the first person. This suggests a discourse of agents and patients as entities interacting within a system, rather than communicative subjects.

There are also three distinct terms in operation: 'candidate', 'student' and 'postgraduate researcher'. Whereas 'student' and to a lesser degree, 'candidate' are more prominent across all policy and practice texts, the designation 'postgraduate researcher' is used comparatively rarely and is omitted completely at institutional level. This may be intended to reinforce a distinction between staff and students as two different entities.

Although regulatory language is common across the dataset, it is significant that 'obligations' are less prominent than might be expected given the concerns surrounding managerialism. Language concerning 'permission' features more frequently, which suggests that both supervisors and students can exercise choice, but subject to protocol.

The discussion of 'health' – primarily in the form of mental health – is less frequent within institutional documentation. Overall, most documents in the dataset address uncertainty to some extent. They focus on external influences on the doctoral project or researcher, sanctions applied to the individual, speculation on the level of awareness that the researcher might possess, and solutions to address their perceived deficit. Each of these cases can be seen as problem-oriented.

8.2 *Doctoral Constructs in Continuing Professional Development*

How these doctoral constructs operate within the context of supervisor CPD demonstrates that pedagogy in national practice and institutional practice are closely aligned in terms of coverage, although both at a lower level than national policy. Across the dataset, however, the interaction of doctoral researchers and supervisors is generally functional, comprising contact, relationship, agreement, responsibility, awareness and communication. Significantly, this is characterised by transmission rather than dialogue. When considering the degree of specificity in discussing the different agents/patients within the university, there is more attention surrounding role definition for supervisors than for doctoral researchers. Supervisors also tend to mediate the institution's responsibilities rather than hold them outright.

8.3 *Pedagogical Affordances and Constraints*

Although the texts in this dataset belong to different genres, perhaps the most significant indicator from CDA concerns those themes that are foregrounded at the expense of others. This may help academic development teams to understand why CPD is designed in certain ways.

The last decade of national and institutional policy and practice documentation remains focused on systemic issues and procedures, and these have also clearly influenced the scenario-based activities used in workshops with supervisors at the University of East Anglia. Although these concern people, they do so within a framework that foregrounds and exemplifies particular procedures, such as failing to prepare probationary documentation, addressing problems of student progress in the event of serious illness, social isolation, frustrated access to resources, and a lack of academic support and guidance.

These scenarios develop supervisors' attention to the 'facts' of a reported case to encourage experiential learning. However, they do not reflect accurately the underlying themes highlighted by this study. For example, 'obstacles' across the dataset are less prominent in the policy and practice texts than might be assumed.

8.4 *A Person-Centred Discourse*

The language of policy and practice changes the perception of what is important in doctoral education. By removing the CDA coding of rhetoric and focusing on the remaining themes, the findings of this study can be mapped to the DLEM quadrants proportionally based on their coding frequency.

The modified DLEM (see Figure 8.4) shows that focus on the person is much more prominent (29% of all coded references). The largest remains the workplace (35%) – the educational environment – with disciplinary themes afforded least attention (13%). The implications of this analysis are twofold.

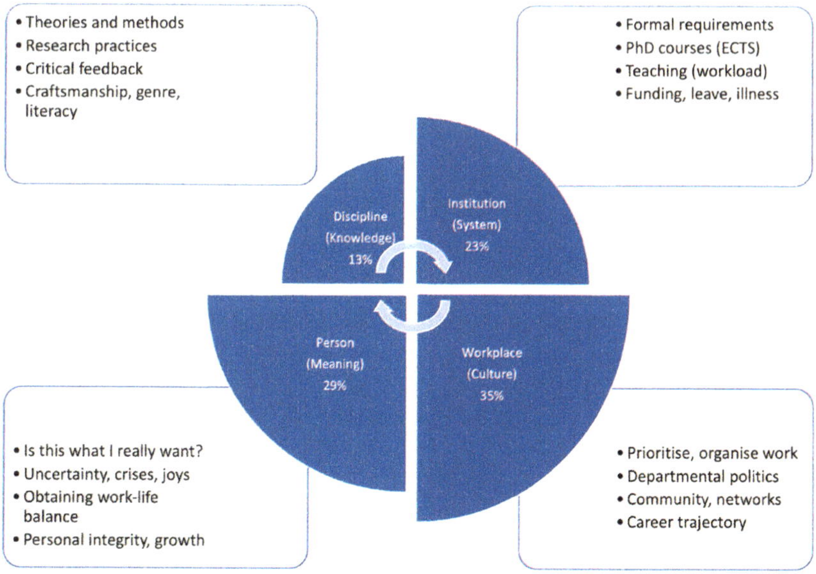

FIGURE 8.4 Modified Doctoral Learning Ecology Model

Firstly, although the two domains most closely associated with managerialism (institution, workplace) account for over half of doctoral education discourse within the dataset, they do not preclude references to the person. Secondly, the disciplinary domain is discussed least frequently, which suggests that there is scope for supervisors to develop this area because of their role in the intellectual development of doctoral researchers.

8.5 *Implications for Supervisor CPD*

In the final part of this discussion, I consider some of the implications of placing the person at the centre of doctoral supervisor development discourse. Rather than focus on briefing supervisors on policy and procedures, and delivering workshop scenarios that are essentially problem-oriented, supervisor CPD can draw on five pedagogical practices to facilitate both alignment and deeper engagement with the disciplinary, workplace and institutional domains of the DLEM.

A person-centred approach begins with active listening to address the communicative oversight in policy and practice documentation. It better reflects the dialogic approach to learning observed in supervisory practice. Furthermore, as the entropic model of doctoral researchers and the doctorate appears to be rhetorical rather than factual, supervisors could benefit from adopting a 'prizing' attitude, viewing students' experiences as formative and contributing to their identity rather than as problems to be solved.

In order to facilitate a disciplinary dialogue, supervisors can introduce the concept of academic literacies to explore the ways that knowledge is enacted in the academy, and cultural practices operate in disciplines. They can also support doctoral researchers by slowing down the thinking process and making behaviours and tasks within the academic workplace much more explicit through the process of 'cognitive apprenticeship'.

Finally, both supervisor and doctoral researcher can use reflective writing in their interactions to better understand their place within the institution. Encouraging the latter to write in this way provides a clearer professional trajectory for both parties, and may serve as a first step towards greater reflexivity, a concept discussed in greater detail by Dowle in Chapter 13 (2022).

9 Conclusion

Placing the person at the core of supervisor development (see Figure 8.5) introduces a syntropic discourse, which highlights growth, complexity and fulfilment rather than one that is characterised by functional and transmissive

FIGURE 8.5
Person-centred CPD model

interactions. The national and institutional documentation used by supervisors in their professional development employ a rhetoric that can appear managerial, but in fact incorporates important issues of personhood. Academic developers in the UK may benefit from reading between the lines of discourse to strengthen this theme in CPD. In doing so, doctoral supervisors and researchers become valued and empowered individuals within the doctoral ecosystem rather than simply subject to it.

Notes

1 Structured self-reflection is key to the national recognition process for supervisors through the UKCGE: https://supervision.ukcge.ac.uk/
2 The text files (named 'ed'/'td') and code books can be found at: https://github.com/matthewsillence/educational_discourse

References

Austin, A. E. (2009). Cognitive apprenticeship theory and its implications for doctoral education: A case example from a doctoral program in higher and adult education. *International Journal for Academic Development, 14*, 173–183.

Barnett, R. (2011). *Being a university.* Routledge.

Barnett, R. (2016). *Understanding the university: Institution, idea, possibilities.* Routledge.

Bastalich, W., Behrend, M., & Bloomfield, R. (2014). Is non-subject based research training a 'waste of time', good only for the development of professional skills? An academic literacies perspective. *Teaching in Higher Education, 19*(4), 373–384.

Bengtsen, S. E. (2016). *Doctoral supervision: Organization and dialogue.* Aarhus Universitetsforlag.

Brew, A., & Peseta, T. (2004). Changing postgraduate supervision practice: a programme to encourage learning though reflection and feedback. *Innovations in Education & Teaching International, 41*(1), 5–22.

Cahusac de Caux, B. K. C. D., Lam, C. K. C., Lau, R., Hoang, C. H., & Pretorius, L. (2017). Reflection for learning in doctoral training: Writing groups, academic writing proficiency and reflective practice. *Reflective Practice, 18*(4), 463–473.

Collins, A., & Kapur, M. (2014). Cognitive apprenticeship. In R. K. Sawyer (Ed.), *The Cambridge handbook of the learning sciences* (2nd ed., pp. 109–127). Cambridge University Press.

Deem, R., Hillyard, S., & Reed, M. (2007). *Knowledge, higher education, and the new managerialism. The changing management of UK universities.* Oxford University Press.

Denicolo, P., Reeves, J., & Duke, D. (2022). Re-framing supervisor development for internationalisation and professionalisation. In M.-L. Österlind, P. Denicolo & B.-M. Apelgren (Eds.), *Doctoral education as if people matter: Critical issues for the future* (this volume). Brill.

Dowle, S. (2022). The role of liminality and reflexivity in transformative doctoral learning. In M.-L. Österlind, P. Denicolo & B.-M. Apelgren (Eds.), *Doctoral education as if people matter: Critical issues for the future* (this volume). Brill.

Eley, A. R., & Jennings, R. (2005). *Effective postgraduate supervision: Improving the student-supervisor relationship.* Open University Press.

Elliot, D. L., Bengtsen, S. S., Guccione, K., & Kobayashi, S. (2020). *The hidden curriculum in doctoral education.* Palgrave Pivot.

Godskesen, M., & Wichmann-Hansen, G. (2013). Aktiv lytning i ph.d.-vejledning – et værktøj til udvikling af dialogiske kompetencer. *Dansk Universitetspædagogisk Tidsskrift, 8*(15), 145–157.

Hill, G., & Vaughan, S. (2018). Conversations about research supervision – Enabling and accrediting a community of practice model for research degree supervisor development. *Innovations in Education and Teaching International, 55*(2), 153–163.

Kelly, F. (2017). *The idea of the PhD: The doctorate in the twenty-first century imagination.* Routledge.

Kumar, V., & Stracke, E. (2017). Reframing doctoral examination as teaching. *Innovations in Education and Teaching International*, 1–9.

Magyar, A., & Robinson-Pant, A. (2011). Special issue on University internationalisation – Towards transformative change in higher education. Internationalising doctoral research: Developing theoretical perspectives on practice. *Teachers and Teaching: Theory and Practice, 17*(6), 663–676.

Manathunga, C., Peseta, T., & McCormack, C. (2010). Supervisor development through creative approaches to writing. *International Journal for Academic Development, 15*(1), 33–46.

Metcalfe, J., Wilson, S., & Levecque, K. (2018). *Exploring wellbeing and mental health and associated support services for postgraduate researchers.* Ghent University and the Institute for Employment Studies. Cambridge, Vitae (CRAC).

Office for Students. (2020). *Coronavirus briefing note* (No. 6). https://www.officeforstudents.org.uk/media/989e5582-cb4b-442e-944b-9cc6c1327d92/coronavirus-briefing-note-postgraduate-research-students.pdf

Owler, K. (2010). A 'problem' to be managed? Completing a PhD in the arts and humanities. *Arts and Humanities in Higher Education*, 9(3), 289–304.

Paltridge, B. (2012). *Discourse analysis: An introduction* (2nd ed.). Bloomsbury Publishing.

Posselt, J. (2018). Normalizing struggle: Dimensions of faculty support for doctoral students and implications for persistence and well-being. *The Journal of Higher Education*, 1–26.

Rogers, C. (1980). *A way of being*. Houghton Mifflin Company.

Taylor, S. (2016). *UK Professional Standards Framework (UKPSF) dimensions of the framework for doctoral supervisors*. Higher Education Academy.

Taylor, S., Kiley, M., & Holley, K. A. (Eds.). (2020). *The making of doctoral supervisors: International case studies of practice* (1st ed.). Routledge.

Taylor, S., Kiley, M., & Humphrey, R. (2018). *A handbook for doctoral supervisors* (2nd ed.). Routledge.

Taylor, S., & McCulloch, A. (2017). Mapping the landscape of awards for research supervision: A comparison of Australia and the UK. *Innovations in Education and Teaching International*, 1–14.

CHAPTER 9

The Role of Supervisors in Preparing Doctoral Researchers for the Final Examination

Gillian Houston

Abstract

This chapter explores the critical advice and guidance provided by supervisors in thesis development and in preparing for the final examination. An underlying theme is how supervisors' interventions can improve the doctoral researcher's output and examination experience. The chapter suggests how the role of supervisors: supports the researcher to become independent and produce high quality research; enables them to generate a well-argued thesis; and contributes to preparation for the examination. It concludes by asserting that supervisors' interventions can raise researchers' awareness of the interdependence of the thesis and oral in the final examination, thereby increasing their confidence.

Keywords

supervisors – independence – thesis – viva – final examination – continuum of judgement

1 Introduction

Numerous research, professional and personal attributes are needed to pass the doctorate. Producing a well-argued, elegantly written thesis is not the only requirement, since success depends on: a research design capable of answering the question; generating sufficient relevant data; conducting rigorous analysis; and drawing meaningful conclusions that enable you to answer the 'so what?' exam question every doctoral candidate dreads.

The supervisor's role in supporting the researcher to succeed is well known (Denicolo, Duke, & Reeves, 2020; Phillips & Pugh, 2010; Taylor, Kiley, & Humphrey, 2018). Supervisors focus on guiding the candidate's research and supporting their 'output': thesis, or equivalent, sometimes referred to as the

 | DOI:10.1163/9789004529304_009

'product '(Tinkler & Jackson, 2004, p. 2). Additionally, they are integral to preparing candidates for the oral examination (viva), which may include role-play as examiners during a mock viva.[1] Thus, during the doctoral training process, supervisors have a dual role as supporter and critical friend. They are responsible for helping the doctoral researcher to learn effectively and efficiently how to become an independent researcher, supporting them through the peaks and troughs of the programme by creating a constructive learning experience during this period of intellectual and personal growth. This rollercoaster of progression through a doctorate is conceptualised by Denicolo et al.'s "Individual journey to independence" (2020, p. 94, fig. 6.5). The role of supporter develops into behaving much more like a 'critical friend' once the researcher has grown in confidence, challenging them to make a strong argument from the data, critiquing their writing, and testing their knowledge of how their research contributes to the field. Only if supervisors fulfil both roles, with the researcher as an active partner, can the degree be completed successfully. This duality can create tensions for the supervisor-researcher relationship when the balance shifts from supporter to critical friend, especially if the supervisee is not growing into the role of independent researcher. The relationship is therefore critical to success in the doctorate.

Reflecting on the need for supervisor styles to adapt during the doctorate, Denicolo et al. (2020, p. 85) reference Gurr's (2001) supervisory styles, suggesting that some supervisors and candidates favour the '*directive*' approach, while at the other end of the scale, there is the '*facilitative*' or '*hands off*' supervisor, which may be preferred from the beginning by more independent doctoral researchers. As Denicolo et al assert, however, whatever model prevails when the candidate embarks on their doctorate, it is not static:

> [Ideally] a dependent researcher starts their doctorate with the supervisor taking on a directive style, who then gradually stands back, becoming ever more facilitative as their doctoral researcher blossoms into independence. (ibid., pp. 92–93)

This encapsulates the dual role of the successful supervisor who is focused on the candidate's eventual success in the final examination, each stage of training and development contributing to the thesis. While the researcher has access to a range of training opportunities, formal and informal, it is their supervisors who are most influential in: shaping choice and design of experiments, or methodology and methods, to answer the research question; advising on conducting empirical research with rigour and integrity to provide sound evidence; suggesting how to undertake analysis that properly represents the results; and deriving impactful conclusions from the findings (and see Chapter 5 for summary of criteria for assessing the doctoral thesis). Completing each stage successfully is fundamental to the assessment of whether the researcher is capable of independent research, normally the stated purpose of the final examination.

My doctoral study (Houston, 2019) explored how doctoral examiners make judgements in the two-part final examination. It involved case studies of ten oral examinations (vivas) observed across six UK universities and eight disciplines, both AHSS and STEM.[2] I interviewed 38 actors from the vivas, conducting supplementary interviews with non-case related examiners and supervisors to broaden the study's scope and subject range, making a total of 43 interviews. Some of the questions I asked concerned the role of supervisors in preparing doctoral researchers for the final examination and the responses contribute to this chapter, comprising two main sections and a conclusion.

2 Supporting the Candidate to Become an Independent Researcher

Supervisors have a challenging role in guiding doctoral researchers to a successful outcome. In addition to supporting the researcher in undertaking research with integrity, supervisors are responsible for ensuring they absorb disciplinary conventions – 'supporting enculturation' (Lee, 2020, chapter 5). Arguably, one of their significant roles in the process is to develop the candidate's academic writing skills to achieve: clarity; conciseness; an analytical approach; and the ability to express oneself clearly – qualities integral to making an argument informed by research.

2.1 *Making an Argument*

If the researcher cannot convince their supervisors of their argument, how will they persuade the examiners? Supervisors consider this at every stage, with the quality of the thesis in mind, the best ensuring that doctoral researchers begin writing in an academic genre early in their candidacy. As Denicolo et al. (2020, p. 102) suggest: "you need to impress on the researcher that they should keep practising their writing skills and technique using your feedback to achieve the required scholarly standard". The ability to make a strong argument is intimately linked to the researcher's writing style. Most important, however, is content and that the research itself is employed analytically to present the argument. Early in my own doctorate, I remember my main supervisor discussing the need for a 'golden thread' to run through the thesis, creating coherence based on argument. This was a seminal moment in learning how to write the thesis.

Flowing organically from the candidate's topic, thesis construction is influenced by disciplinary considerations and whether the researcher is authoring or co-authoring publications. 'Publishability' is a quality many examiners and supervisors believe is important; in disciplines where the convention is for the thesis to contain one or more recent peer reviewed publications, researchers have already met this criterion:

> Usually ... we expect PhD students to have a number of completed studies which could each be a thesis chapter and, alternatively, a publication in a good scientific journal ... what I expect in my field is a minimum of four ... completed experimental studies for which the ... student has been leading the work and, partially at least, designing it and evaluating it independently. (STEM supervisor2)

This is a good example of how examiners in subjects such as biological sciences expect doctoral researchers to exhibit significant leadership and analysis in both thesis and viva and which publishing during the doctoral programme helps to develop.

Ideally, supervisors are both supporters/developers and critical friends, providing advice and guidance, but allowing the researcher to make their own decisions, including readiness to submit. Most doctoral researchers would not consider submitting their thesis if their supervisors advised against it, but most supervisors do not have the right of veto and examiners do not know how they have advised the candidate.

2.2 *Readiness to Submit*

I asked doctoral researchers and supervisors how they knew the thesis was good enough. Part of the rationale for these questions was to establish to what extent the researchers had reached a stage of independence where they knew their work was ready for examination.

- *Question for candidates*: Having met the progress hurdles (e.g., transfer and confirmation of status), during your programme, how did you know when you were ready to submit your thesis for the final examination?
- *Question for supervisors*: Assuming the candidate has met all the progress hurdles in previous years, how do you know when to advise him/her that s/he is ready to submit for the examination? On what evidence do you base your judgement?

The questions elicited interesting responses, confirming the central role of the supervisor in thesis development, and the need for agreement between all parties.

2.2.1 Case 1

"My supervisor said [it] was ready" (STEM candidate4). This researcher acknowledged they had perfectionist tendencies and needed to be encouraged gently by their supervisors to submit: "they gave me a deadline and I had to finish it by that ... after having been told it was ready". They had struggled to agree "It was ready a lot longer before I was ... They kept saying, 'Okay, it's ready, just submit it', but I kept changing things ... and eventually they said, 'No, it's ready – submit it!'". The researcher added "I've learnt during the PhD that it's not possible to achieve [perfection]. You can work towards it but you'll never achieve it". The researcher's supervisors had supported them to produce a high-quality thesis (pass with minor amendments) and in the process the researcher had acquired more pragmatism. The examiners' concluding comments were highly positive: "We were particularly impressed with the thoroughness of the stats" and "A very impressive piece of work, very worthy of a PhD". Although this candidate had been reluctant to submit, they and the supervisors were finally in agreement about thesis readiness.

2.2.2 Case 2

It was a common agreement with the supervisors. "Yes, I had it done and we mutually agreed that it was mature enough to submit" (AHSS candidate3). In this case, although all parties had been in agreement about submission, the examiners were critical of elements of the thesis, especially the researcher's choice of the countries involved in the comparative study. However, they were in no doubt about the extensive work undertaken or the contribution to knowledge. In addition to correcting typographical errors and referencing, the candidate was required to undertake substantial minor corrections within three months, including: re-writing the abstract; stating clearly the contribution to knowledge; revisions to strengthen the argument and make the thesis more analytical; and re-writing the conclusions. The context in this case was revealing:

> We [brought] some of our own examining experience to bear, to decide whether the thesis would meet examiners' criteria ... informed by University regulations, our experience and other factors such as "Could the candidate submit without our support?". The timing was a reason why we needed to have this discussion when we did. The candidate had to show the [country] government they'd completed the work. This was ... an unusual situation – in most cases you don't have that kind of pressure. (AHSS director of studies1 (main supervisor))

This conveys the competing influences affecting readiness to submit, confirming the external influence of the sponsor as a major factor. That many supervisors also act as examiners gives them a particular insight although the uniqueness of each examination means they cannot predict the viva outcome precisely. It was a situation where both supervisors and researcher had agreed the thesis was 'good enough'. Compared with some of the other cases, it was surprising that this amount of amendment and restructuring did not warrant major corrections, but the examiners' recommendations possibly reflected their knowledge of the pressure being applied by the candidate's sponsors for completion within the shorter time period signified by minor amendments.

Cases 1 and 2 are interesting for the contrast between the decisions about thesis readiness, with supervisors being influential in both. On one hand, the doctoral researcher was reluctant to submit, wishing to continue improving the thesis, yet the supervisors encouraged submission as they considered it ready, while in case 2, the imperative for the researcher to return to employment with their sponsor influenced timing of thesis submission. The main supervisor, however, endorsed the candidate's statement concerning mutual agreement: "as a group the supervisors and the candidate have talked through whether the goals and aims set have been completed … The student also has to feel they've achieved this". In another case, a candidate showed considerable insight concerning the readiness of the thesis:

> It doesn't have to be perfect, it just has to be done and done by the end of the three years … that was my goal … But, if I had timed myself better … I would have left myself two or three weeks after I'd finished … before handing in … so … I could think about the things that were in it … in a holistic way, having been too close to them before. (AHSS candidate1)

This researcher encapsulates the feeling of time pressure alongside the need to allow an interval to reflect on the findings to produce a coherent thesis, together with an understanding it needs to be 'good enough' rather than perfect.

2.2.3 Case 3

> "I had just completed a research paper and was accepted [for a post-doctoral position] and my four years was starting to go to its end, so… that's why I started to write up my PhD" (STEM candidate3). When asked if their supervisors had helped them to know it was the right time to 'write up', the researcher added "Yeah, it was probably by mutual agreement and nobody had to say 'You need to write up now', really. It was

kind of, we both knew it". To some, this will appear a 'hands off' approach (Denicolo et al., 2020) that defies received wisdom about early drafts of the thesis, but the researcher had published papers which contributed to the thesis, so had already captured the academic writing genre and was adept at making an argument on the basis of research results. This was evident during the viva, the researcher demonstrating high levels of 'doctorateness' (Denicolo & Park, 2010) and research leadership in the kind of peer-to-peer discussion that marks a successful examination. Minor amendments were recommended, concerning presentation of the statistical analysis. The case suggested the researcher had instilled considerable confidence in their supervisors and examiners that they had the capacity to lead their research and required minimum direction, an example of a highly facilitative style (Gurr, 2001) that enabled the researcher to flourish.

2.2.4 Case 4

> "I didn't know until ... really near the end of the process ... I ... almost gave up responsibility for knowing whether I was ready or not and I relied on my supervisors to say 'Yes, this is what you need to do now and then you'll be ready for it' ... and the other thing I relied on [was] the deadline ... I had the deadline and then I actually went over [it] by 3 months – I got an extension". (AHSS candidate4)

This researcher describes a completely different approach to thesis readiness, suggesting a less confident candidate who was unsure about the quality of their work, for example "I did worry that my work wasn't good enough ... all the way through ... but I knew what I wanted to get in [the thesis]". This was someone who relied on the wisdom of their supervisors to advise them about thesis readiness because they "felt a bit ambivalent" and also "I knew ... there were weaknesses with it that, if I had more time, I'd have put right". Their concerns were unfounded (minor amendments) but their testimony emphasises the critical role of supervisors in building confidence. This researcher had been downcast when advised by their supervisors to re-write the final chapter. While this happens relatively frequently, given that much rests on the extent to which the researcher is able to draw conclusions from their findings, candidates may not be aware of this since they only complete a doctorate once and may feel discouraged by being asked to revise the final chapter significantly when they thought the thesis was ready.

All four cases show the complexities of judging when the thesis is ready and the pressure on candidates and supervisors in making that decision. My study showed researchers had faith in their supervisors' judgements. It suggested that all candidates had been open to taking advice from their supervisors but also that they were sufficiently independent to make a decision about thesis readiness. The mutual agreement suggests successful researcher-supervisor relationships and that the progression from 'direction' to 'independence' was well managed, some being more challenging than others. Supervisors had more or less successfully relinquished their 'directive' role by the time of submission and candidates were more than able to argue their case in the viva, some displaying more confidence than others. Supervisors had guided the researchers through each step in their training, supporting them to become independent research leaders who met the doctoral threshold.

In three different cases involving recommendations for major corrections, supervisors were perhaps not sufficiently aware of: lacunae in the researcher's knowledge or understanding; subject conventions for thesis format; or in one case, had insufficient time to enculturate the candidate in the conventions for writing a thesis by published work. In all cases, however, the researchers appreciated the advice received, including the formative assessment during the viva that would improve the quality of their thesis.

3 Preparing the Candidate for the Viva

The supervisor is critical to ensuring the doctoral researcher is well prepared for the viva, irrespective of thesis quality. Respondents noted the increased emphasis on the viva in cases where the thesis raises concerns, for example: "There are situations where a rather 'wobbly' thesis is well defended at the viva and so a candidate convinces the examiners that actually they're much better than the written thesis" (AHSS external examiner1) and "The judgement about the written thesis has to affect the viva" (STEM independent chair3).

3.1 *Continuum of Judgement*

The process that characterises examiners' judgements in the doctoral examination is not overtly emphasised by supervisors. While the thesis is the principal source of evidence for examiners' judgements, a complex and integrated relationship exists between the two elements of the final examination, which should be considered together as part of a "continuum of judgement" (Houston, 2019, p. 106):

> In this ... example, the first chapter was published but [the candidate] didn't say so in the written work ... we actually knew that before but that came out in the viva. [The] statistical analysis was inadequate, but it wasn't totally clear why that was ... what came out pretty strongly was that [the candidate] literally didn't know enough. So there are things you have to elicit in the viva. (STEM internal examiner2)

This case illustrates the viva's role in moderating examiners' judgements, enabling them to ask questions arising from reading the thesis, for clarification and helping to avoid misunderstandings. Here, the viva led to major rather than minor amendments because it revealed significant gaps in knowledge, but the reverse can also occur. The continuum allows examiners opportunity to reflect and change their views, both essential in such a 'high stakes' examination.

3.2 *Preparedness of Doctoral Researchers to Defend the Thesis*

My study suggested that, while no-one can pre-judge the outcome of the examination, if supervisors consider a thesis to be ready for submission, the candidate is likely to pass, even if they must complete major rather than minor corrections – respondents confirmed minor amendments are the most frequent outcome of the examination. Perhaps surprisingly, some doctoral researchers did not seem to have this concept in mind before the viva and most appeared nervous. One researcher (minor amendments), however, showed in-depth understanding of the overall process, partly engendered by their supervisors:

> It's quite ... hard to know when you are writing your thesis exactly what [examiners] are after, [but] ... my supervisors would tell me if I'm doing something ... wrong. Whereas, in the viva, I always had the feeling that most of the judgement would be on the thesis and ... that ... it wasn't really possible to mess up your viva ... if they liked your thesis already, that they would ask you questions to clarify certain things ... in my viva, it happened several times, when I clarified it, they kind of took that off the corrections list ... I think it's ... not really possible to completely not pass ... I suppose it depends on whether your supervisors agree with you submitting your thesis or not. (STEM candidate1)

This candidate entered the viva confidently, well able to explain and defend their work. Another researcher also showed insight into the relationship between thesis and viva: "I think a larger proportion [of the judgement] is on the thesis ... given [that] more work ... goes into it, and ... the viva would not exist without the thesis. So, I think ... [examiners] give a much greater weight to the thesis" (STEM candidate5).

These two researchers' judgement about the significance of the thesis was borne out by other respondents. Most cases suggested that doctoral researchers and their supervisors were well aware of any weaker thesis elements and had been realistic about any elements they would need to explain. In one case, however, the supervisor was surprised the researcher had been asked to undertake major rather than minor corrections, while the candidate was appreciative of the examiners' formative feedback. The corrections were based primarily on a statistical analysis that in parallel exposed the candidate's lack of knowledge and understanding of statistics and showed insufficient use of data, failing to exploit its richness and variation.

Most candidates appeared well prepared for the viva, if nervous, and some said they had enjoyed it, for example:

> I think ... my impressions and my expectations of the questions and ... and what they were looking for was the same [as] what I found in the exam ... it was very enjoyable and I really liked it much more than I thought I would ... my examiners ... were really nice and ... without looking at the amount of work I have to do ... the viva itself was good ... they gave each part ... considerable importance ... I think they read everything. (STEM candidate5)

This was a mature candidate who, despite having to undertake major corrections, understood what their examiners were seeking and appreciated the opportunity to discuss their research during a lengthy viva of more than 3 hours, with examiners who had read their thesis thoroughly and understood the work.

None of the doctoral researchers interviewed was completely surprised by the examination outcome, although one or two anticipated fewer corrections, or were taken aback by the questions. One candidate, when asked if the examiners asked questions they had expected, responded: "No, they didn't ... in some ways the things that they did ask me should have been totally obvious and I should have thought about things like the impact of the research and putting yourself out there and reflexivity [etc.]" (AHSS candidate1). While this researcher might have anticipated the question concerning impact, their comment underscores the impossibility of knowing what questions examiners will ask: "they didn't ask me the questions I expected but then I don't think anyone ever does get asked the questions they expect".

Some of the doctoral researchers were better prepared and able than others to defend their work, although the majority demonstrated the ability to argue their case non-defensively, when challenged by the examiners, while accepting suggestions graciously. These are attributes that signal readiness for independent research: knowing you have undertaken research with integrity that stands up to scrutiny, while being open to other ideas, suggesting candidates were well advised and prepared for the examination.

3.3 *Mock Vivas*

Mock vivas can be instructive in preparing researchers to defend their thesis, provided they appreciate it is the experience itself that is important, rather than expecting the practice to mirror the real thing, especially the examiners' questions. While I did not ask about mock vivas in my study, two candidates had experienced them.

> I did a mock viva with [supervisors] which was about an hour long and basically just consisted of them taking elements of my supporting statement and asking me questions about it … [This] was … what I expected of the viva, that they would take … my supporting statement as a jumping-off point and almost just test me or expand on that to make sure that what I'd written was deeply felt and deeply thought about, in terms of how I would come across in an oral examination. (AHSS candidate5)

Using their knowledge of the work and supporting statement (PhD by published work), this researcher's supervisors had also acted as 'examiners' in the mock. While this was excellent preparation, the researcher added:

> [The supervisors'] reaction and feedback on my supporting statement was quite different from the two examiners … that was interesting because they brought up a lot of stuff that had never even come up during the supervisions … in terms of preparing, it was the mock viva, it was having a look at a video of what a viva's normally like.

Here, although the experience itself had been helpful, inevitably, the actual examiners had identified different questions from the supervisors. It was surprising that the supervisors, when acting as examiners, raised points that had not been discussed in supervision meetings: perhaps in taking on the role of examiners, they had read the supporting statement differently. If so, this would be an interesting area to research. The researcher subsequently confirmed that they had worked very hard to prepare prior to the examination but realised that: "questions were going to come up that I'd have to react to spontaneously", an informative outcome of the mock viva.

The other researcher who had experienced a mock viva was in a completely different discipline. They had a job interview about a month before their viva that had gone well and considered that had been good practice as it included a presentation. Subsequently, however, they had a mock viva with their supervisors "which was horrendous and I couldn't speak" (AHSS candidate4). Despite the ordeal of the mock viva, this researcher concluded "it really focused my attention and the week before the viva I did loads of work ... and I took a day off work ... to do it". This candidate confirmed that some of the questions in their mock viva had come up in the actual event and had increased the intensity of their preparation for the viva, leaving them well prepared to answer the examiners' questions with confidence.

It is beneficial if supervisors constructively support researchers in analysing the outcome of the mock viva, especially the parts that appeared not to go well, so the candidate has a strategy for the viva itself.

As a result of my study, I would advise doctoral researchers to arrange a mock viva *with their supervisors* within two weeks before the actual examination, which fulfils several purposes. Here as in previous stages, supervisors have a crucial role to play. They can probe any weaknesses, thus helping the candidate to prepare for difficult questions from the examiners; a short interval between the mock and the viva gives the researcher time to consider the thesis in a way that may be more effective once they have experienced alternative perspectives in a mock viva; and the general experience of answering examiners' questions is good practice in itself. On the other hand, however, it might be that a challenging mock viva would mean the candidate's confidence was dashed prior to the real examination, even though by this stage, they should be well prepared for their work to be constructively challenged by peers.

4 Conclusion

Conducting the study engendered immense respect for supervisors and the fundamental role they play in thesis formation, preparing diverse doctoral researchers to defend their research successfully in the final examination. Candidates impressively defended their research and showed insight into the examination process. Analysis for this chapter, however, suggested supervisors could help increase candidate confidence, particularly with respect to the viva, so more can enjoy the experience and make the most of having the undivided attention of two experts in the topic, enthusiastic to discuss their research. My conclusions are as follows.

It should be instilled in all doctoral researchers that, from their first day of registration, they are working towards the final examination. No doubt many supervisors already take this approach, but may not articulate it. Early on, as part of researcher training, an overview of how all the elements of the thesis, or equivalent, form a whole that demonstrates the qualities outlined earlier in this chapter, enables researchers to be thinking of the end point while they complete various stages. Mentioning the 'golden thread' of coherence is particularly helpful.

Supervisors could increase researchers' awareness of the interdependence of the thesis and oral in the final examination, building confidence while focusing on constructing an excellent thesis. Greater emphasis on this interdependence and raising awareness of the continuum of judgement could increase understanding and preparedness for the final examination.

While it would be highly inadvisable for candidates entering the viva to be over-confident or complacent about passing, it is important to remind them that:

- Producing an excellent thesis is the best preparation for a successful viva.
- Having passed the progression hurdles at each stage, it is unlikely that they will fail outright at the final examination, unless they have cheated.
- Most doctoral candidates pass with minor corrections or amendments.
- Irrespective of expectations, the viva can affect the extent of corrections to the thesis, i.e. whether major or minor.
- As one element of the judgement of their suitability to undertake research independently, the viva is an opportunity for candidates to: add anything they had for whatever reason to omit from the thesis; correct any misapprehensions on the part of the examiners; receive formative feedback to improve the quality of their thesis; and convince the examiners of their contribution to the field.
- Most examiners are genuinely fascinated by each researcher's work and relish the opportunity to discuss it, therefore they will have read the thesis thoroughly, perhaps several times.

The study confirmed the myriad responsibilities of supervisors in the candidate's transformation from doctoral researcher to doctoral graduate. Specifically, supervisors significantly influence researchers' preparedness for and confidence in their ability to pass the final examination.

Notes

1 The oral element of the UK doctoral examination (viva) involves the candidate, 2 or 3 examiners and takes place in private; it may include an independent chair. Supervisors may offer candidates mock vivas in advance of the examination.

2 AHSS: Arts, Humanities and Social Sciences; STEM: Science, Technology, Engineering and Mathematics.

References

Denicolo, P., Duke, D., & Reeves, J. (2020). *Supervising to inspire doctoral researchers*. Sage.

Denicolo, P., & Park, C. (2010). *Doctorateness – an elusive concept?* QAA.

Gurr, G. (2001). Negotiating the 'rackety bridge' – a dynamic model for aligning research student needs and supervisor style. *Higher Education Research and Development, 20*, 81–92.

Houston, G. (2019). *A study of the PhD examination: Process, attributes and outcomes* [DPhil.]. Oxford University. Retrieved April 5, 2021, from https://ora.ox.ac.uk/objects/uuid:07291f0e-e80b-4b06-a6af-b3ac8b90a00e/download_file?file_format=pdf&safe_filename=Houston_2018_A_study_of.pdf&type_of_work=Thesis

Lee, A. (2020). *Successful research supervision: Advising students doing research* (2nd ed.). Routledge.

Phillips, E., & Pugh, D. (2010). *How to get a PhD: A handbook for students and their supervisors* (5th ed.). Open University Press.

Taylor, S., Kiley, M., & Humphrey, R. (2018). *A handbook for doctoral supervisors*. Routledge.

Tinkler, P., & Jackson, C. (2004). *The doctoral examination process*. Society for Research into Higher Education and Open University Press.

CHAPTER 10

New Beginnings or Same Old Ending for Researcher Development?

Julie Reeves

Abstract

This chapter will review the progress researcher development has made in the UK since it was initiated nearly two decades ago. Standing in the midst of the coronavirus pandemic, the author asks how researcher development came about and what lessons, especially with respect to culture change, can be learned. The success of researcher development is viewed as the result of a combination of talented individuals and external interventions, notably from funders. Contemporary challenges about an unhealthy research culture and concerns about doctoral wellbeing, raise questions about the robustness of researcher development and the structural limitations of the profession to effect change. There is, though, an opportunity here for positive change and the chance to create a new future.

Keywords

skills training – Roberts funding – researcher developers/development – Third Space professionals

1 Introduction

Stay around in any profession or sector long enough and one is bound to see initiatives wax and wane like the moon, and higher education is not an exception in this respect. Sadly, many initiatives, despite seemingly worthwhile at the time, often fail to obtain structural support and the traction needed to ensure their longevity and sustainability; 'records of achievement' and 'professional development planning' or PDP for doctoral researchers in the noughties, are illustrative of the point. Researcher development (the specialist support provided to researchers, their supervisors and/or line managers), however, has been a genuine success story, certainly in the UK. Since 2003/04, researcher

 | DOI:10.1163/9789004529304_010

development has itself developed and evolved, seen funding come and go, and yet in spite of this has endured.

This chapter reflects on the progress researcher development has made in the UK nearly two decades on. Looking beyond the pandemic, it queries whether there is sufficient institutional commitment to face the cultural change brought about by the impact of the coronavirus and, more importantly, to support the professional and skill development needs of doctoral researchers in the 2020s and beyond.

2 How Did PGR Researcher Development Come about in the UK and What Are the Lessons Learned?

The activities associated with developing doctoral researchers have evolved considerably in the UK since 2003/4 when a national initiative and funding scheme for 'Career Development and Transferable Skills Training' began in response to a report by Sir Gareth Roberts (2002). Roberts called on the government to better equip doctoral researchers for a range of careers. 'Currently', Roberts noted in the report, "PhDs do not prepare people adequately for careers in business or academia. In particular, there is insufficient access to training in interpersonal and communication skills, management and commercial awareness" (Roberts, 2002, p. 111). Roberts suggested this transformation could be achieved by developing the generic or transferable skills of researchers and through raising awareness of the skills they could offer to prospective employers (see also Chapter 2, this volume). Rather than adding to the supervisory role, Roberts proposed a supplementary 10 days per annum for training in transferable/generic skills, in addition to research methods training. The government responded positively to his proposal, whilst the main response by institutions who received the additional funding, colloquially called 'Roberts money', was to recruit staff to implement the policy of developing these transferable skills in researchers – although, it should be noted that not all institutions received this funding since it was distributed pro rata with government research funding.

Suites of training courses quickly emerged, with a common core set focused on: communication skills (presenting and writing); project, time and people management (including 'how to manage your supervisor') skills; professional conduct (including research ethics, attribution and integrity); understanding the doctoral process; viva preparation; leadership; and career management. Today, such programmes may also offer public engagement opportunities and engagement with other sectors, and sessions on the wider impact of research.

Whilst supervisors, graduate schools and doctoral colleges around the world had long standing histories of providing training to doctoral researchers this had been dominated by the production of the thesis, with training predominantly in research methods and academic writing, and based on the assumption of a subsequent career in academia. The latter fuelled training in getting published and skill development through seminar presentations, conference participation and, sometimes, journal clubs. What was new about Roberts funding was that it was firmly focused on the development of transferable skills (in addition to those skills required for thesis production) and on career development/management in careers outside of academe. These were not topics doctoral supervisors or graduate schools were familiar with, neither were they initially much interested in. In addition, Roberts funding placed an annual reporting requirement on institutions to account for and evidence the impact of funding spent, which was also novel.

Undoubtedly, thinking in the UK was influenced by developments in Australia. Australian institutions had paved the way for broader training following policy discussions led by the Minister for Education, Training and Youth Affairs' in 1999. This established the Research Training Scheme which aimed at improving doctoral completion rates and, similar to Roberts, ensuring graduates had a smooth transition to the workplace (Kearns, Gardiner, & Marshall, 2008). Correspondingly, 'generic capabilities' programmes for researchers expanded across Australia, and Hugh Kearns and Maria Gardiner were early leaders with an innovative programme at Flinders University. Their practical advice on "The Seven Secrets of Highly Successful Research Students" was extremely useful for doctoral researchers and researcher developers alike as Roberts activity got underway.

In the UK, Roberts funding was concerned with transferable skills and transitioning to the workplace. Not only did it generate an innovative range of activity but also led to the birth of a new profession, one that might have been viewed as complementary to existing supervisory practice. However, the very advent of generic/transferable skills training challenged the monopolistic hold some supervisors had over their supervisees. Not surprising then that, at least initially, the idea of developing transferable skills was met with a mixed reaction among the doctoral community, including those who had until then been largely responsible for doctoral development – supervisors.

Transferable skills development proved novel for both doctoral candidates and institutions not used to provide such activities or programmes. Within academe the agenda encountered a range of response from enthusiastic support from researchers (especially among international researchers) and some supervisors, through 'tepid tolerance' to 'outright hostility'. Richard Hinchliffe (in Hinchcliffe, Bromley, & Hutchinson, 2007, p. 8) observed that there were "three main issues that [made] generic skills training a contested area for some academics: Time pressure … distrust of the generic skills vocabulary … [and from an educational standpoint the view that] 'It's not our job …' [to train researchers for other sectors]". Notably it was the twin expressions of tolerance and hostility among doctoral supervisors that those newly tasked to implement the initiative largely encountered (see Reeves in Hinchcliffe, Bromley, & Hutchinson, 2007). Overt enthusiasts, like all early adopters, were not dominant initially. And supervisors were not the only source of opposition; some institutional (Human resources/HR) staff and educational development units similarly felt threatened by the new wave of 'bright young things' entering the professional development space, often with more funding, especially in the research-intensive institutions, and with 'wild ideas' and experimental approaches.

The years from 2003, when Roberts funding was introduced, to 2011 when it ceased, were exciting times for researcher development; a national programme of intensive workshops (called 'GRADschools') providing 3 to 4 days of experiential training to doctoral researchers expanded considerably as a result of the funding – with some research funders making attendance compulsory for their researchers; regional hubs representing all institutions were established by 2005; and there were lots of experimental workshops and programmes in individual institutions. Arguably, the Roberts agenda revitalised training and professional development in the higher education (HE) sector. The period also saw the rise of specialist external provision, frequently set up by academic staff. For instance, Incus Associates was established in 2004 by Professor Norman Staines, a Professor of Immunology at King's College London; Vox Coaching was co-founded in 2005 by University of Bristol lecturer Pete Bailie; and in 2010, Dr Joanne Young founded the Scientific Editing Company after her doctorate and postdoctoral research at the University of Edinburgh. Epigeum, an early provider of online training, was a 'spin-out' company, from Imperial College London, and was founded in 2005. With so much transformational activity, research and publications were inevitable, for instance Hinchliffe, Bromley and Hutchinson (2007) was one of the early edited volumes to focus on *Skills training in research degree programmes*. The *International Journal for Researcher Development* was launched in 2009, renamed *Studies in Graduate and Postdoctoral Education* in 2017.

Nearly a decade on from Roberts' initial report and the picture and attending attitudes had altered considerably; transferable skills training and researcher developers were not so novel, and there had been a palpable change in the culture surrounding doctoral training. A report by Alison Hodge et al. (2011) into the impact of the transferable skills training agenda found that whilst there was some variability, there had been increased support for doctoral skills training since Roberts' initial report, although this was less discernible with respect to the postdoctoral community whom the initiative had also targeted. "The activities funded", the report stated in its dedication to Sir Gareth, "have come to represent a programme of major cultural change in the level of provision of skills and career support for researchers in UK Higher Education Institutions" (Hodge et al., 2011, p. 1). Indeed, with respect to doctoral education, researcher development was being embraced with greater enthusiasm and less hostility than it had encountered in the early days. In large part, this change was because the activity was not only funded by the research councils (the funding bodies in the UK) but in 2010 the funding councils (now part of UK Research and Innovation – UKRI) collectively issued a 'statement of expectation of doctoral training'. Thus, providing external direction and further structural support in addition to funding.

When central funding ceased in 2011, there was an expectation that institutions would continue where the 'Roberts money', originally intended as pump-priming, left off. Inevitably, the response was uneven across the sector with some institutions expanding their provision and others contracting theirs. The Roberts agenda experienced a momentary 'wobble'. However, on the whole all UK institutions with doctoral researchers, even if they only had a small community of researchers, continued to provide researcher development in some form. Frequently this provision drew on internal expertise and with academic staff either drawn into researcher development via Graduate Schools/Doctoral Colleges (Denicolo, Fuller, & Berry, 2010) or through cohort training by doctoral training centres or partnerships. Often, such staff would perform several roles as an academic, supervisor/PI and in delivering researcher development workshops, courses or programmes. In addition, many institutions continued to employ staff directly to wholly design and deliver researcher development to doctoral researchers, while some continued to rely on external providers. Over the years researcher developers had commonly collaborated with librarians, careers advisors, research managers and funding specialists, public engagement, research impact and policy managers and advisers, to offer a range of provision to doctoral researchers. All of which confirmed the changing nature of expectations surrounding the doctorate (see also Denicolo, Reeves, & Duke, Chapter 6, this volume). The professional and career development landscape surrounding and supporting doctoral researchers had become a rich and varied one.

The combination of the national policy initiative following Roberts' recommendations, supported with dedicated funding, reinforced by the funding bodies and learned associations (such as the Royal Society) stating their expectations of doctoral education (RCUK, 2016), all served to underpin local researcher development activity. In addition, the researcher developer community were supported by a few key national organisations including UK Grad (subsequently reformed as Vitae), the UK Council for Graduate Education (UKCGE), and Postgraduate Issues Network (PIN) of the Society for Research in Higher Education (SRHE). Against the backdrop of a wider debate about 'doctorateness' (Denicolo & Park, 2013), these organisations played an instrumental role in bringing about a change of culture, providing scaffolding for an environment in which the training of doctoral researchers became accepted as not only normal, but expected as a right.

The success and extent of the researcher development model have proven influential beyond the UK, with experienced researcher developers often invited to deliver workshops around the world (and some of the contributors to this volume met as a result of such workshops). For instance, the Medical Research Council's *Researcher Development Programme*, with Manchester University and Vitae, provides training to doctoral researchers in and from the Gambia. The Africa Research Excellence Fund, established in 2015 and supported by the MRC, offers grant writing and leadership training to researchers across Africa, as well as fellowships. Vitae continues to work on the international level, with the mission of 'realising the potential of researchers, globally'. At the same time the *Researcher Development Framework* is used by researchers on all continents these days. Until the coronavirus pandemic, workshop invitations to UK researcher developers were commonly received from European and African institutions, with some developers becoming established annual contributors to local doctoral programmes. However, the pandemic affords the possibility of even greater global reach and collaboration with the shift to online delivery (we will return to this point below).

3 Were the Changes Sufficiently Robust and What Are the Current Structural Limitations/Weaknesses?

Despite the growth of researcher development, troubling reports on the well-being of doctoral researchers began to emerge in the late 2010s (Levecque et al., 2017; Guthrie et al., 2017; Vitae in partnership with the Institute for Employment Studies (IES) and the University of Ghent, 2018), revealing that doctoral researchers were at risk of experiencing serious mental health problems (see also chapters 11 and 12). Katia Levecque et al in a study of PhD students in Flanders, Belgium found that "one in two PhD students experiences psychological distress [and] one in three is at risk of a common psychiatric disorder". A study into the UK research culture inhabited by postdoctoral researchers (Wellcome, 2020) sadly confirmed that the research environment was not a healthy one for a wide range of researchers.

The UK studies were particularly worrying as they implied the structural support and changes envisaged in those early and heady days of Roberts funding had not been as supportive or transformational as had been hoped. Undoubtedly a lot of researchers have been trained, along with their supervisors, yet it does not seem to have led to profound and enduring positive change in the nature of the researcher experience, particularly the doctoral experience. Something is not quite right here; this is especially concerning as we would all hope and desire that undertaking a doctorate would be one of the highlights of one's career, if not one of the most joyous events in one's life. However, the fact that so many researchers are struggling or are unhappy must cause us to enquire more deeply into the matter and search for a more profound response than sending researchers on 'resilience training' or for counselling, and their supervisors on 'mental health first aid training' (see Chapter 11 for a philosophical discussion of this turn). These deal with the symptoms but do not address the problem. These reports confirm that we need to look away from individuals and towards a wider structural institutional response. Whilst researcher development was not explicitly directed towards mental health and wellbeing, it did aim to provide better structural support on the doctoral journey. Effecting a quiet revolution in the development of researchers, including their levels of confidence and competence in a broad range of skills as Roberts sought to achieve, has, arguably, not been quite the victory it seemed. This raises the question of the place of researcher development within institutions.

The Higher Education (HE) sector can be rather haphazard in its implementation of training and development, for instance, see Taylor et al. (2021), whose case studies indicate that few countries have compulsory training beyond that required for new supervisors – three from the 21 countries they studied. Seldom, in UK HE at least, is much training compulsory, unless it is associated with issues of 'risk' such as health and safety concerns, or equality, diversity and inclusion (EDI) to ensure fairer recruitment and promotions practice. For staff, formal training is largely deficit focused, often aimed at meeting regulatory requirements. Whilst acknowledging that many individuals maintain professional good standing, this along with licensing are not regulatory features for academic staff (see also chapter 6 in respect of supervision) although they are for some professional service roles in institutions, for example, in finance and human resources (HR). Whilst departmental away days are not unheard of, INSET days (In service training) such as those found in the compulsory education sector are less evident. Although medical doctors, pharmacists, lawyers and other professionals must maintain a Continuing Professional Development (CPD) profile as a license to practice, academic and academic support staff, including researcher developers do not have such professional obligations. Institutions rely heavily on individuals self-identifying and finding ways to service their own needs (see Sillence, Chapter 8, this volume, on the language surrounding doctoral supervision and relationships). This includes doctoral researchers who often attend training without their supervisor's knowledge. A matter of too much agency and not enough structured support, perhaps?

Against this cultural backdrop, professional development programmes and training courses for academic staff often struggle to achieve credibility and attendance. Worse, Universities seem to lack the kind of structural support one would commonly find in other sectors. Notably institutions do not uniformly or even regularly train the staff who train or develop others, which includes doctoral supervisors, researcher developers and many in the wider researcher development community, and this may have placed researcher development at a disadvantage, a point we will return to below. Cally Guerin et al. (2016, p. 95) observed, with reference to responsibility for the design and delivery of supervisor training, "… these decisions appear to be within the purview of Graduate School staff … [who] may or may not be academics, nor have learning and teaching specialist skills themselves. We noticed that programmes were often reliant on the personal drive and commitment of individuals, rather than a result of sustained institutional policy or practice". This observation is made in the Australian context, but the UK appears no different.

Professional standing is usually recognised through achieving an agreed standard as specified in a relevant framework, code of practice and/or through accreditation, such as chartered status. However, in the UK, there is a limited range of options for formal recognition in HE. Staff are expected, by virtue of working in HE and holding higher degrees and/or other professional qualifications, to be able to design and deliver training. For supervisors, whilst formal training focuses, frequently, on regulations and requirements (Taylor, Kiley, & Holley, 2021, and see also Huet et al., 2022; Sillence, 2022; Österlind, 2022, this volume), the experience of supervision can be used as evidence for gaining professional recognition against AdvanceHE's (the body supporting UK HE) professional standards framework (PSF), the framework guiding educators' practice in the UK (Taylor, 2016). Although this needs considerable updating in the light of recent developments, it does provide a route for the recognition of specialist practice. Educational developers, also, might be expected to be members of AdvanceHE if they are going to teach education staff how to teach, although the training they offer to those staff may not extend to doctoral researchers. Doctoral researchers may or may not receive the same level of training as new lecturing staff, despite oftentimes being as important to the undergraduate student experience through their close regular teaching contact with students, especially in the early stage of undergraduate study. Neither are there similar requirements or expectations of those supporting researcher development, excepting those qualified as librarians and careers advisors who offer specialist advice, and even these staff may not be trained in designing and delivering training or professional development programmes.

Some researcher developers, like supervisors, are members of the AdvanceHE, however, the focus of the PSF means it does not address personal qualities, behavioural change or the research culture in a similar way that, say, the Vitae *Researcher Development Framework* does for researchers themselves.[1] The most frequent qualification of researcher developers is that of the doctorate. A survey of researcher developers by Anna Price and Richard Freeman (Price and Freeman, 2016) found 68% of respondents held a doctorate, had a variety of roles and were highly motivated to help researchers. As a profession, researcher developers rely heavily on their own experience, with few formal opportunities for CPD and career progression. Although, in 2019 Vitae trialled a professional framework for researcher developers, the *Career Framework for Researcher Developers* (CFReD). Similar to Advance HE's PSF, it provides a framework of standards and submission for recognition requires a portfolio of evidence. At the time of writing, the sector was waiting for this to be made more widely available. On the whole, the sector has supported the professional development of researcher developers through membership bodies such as the UKCGE, Vitae, and the SRHE-PIN, and networks such as the Researchers14 group (comprised of researcher developers in the UK research intensive organisations) and regional groupings, such as the UK South East Researcher Developers network. Being personally motivated to help others, perhaps as a result of one's own doctoral experience, is an admirable quality, it is, though, fair to note that institutions have benefited considerably from the profession, while having provided very little career recognition to this professional group in return. Price and Freeman found that the researcher developers experienced professional 'uncertainty', especially in terms of a lack of a clear career pathway.

Providing appropriate training to researcher developers is an issue institutional leaders have not deemed as vital for the support of researchers as they might do for staff in HR or Finance departments – and this matter has not been pursued at the policy making level either within institutions or across the sector. The closest the sector comes to establishing structural requirements or obligations is in the *Concordat to Support the Career Development of Researchers* (which also contains the *European Charter for Researchers* and a *Code of*

Conduct for the Recruitment of Researchers (EC, 2005)). Although this obliges institutions to ensure that the line managers of researchers are equipped to carry out their roles, formal training is limited to 'leadership/line management' and 'project management', and ensuring managers are "effectively trained in relation to EDI, well-being and mental health" (Concordat, 2019, pp. 4, 8). The standing of those providing this training and supporting line managers and researchers is implicit in the document and only mentioned generally in terms of providing researchers with "opportunities, [and] structured support … to engage in a minimum of 10 days professional development" and access to "professional advice on career management" (Concordat, 2019, p. 8).

Institutions have a responsibility to enhance the skills of their researchers as indicated by the Concordat and 'statements of expectation'. Researcher developers, who design and deliver the relevant training, contribute considerably to their fulfilling that responsibility. Institutions have benefitted extensively from researcher developers' experience, enthusiasm, creativity and expertise but there has been little acknowledgment, recognition and reward in terms of either a clear career pathway or inclusion in the strategic decision making that affects researchers (Connie Schroeder (2011) made a similar point with respect to educational developers and Richard Watermeyer and Gene Rowe (2021) have made comparable observations with respect to public engagement professionals). Researcher developers may have unwittingly been party to their strategic marginalisation or invisibility within institutions by virtue of their focus on the outcomes for researchers rather than on the internal politics and business planning processes related to their own employment prospects. Indeed, Price and Freeman found an absence of CPD planning among researcher developers and suggested they needed to engage their institutions more to secure this. The question now remains whether researcher development can reposition itself to meet contemporary challenges in a sustainable way, or whether financial constraints as a result of the pandemic will lead to retrenchment and further marginalisation?

4 New Structures of Responsibility?

In many respects, the story of researcher development over the past two decades has been one of repositioning and adapting to a rapidly changing environment. Whilst some aspects of researcher development contracted when the Roberts funding was withdrawn, notably the number of 'GRADschools' diminished, many institutions continued to expand their offer and commitment to doctoral researchers. The GRADschool model of several days' intensive and experiential activity resurfaced in new guises, for instance a Consultancy Challenge was developed for the South East Physics Network by Dawn Duke and became an annual regional event where doctoral researchers produced solutions to real-world problems posed by local employers. In this way each group learned much about the benefits and needs of the other. The challenge model was itself reworked in 2021 for an international research project team (BRECcIA-GCRF) and turned into an online two week 'research output challenge'. Programmes with a longer timespan appeared alongside shorter workshops. Accreditation has emerged for doctoral researchers, with postgraduate certificates in researcher development offered by Robert Gordon and Strathclyde universities, for example. What has been interesting to observe in the doctoral community over the years is the way extra-curricular activities, such as public engagement, have afforded these researchers the opportunity to develop personally and professionally, supported by 'third space' professionals (see Whitchurch, 2008) such as researcher developers. Leveraging informal learning opportunities, including public engagement, to expand the doctoral experience is another lesson obtained from doctoral training, and one of the most exciting developments combines this kind of 'on-the-job' learning with international collaboration. The University of Surrey co-delivers and shares the *23InternationalThings programme* with universities in New Zealand, Australia, USA and UK, enabling doctoral researchers from all countries to be trained and work together.

In the midst of the pandemic, it is encouraging to note that researcher developers are looking for new ways to collaborate and share costs, and this model looks set to grow further. All these activities demonstrate the adaptability of the researcher development community and the importance of sharing best practice with and learning from each other. They demonstrate another key element in the researcher development story, one of achieving culture change through collaborative effort. Of course, this kind of creativity and practice sharing assumes the continued professional existence of researcher developers, which the coronavirus pandemic may place under threat as institutions look to streamline activity. In business organisations staff development is often among the first activities targeted as expendable in financially stringent times and, since the 2008 financial crisis, universities have been increasingly working like businesses.

In contrast, institutions are facing challenges to be inclusive in their people management, to increase the diversity of thinking in all disciplines, to ensure the good mental health and well-being of doctoral researchers specifically and of all staff in general. This more than indicates that this is not the time for less investment of resource (including people, time, the gathering of internal data, and funding), but for more. What we learned from the Roberts era about effecting culture change was that it required sustained and determined effort by staff dedicated to the broader cause of researcher development, as opposed to focusing on the researching and scholarly ability of an individual, which is and remains the concern of supervisors. In turn, these staff developed specialist knowledge and became adept at collaborating with other specialist staff in their institutions, librarians and careers advisers among others, and with external organisations to link into the external world of work to provide a wide variety of professional development interventions. The success of researcher development required external pump-prime funding, scaffolding in the form of directives from the key funders and, most of all, time. Key funders have indicated that further culture change is required. The policy documents and directives (such as the Concordat, RCUK/UKRI statement of expectations and focus on positive research cultures) are already in place, the researcher development community has the expertise necessary, but ultimately only senior managers with the support of all the staff can make the required change happen.

The call for further change to the research culture is echoed in the shifting needs of doctoral researchers. It is most likely that future doctoral researchers will need to be able to work in an inclusive and collaborative way, be aware of the contributions diverse peoples and disciplines make, and be ethical and globally minded researchers. They will be comfortable communicating with a variety of sectors and publics; they already expect equality and respectful treatment of people and the environment. Doctoral researchers are passionate about their topics and will want and need opportunities to meet and work with others, yet they also want to do this in a sustainable way and one with a low carbon footprint. They have been raised by the internet and are at ease with online interactions and training. A group of eight doctoral researchers at the University of Waterloo, Canada, neatly summed up what they believe the future will look like:

> We conclude with our vision of the PhD student of the future as one who thrives in transdisciplinary settings, links society and science through knowledge brokering, spans boundaries between multiple epistemologies to communicate and collaborate through uncertainty, and prioritizes societal impact. (Lazurko et al., 2020)

This impact will need to be assessed alongside celebration of the benefits brought to institutions by doctoral researchers through their public engagement, teaching, mentoring and other informal (and invisible) contributions.

As the needs of researchers are changing, so will the roles of the researcher developers who support them. That researcher development has become such an important feature of the UK HE landscape is testament to the determination and commitment of everyone associated with it. Nearly two decades of researcher development indicates that this is not just a 'nice to have element' of provision but an essential function. However, what seems to characterise researcher development, and is another element in the story, is the vulnerability of it as a business activity and function within HE. Often this vulnerability is only revealed when an individual senior champion or sponsor moves on or changes roles. The lack of strategic presence, or inclusion in university level decision-making speaks further to the structural limitations the activity and profession face. Institutions have recruited and created researcher developers but have not yet established appropriate career pathways, training programmes or support structures for them. Whilst many 'third space' professionals share this fate along with their professional service colleagues, one must question this as a sustainable and fruitful employment practice. Waiting to be noticed and appreciated, however, will not suffice. Instead, trumpets must be blown as cases are made for this important activity.

Now is the time to ensure that new forms of support for researchers and those who support them is provided. We need to pool our collective expertise to be impactful and collaborate within and beyond our institutional boundaries if we are to adequately support and prepare our doctoral researchers for the post-pandemic future. Collaborative professional development models are emerging on regional, national and international scales. For institutions that do not have the capacity for their own full-service programme, either in terms of funding or staff, sharing the cost of delivery is worth considering. Moving online and being able to reach researchers around the world is opening up a host of new opportunities and brings a whole new dimension to researcher development. It is up to all of us who care about researcher development, no matter what our institutional role, to ensure that structural support for it is established and sustained despite the need for careful institutional budgeting. Rather than allowing the good work to be lost by default and inaction, the Covidian era can be taken as an opportunity for fresh approaches and new beginnings. We must work together to make a strong case that researcher development has and can continue to make a significant contribution to universities and society at large.

Note

1 Some researcher developers are members of the HR professional body, the Chartered Institute of Personnel and Development. However, like AdvanceHE, this organisation's requirements do not address the specialist needs of researchers.

References

Denicolo, P. M., Fuller, M., & Berry, D. (2010). *A review of graduate schools in the UK.* UK Council for Graduate Education.

Denicolo P. M., & Park, C. (2013). Doctorateness – An elusive concept? In M. Kompf & P. M. Denicolo (Eds.), *Critical issues in higher education.* Sense Publishers.

European Commission. (2005). *European charter for researchers and a code of conduct for the recruitment of researchers.* Retrieved March 27, 2021, from https://euraxess.ec.europa.eu/sites/default/files/am509774cee_en_e4.pdf

Guerin, C., Walker, R., Aitchison, C., Laming, M., Padmanabhan, M. C., & James, B. (2017). Doctoral supervisor development in Australian universities: Preparing research supervisors to teach writing, *Journal of Academic Language & Learning, 11*(1), A88–A103. https://journal.aall.org.au/index.php/jall/article/view/446

Guthrie, S., Lichten, C.A., van Belle, J., Ball, S., Knack, A., & Hofman, J. (2017). *Understanding mental health in the research environment: A rapid evidence assessment.* RAND Europe RR-2022-RS. Prepared for the Royal Society and the Wellcome Trust.

Hinchcliffe, R., Bromley, T., & Hutchinson, S. (Eds.). (2007). *Skills training in research degree programmes: Politics and practice.* Open University Press.

Hodge, A., Bownes, M., Burgess, R., Chambaz, J., Dodson, E., Johnes, G., Loving, C., Mcvitty, D., O'Carroll, C., & Ritchie, E. (2011). *Review of progress in implementing the recommendations of Sir Gareth Roberts, regarding employability and career development of PhD students and research staff.* A report for Research Councils UK by an independent review panel. Research Councils UK (Hodge review).

Kearns, H., Gardiner, M., & Marshall, K. (2008). Innovation in PhD completion: The hardy shall succeed (and be happy!). *Higher Education Research & Development, 27*(1), 77–89.

Lazurko, A., Alamenciak, T., Hill, L.S., Muhl, E-K., Kwame Osei, A., Pomezanski, D., Schang, K., & Sharmin, D. F. (2020). What will a PhD look like in the future? Perspectives on emerging trends in sustainability doctoral programs in a time of disruption. *World Futures Review, 12*(4), 369–384. https://doi.org/10.1177/1946756720976710

Levecque, K., Anseel, F., De Beuckelaer, A., Van der Heyden, J., & Gisle, L. (2017). Work organization and mental health problems in PhD students, *Research Policy, 46*(4), 868–879.

Price, A., & Freeman, R. (2016). *Researcher developer: An evolving third space profession in higher education* [Presentation]. Researcher education and development scholarship conference. Retrieved March 27, 2021, from https://www.sheffield.ac.uk/rs/ecr/events/reds2016

Research Councils UK-RCUK/UKRI. (2016). *Statement of expectations for postgraduate training.* Retrieved March 28, 2021, from https://www.ukri.org/wp-content/uploads/2020/10/UKRI-211020-StatementOfExpectationsPostGradTraining-Sep2016v2.pdf

Roberts, Sir G. (2002). *SET for success: the supply of people with science, technology, engineering and mathematics skills: The report of Sir Gareth Roberts' review.* HM Treasury.

Schroeder, C. (Ed.). (2011). *Coming in from the margins: Faculty development's emerging organizational development role in institutional change.* Stylus Publishing.

Taylor, S. (2016). *UK Professional Standards Framework (UKPSF) dimensions of the framework for doctoral supervisors.* Higher Education Academy.

Taylor, S., Kiley, M., & Holley, K. A. (Eds.). (2021). *The making of doctoral supervisors: International case studies of practice.* Routledge/Taylor and Francis.

The Concordat to Support the Career Development of Researchers. (2019). Retrieved March 28, 2021, from https://www.vitae.ac.uk/policy/concordat

Vitae blog. (2017). *The future of doctoral education.* Retrieved March 28, 2021, from https://www.vitae.ac.uk/news/vitae-blog/the-future-of-doctoral-training

Vitae in partnership with the Institute for Employment Studies (IES) and the University of Ghent. (2018). *Exploring wellbeing and mental health and associated support services for postgraduate researchers.* Retrieved March 27, 2021, from https://www.vitae.ac.uk/doing-research/wellbeing-and-mental-health/HEFCE-Report_Exploring-PGR-Mental-health-support/view

Watermeyer, R., & Rowe, G. (2021). Public engagement professionals in a prestige economy: Ghosts in the machine. *Studies in Higher Education, 47*(7), 1297–1310. Retrieved May 15, 2021, from https://www.tandfonline.com/doi/full/10.1080/03075079.2021.1888078

Wellcome. (2020). *What researchers think about the culture they work in.* Retrieved March 27, 2021, from https://wellcome.org/reports/what-researchers-think-about-research-culture

Whitchurch, C. (2008). Shifting identities and blurring boundaries: The emergence of Third Space professionals in UK higher education. *Higher Education Quarterly, 62*(4), 377–396.

PART 3

Challenges and Opportunities for Doctoral Researchers' Wellbeing

CHAPTER 11

Dimensions of Wellbeing in the Doctoral Research Environment

Implications for Quality

Martin Gough

Abstract

As higher education institutions adopt their own versions of the Wellbeing Agenda, the accompanying discourse inevitably pervades the doctoral research environment. Please join me into an exploration of the concept of Wellbeing relevant to this context. I cannot in this abstract give away very much of the argument towards my recommendations, for fear of undermining the exploration, which is now our joint endeavour. Suffice to say that that there is a paradox at the heart of this concept, in that pursuit of the Wellbeing Agenda in the higher education sector and beyond is, under a certain categorisation of wellbeing, tending to undermine actual wellbeing in the richest, and more desirable, sense. And the effect of this is most acute in the doctoral research environment.

Keywords

Wellbeing Agenda – utility – flourishing – Essentially Contested Concepts

1 Introduction

I set the scene with a vignette:

> It is mid-Winter, some time after the short hours of daylight have faded. The mist hangs heavy above the river estuary which opens out near the campus. It is now mid-evening, most campus staff have departed home, but not the conscientious doctoral researchers who are continuing to beaver away in the lab. They are certainly self-consciously concerned not to exhaust themselves, and their supervisors are not tyrants (relatively speaking), but the researchers are keen to impress through demonstration

 | DOI:10.1163/9789004529304_011

> of their industrious presenteeism. There is one of their number whose project has been faltering a bit over the last couple of months. He has not been saying much to his peers when in the lab (to be honest, he was never the talkative 'type'), and he is found staring into space quite a bit of the time. He has been leaving the lab towards the end of the day but somewhat early (that is, by the standards of his peers), when the others are still immersed in tasks some way off before being brought to a suitable pausing point. This evening, after he leaves, two of the group share that someone had told them that he has been occasionally spotted wandering around on the bridge over the estuary. It is not his usual route home. They all acknowledge that they have all noticed that something is not quite right with him. With thought of his welfare, and also more excited thought this evening of some 'out-of-the-ordinary' intrigue and trepidation, they quickly decide that they should follow him to see where he goes, whilst, of course, keeping a discreet distance and exchanging just whispers. Before long, through the mist, they manage to make out his figure on the bridge ("I think it is …", "No, I'm sure it is him …"). He is spending a while looking over the railings and into the distance. They turn to each other and share a similar thought, in an almost synchronous communal whisper: 'Will he jump?' …

I have added some frills for dramatic effect but this is a story of an actual episode, set well before Covid-19 times, relayed to the class of a workshop, which I was running in aid of the development of new supervisors.[1] The context is a development activity for doctoral supervisors designed, following enquiry by Anne Lee (2007, 2008), to assist in uncovering (often largely implicit) tendencies in approaches by supervisors towards the supervisory relationship.

In discussion of the activity and the surrounding issues in the workshop I report here, one participant, prompted by a questionnaire statement,[2] related the experience represented in the vignette. The story did not continue with report of the fellow laboratory researcher colleague actually jumping, which would be detrimental to his wellbeing. Issues of wellbeing are clearly raised in this story anyway, but they are not straightforward and this in turn gives the purpose to writing this chapter about them.

2 Scenarios for Wellbeing Considerations

Staging discussion of an issue in a workshop, workshops being a form of teaching, is an effective method of general open-ended enquiry into that issue.[3]

So I continue here with a series of scenarios, which I have in another workshop environment put to a wider group of participants whose own work roles encompass concern about the environment for doctoral researchers, a concern which has been growing across the sector. Reports (e.g., Guthrie et al., 2017; Levecque et al., 2017; Panger et al., 2014) investigating the phenomenon of mental ill-health and causes underneath it finds that the issue is more acute in this environment than in most other domains of society. Indeed, a higher proportion of the doctoral researcher population than other student populations is reported as experiencing problems in this way, prompting discussion and recommendations for targeted response (e.g., Ayres, 2019; Lane et al., 2019; Pierson, 2019). But our priority here is to investigate in what ways, conceptually speaking, this phenomenon is or is not so acute in this environment.

So, the question posed to my workshop participants is whether or not a wellbeing issue is hereby represented in the scenario in question. And if so, then what sort of wellbeing issue is it, is there a useful further system of re-categorisation of the issues? – and it would be the different sorts that I would really want to tease out. Additional questions could include whether the binary options 'positive' vs. 'negative' help in describing emotions and other feelings alluded to in the scenarios. So, reader, feel free have a go at this task yourself before reading beyond the following list (scenarios A–N).

A. "My GP has diagnosed me with chronic stress and clinical depression".
B. "One of my lab group members has started to harass me".
C. "I've been working in jobs for 50 hours a week to fund my studies and try to keep up with the bills – I am troubled by where the money will come from next".
D. "I'm working such long hours in my lab but my results are not showing up anything. I feel so tired and depressed".
E. "I am struggling to articulate what my thesis is. What shall I do? It's like I've been abandoned to endless torment, since my supervisor does not seem to care".
F. "I am trying to write critically about my area but it is so hard and my supervisor keeps sending my efforts back for re-writing".
G. PGR Questionnaire:
responses on a scale of 0 (it bothers me not at all) to 10 (I am extremely bothered) […]
41. My supervisor waits at least a week before responding to my queries
H. "I'm so angry that the University has decided to close down my department".
I. "I've got to read all this tortuous Middle English literature and finish this chapter by the end of the month and I feel so stressed out".

J. "I am deeply troubled by this Interpretivism business: it does not seem right to me and I don't get it".
K. "I don't feel like I really belong in my research group. Am I an impostor?"
L. Code of Practice for course materials, classroom conduct, research seminars and theses [...]
3.k.xxiv Trigger warnings will be issued in advance if any material is to be viewed or expressed which may cause distress or offence to any participant or viewer.
M. "It's really brilliant that you can drop in to the Campus Mindfulness Centre and play with a puppy. It stops me fretting about this horrible Annual Review".
N. "I suffer from panic attacks and I'm so anxious about the thought of my viva, which will be coming up before long. Could I have exemption from it?"

Scenarios (E, F, G) are more explicitly about the supervisor, which is certainly one sort of categorisation. (G) is in the form of an institutional questionnaire that asks doctoral researchers to rate the questionnaire statement according to how much they're 'bothered', or dissatisfied, by the matter that it represents; and (L) is also an institution-like document; whereas all the rest are as if uttered by a doctoral researcher themselves.

Doctoral supervision pedagogy, at least no less than general academic pedagogy, has always had a pastoral dimension (whether or not observed well by all supervisors). Following through the expectations of the Wellbeing Agenda, should supervisory practice, as individual supervisor action but also as an institutional framework for developer and support functions, now become mainly about ensuring the continued wellbeing of doctoral researchers? My response to this question, which I explore in the rest of this chapter, is, variously, no and yes, as in accord with the more fundamental categorisation which I am interested in, and which may apply to the scenarios (A–N) directly but is more about what we mean by wellbeing and the model of it which we should follow.

3 The Utilitarian Conception of Wellbeing

The answer which the question posed in the final paragraph of the previous section demands will at any one point depend upon the particular dimension of wellbeing under consideration. Few would equate wellbeing and mental health together, for instance, even though much literature on the topic finds itself using the terms interchangeably: for one thing physical health, with components not co-extensive with those under mental health, is in turn part of wellbeing. I am certainly happy to assume that mental health, and mental ill-health, are real states of persons. And I shall not try to establish that there is nothing intrinsic to the nature of doctoral research study that may precipitate states of actual mental and other ill-health,[4] by comparison with undergraduate study and other common processes of life (Gough, 2006).

Nonetheless, the Wellbeing Agenda, as illustrated in much discourse, including some higher education institution documentation, tends to approach all issues contained under the concept of wellbeing somewhat uni-dimensionally, and this is where the problem lies for the doctoral research environment, and for higher education practice generally. Not only does the Wellbeing Agenda tend to equate the wellbeing which is at issue with mental health but its theoretical metaethical assumption is, at root, Utilitarian.

Although there are more modern and sophisticated revisions of Utilitarianism as a system of grounding ethical value and for normative ethical decision-making (such as the degree of 'desire-satisfaction' across a population), Jeremy Bentham's (1823) original formulation is more illuminating for working through the issue at hand. His 'Greatest Happiness Principle' proposes that we judge the ethical value of a situation, or of an act by someone, and that we decide what is the right course of action to take from now on, according to the actual (or expected) consequences. More specifically, the more we find happiness (or pleasure), and the less we find unhappiness (or pain), present or resulting, the better is the situation or the act. The experiential state of happiness/pleasure is what Bentham assumes is ethically relevant. As a universal ethical theory, his Greatest Happiness Principle means that we should all aim to bring about the greatest happiness of the greatest number. The intensity of happiness/pleasure and the quantity of sentient beings experiencing it are the main focus.[5]

Who would be against all that, and who would be against wellbeing based on that? – you, reader, might ask. Bentham's theory provided a philosophical foundation for the classical liberal laissez-faire capitalist economics of his time. Both in his original form and in more recent revised forms, Utilitarianism similarly provides a basis for modern economic theory coming under a neoliberal banner.[6] The assumption is that accruing units of value, i.e., units of utility,[7] which Bentham equates with experiential states of happiness/pleasure, is *prima facie* good. Following the Greatest Happiness Principle, the more for all sentient beings is the better. But it is an individual accumulation model as well.[8]

The experiential states of happiness/pleasure or unhappiness/pain are, uncontroversially, psychological states. Psychological states are mental states. When you combine all this with issues to do with the individual's health, then this framework of thinking takes on a medical hue as well. I take the term 'medical' in a broad sense, to cover any health-related matter which may require an intervention, whether surgical, drug or other therapeutic. So ill health is real when it happens. It is not very nice. You are not going to be very happy. If it is chronic, afflicting you as more than a fleeting condition, then it can certainly come to be recognised as a medical matter of concern. Quite quickly we move from episodes of you being in pain, or just unhappy or dissatisfied, to (following Utilitarian logic) identification of 'harm' to you, a reduction of your wellbeing, as constituted by the pain/unhappiness/dissatisfaction or by prospects of future absence of pleasure/happiness/satisfaction, now *prima facie* medical in nature.[9] It is effectively an equation between unhappiness itself and harm. And this then gives licence for institutional intervention to rectify the 'harm', by any means necessary, if that is what it will take, as a priority over other concerns.

What this Utilitarian framework offers is a linear as well as a homogeneous scale of utility, or happiness, which necessarily each individual is trying to maximise for themselves as an *a priori* 'positive' good, maximise their accumulation of 'utils'. As John White (1990, p. 31) puts it, the accumulation of satisfactions is "the flattened-out, uni-dimensional account of the utilitarians and economists". This way of thinking comes through clearly in Education literature. There is (albeit bi-dimensional) "the mood meter tool. Its y-axis represents energy levels and its x axis the pleasantness of the emotion. [... individuals] now know how to regulate their emotions and how to live healthier and happier lives" (Eggleton, 2021, pp. 8–9). "... trainees to record their perceived resources and challenges and draw a timeline of their programme experiences, marking where their wellbeing was higher/better, or lower/poorer. [...] where trainees had to form new relationships as part of the programme [...], wellbeing dipped on most timelines" (Quickfall, Clarke, & Thompson, 2021, pp. 20–21). By way of example of university documentation: "When individuals have more challenges than their personal resources enable them to deal with, the balance may dip, which may affect their feeling of positive wellbeing".

4 Wellbeing as Flourishing

In order to establish the inadequacy of the utilitarian approach, let us consider more specific substantive issues, such as those represented in the scenarios from my workshop list above. Paranoid delusion, as well as more common stress, and of course other ill-health precipitated by poverty, substance abuse, or lack of sleep, are definitely wellbeing matters (cf. scenarios A, C, D) and also in the medical domain. Is medical language concerning belonging (in relation to its opposite, impostorism, cf. scenario K, restated for doctoral research and higher academic levels) likewise appropriate?

To answer this, we need to consider whether belonging and the experience of it are or are not part of wellbeing. If belonging is not itself a medical matter and wellbeing is entirely medically defined then belonging would not be relevant to wellbeing. Self-doubt about what you are able to contribute to your community is a healthy self-check on bombastic presumptions. Often what you produce is not at that point academically very good. But either you can work it up some more or you are in the wrong group and you would do well for yourself to develop your talents elsewhere. So you may be right about the importance of your contribution (and peers are being exclusionary) or you may be wrong, at various points in time, but you are not ill.[10]

It might seem sad, especially as a doctoral researcher new to a programme of study at a university, if you've got no friends to hang out with, a group to belong with: an active social life is reported on balance to have benefits, but not necessarily for all in all contexts and there is a danger in pathologising minority lifestyle choices. If we can re-imagine wellbeing and belonging through a different paradigm of thinking then there may be prospects for a clearer rationale for their importance, generally but especially in higher education, and at higher academic levels even more so.

The most theoretically robust account of wellbeing draws from Aristotle's thesis of *Eudaimonia* (or flourishing,[11] for short), which offers a framework for all to have the opportunity to fulfil themselves and lead the Good Life. The framework necessarily has a strong epistemic dimension, although how this is constituted will have an individual aspect. You cannot flourish without seeking and attaining wisdom suited to your interest, even if individuals' more specific interests will differ. For Aristotle (1925 edition, Book X.7, 1177a, 12ff), *Noûs*, or intellectual contemplation, will offer the highest and most perfect happiness if attained. Because people are different, the pursuit of the heights of intellectual wisdom will not suit all, they can flourish pursuing heights of wisdom in other walks of life.

The above notwithstanding, for those pursuing proficiency in academic disciplines the university sector will be failing them shockingly if opportunities for intellectual development are obstructed.[12] This allows us to see how wellbeing with a necessarily intellectual character is so important for those who are at university in order to learn. And belonging, in the relevant context meaning to belong to a scholarly academic community, has a necessarily disciplinary (rather than institutional or just social) dimension. So what it means for the student/scholar to flourish will vary by discipline as well as by individual. Forces working against belonging are therefore not medical but cultural, so we can recommend that situated academic cultural behaviours do need to be more inclusive (cf. scenarios B, K). But it does mean that unhappiness through frustration with progress in studies and trepidation and discombobulation in the face of the epistemic and academic process challenges[13] are typical aspects of developing wellbeing rather than clearly detrimental to it (cf. scenarios D, E, F, G, I, J, M, N – regarding N, an intellectually challenging viva is not an episode of harassment of the candidate and is not undermining their wellbeing like scenario B would be).

5 Emotional Epistemology

The picture conjured from the typical 'Wellbeing Agenda' publicity (e.g., 'Wellbeing Week') is that work and study in higher education may be necessary (if only for economic productivity outcomes) but are necessary evils in being detrimental to health, and that you should therefore redress the (linearly defined) balance by doing something else in addition which is pleasurable. So the sanctioned extra-curricular pursuits or interventions are then proposed as the means to mitigate the harmful exposures (cf. scenario M).[14] Even if work (for staff, at least) is so oppressively structured, cynically or not, that it does harm our health, this Wellbeing Agenda picture broadcasts the worst possible message about the value of higher education to students and those who would support decisions to study and research. It is a palpable threat to quality in higher, including doctoral,[15] education since it seems purposively to distract from learning and achieving intellectually as an end in itself and as a means to wellbeing as flourishing, which depends upon integration into the scholarly disciplinary community (i.e., not primarily the general community of a particular institution). I echo, to some extent, a thesis of those who highlight and oppose what they term 'emotional epistemology':

> [...] the idea that educational institutions must address affective, emotional and personal aspects of learning and subject content is changing the purposes, processes and content of education [...] the current shift [...] not merely puts the emotional first but is undermining the cognitive. (Ecclestone & Hayes, 2008b, p. 1)

> In attacking [...] academic authority (expertise), acknowledging the value of subjective experience, accepting failing and frailties, [... the therapeutic alternatives] undermine the central ethical value of the university, namely, the disinterested pursuit of knowledge. [...] the political consequence of a therapeutic education, from the early years curriculum

> to the postgraduate course, will be social passivity because a diminished and uncertain self can pose no questions and offer no challenge to anyone. (Ecclestone & Hayes, 2008a, p. 104)

Williams (2016a) develops this line of thinking in making the 'fear of knowledge' a framework of explanation for an analysis of where, in particular through stifling academic freedom (of both staff and students), higher levels of education are heading down the wrong path, as follows. If a certain knowledge might challenge the neatness of the student's prior worldview, the student may themselves be caused to be upset and threatened, so they would need protection from this knowledge out there which they would find they do not want to be informed about, e.g. with 'trigger warnings' (cf. scenario L), or even more draconian censoring of the curriculum, 'no-platforming' of invited speakers, etc.

Williams illuminates certain phenomena, highlighting how emotional epistemology will discourage intellectual boldness in undergraduate students. Different factors do also come into play at doctoral level for those who have spent a few years in HE and are already happy with more of it.[16] I suggest that the boldness issue is especially pertinent for doctoral research but needs different framing from what Williams's account can provide. It would be possible to fear potential outcomes of research you happen to be conducting, from the point of view that the new knowledge might be used as a weapon by someone else to carry out harm to others, but the fear here is not of the knowledge itself. More importantly, the requirements of doctoral research to accept significant freedom and responsibility to make an original contribution to knowledge mean that the researcher is the one producing the knowledge, not having it forced upon them.

This freedom can be exciting but the sudden realisation that it is ultimately down to you, as doctoral researcher, to sort out your thesis can be a debilitating moment (cf. scenario E) if you are conditioned to being directed in your studies, as in the more tightly controlled taught programme curriculum.[17] Although chronic paralysis as an affliction may well evolve into something more clinical, such a moment, as a natural feature of freedom, even if troubling, cannot be treated as a wellbeing matter on the medicalised utilitarian deficit model.

6 Conclusion and Recommendation

To summarise what I have attempted to achieve here, commentators on the state of higher education and the way that it is going do tend to be broad brush, which normally means assuming undergraduate education is the chief issue. So it is important that I have the opportunity here to focus on the doctoral research education level. The further step is to offer more theoretical depth in analysis of the general problem.

Manuela Schmidt and Erika Hansson (in the next chapter in this volume, Schmidt & Hansson, 2022) are also concerned about the concept of wellbeing. They allude to competing conceptions similar to the two I have explicated. But they then quickly assume a unitary conception which remains rooted in the purview of Psychology, as well as being concerned only with the doctoral research stage of life, rather than thinking lifelong. Their review brings out interesting facets of doctoral experience but drawing clear conclusions is hampered by this: indeed they admit that the literature shows "a growing awareness of the lack of a unified definition". Instead of their preferred 'holistic' conception, we need to realise that wellbeing is an essentially contested concept (Gallie, 1955–1956). Here the different and incommensurable theoretical positions claim unitarily to be owning the concept and compete permanently without 'winning', and so will be perceptibly in tension with each other in practice. I have certainly been promoting one dimension of wellbeing as superior to the other but, through theoretical and conceptual analysis, find that we need to accept that both make a contribution in explaining and resolving situations.

All the workshop scenarios (A–N) are about wellbeing in one way or another. Happiness or unhappiness, as psychological episodes, are relevant in judging so, *ceteris paribus*. But … *ceteris non paribus*, if this approach does not recognise prospects and obstacles for wellbeing as flourishing. Returning to my overarching question whether supervisory practice should now become mainly about ensuring the continued wellbeing of doctoral researchers, the answer is: of course, yes, to enable personal intellectual flourishing within the context of developing the academic discipline; of course, yes, to do this in a way which is respectful of persons and their psychic life; but no to prioritising psychological states of happiness above academic integrity and quality.

Utilitarian thinking has its place in rational decision-making in certain contexts but can only explain a part of human experience. The key philosophical mistake of the Utilitarian model is the exclusive presumption of a linear and homogeneous scale of utility and value, combined with seeing experience in terms of discrete ontologically independent psychological states. Insofar as the Wellbeing Agenda assumes this model then it is wrong-headed.[18] The nature of an experience, and state of the experiencer, is instead intrinsically tied up with what is the focus of the experience. This is because of the intentional structure of consciousness.[19]

The same applies to emotions and attitudes. To return to one of my workshop enquiry questions, since the Utilitarian framework requires everyone to try to maximise happiness for themselves as an *a priori* 'positive' good, unhappiness is *a priori* 'negative'. So a state of unhappiness, an "oppressive psychic harm" (Williams 2016b, p. XIV), resulting from any cause demands to be countered by any stimulus (which could therefore be a therapeutic intervention) which would relieve the state, thereby allegedly solving the 'problem',[20] which in turn equates to a mental health problem because there is no other criterion in this model for measuring wellbeing or mental health.

Against this picture, we are not just unhappy or angry, not just having a mood on a metered level, but unhappy or angry about something in the world which we judge needs addressing, and so these states can be conceived not as intrinsically 'negative' (i.e., lowering the utility level of individuals experiencing them) but as 'positive' towards this end of addressing and then maybe changing this part of the world. The (toxically combined) Utilitarian/Economic/Medical/Psychological model falsely drives a wedge between rationality and emotion. The appropriate response from those in power should be to address what is seen to be needed in the world, not to attend primarily to your psychological state in itself to 'cheer you up' or 'calm you down' (cf. scenarios C, G, H).

Higher Education practitioners should be recognising the above nuances. To underpin prospects for developing intellectual wellbeing and enhancing belonging in the Academy, are we going to see a clear prioritised recommendation from the Wellbeing Agenda process to the effect that we need mainly to resource teaching, supervision and researching better, such as by reducing the student:staff ratio, or by allowing more time and space for the disinterested pursuit of knowledge in order to make our contributions and supervise novices to assist them to find their place in the community? This rhetorical question expects the answer 'no' in practice from the powers-that-be but stands in principled support of the answer 'yes'.

Notes

1 The University where I ran the workshop and the University where the participant conducted her doctoral research shall remain nameless.

2 "My students go through a 'dark night of the soul' whilst doing their research, but emerge stronger for it" (Lee, 2012, p. 161).

3 For instance, I integrated workshops into the method of the following project: "Evaluation of researcher support programmes: assessment within development events, and the attitudes and experiences towards academic careers provision, of early career academics (ECAs)", Report of the project to the Centre for Excellence in Preparing for Academic Practice, published March 2010 @ http://www.learning.ox.ac.uk/cetl.php?page=208. My position on this pedagogical matter draws from Yrjö Engeström's (1987) 'Expansive Learning' theory. It is especially relevant for professional learning, in the sense that an effective development

strategy is not just about instilling useful 'skills' and presenting codified knowledge all predefined for consumption and assimilation. Rather, it is about encouraging participants to see where the more problematic issues in their practice lie, as emerging from the 'activity system' as a whole, and to learn by setting about tackling them. And this in turn generates some level of findings by means of such enquiry, moving the debate forward. If the reader wonders whether this also draws from the Socratic method of enquiry then I would respond that it certainly aspires to.

4 Such as those reported by Marie-Louise Österlind (in Chapter 14 of this volume).

5 There are actually seven dimensions feeding into Bentham's 'Felicific Calculus' but I shall not explain his theory in its full detail just for the sake of it here.

6 Even if endorsing Utilitarianism does not commit you to only one economic or political system.

7 'Utils' perhaps: Martin Hollis alluded to this occasional term of economists (cf. https://www.amosweb.com/cgi-bin/awb_nav.pl?s=wpd&c=dsp&k=util accessed 20 October 2021), but to show the incoherence of this general approach, at the *Analysis 50* conference (Newnham College Cambridge, 30 March–1 April 1990).

8 The neoliberal economic theorists use units of financial value as proxy for utils, so they aim to demonstrate both the value of the pursuit of individual wealth and also, as sum of such parts, the collective wealth resulting, as in Gross National or Domestic Product.

9 And if the cause is 'bad education' then it will be seen also to amount to economic harm, if education is the production of human capital (Becker, 1964), since it will limit your own individual earning power and productivity and thereby macro-economic collective wealth as well.

10 Any chronic debilitating condition related to this would, of course, be a different matter.

11 A not dissimilar term in use is 'thriving', to be contrasted with 'surviving', for instance. After numerous somewhat cryptic allusions earlier in the book to wellbeing being important but without much explanation, Elliot et al. (2020) explain in the final chapter what they (presumably not separately) mean by thriving in the doctoral context. They offer at the same time no theoretical underpinning themselves, which is my aim here.

12 Such obstruction can be seen as a concrete realisation of the Marxian alienation which Alistair McCulloch (in Chapter 2 of this volume) argues is the general feature of contemporary doctoral education when considered as 'work'. Alienation here is not the psychological state of feeling 'left out' somehow, even if that may also happen as a result (and whether or not that counts as 'negative' on the utilitarian wellbeing scale). The intellectual endeavour I conceptualise here is both the part of you which goes into your doctoral creation (then to be expropriated by the mechanism of the knowledge economy) and also your self-development towards (intellectual) flourishing. This is not just true for those then taking their attributes (human capital) in to other sectors of the knowledge economy but true even if you are heading into an academic career. Indeed, this stifled creativity and independence (as observed by Britt-Marie Apelgren, Sverker Lindblad and Gun-Britt Wärvik in Chapter 3 of this volume) ought to be important otherwise for most careers. Wellbeing as flourishing, when it can happen, is more of a lifelong project and not a state of the person which can be rectified in the moment.

13 Such as the sometimes distressing experiences of liminality, as explained by Shane Dowle (in Chapter 13 of this volume).

14 As Julie Reeves (in Chapter 10 of this volume) suggests regarding relatively more purposive 'training' for researchers and their supervisors, similarly these more tangential, possibly mood-raising, wellbeing initiatives aim to deal with symptoms which higher education management would rather were not there. And they do anything but address the real problem of wellbeing. I do not at the same time demand abolition of such facilities understood on their

own terms. People have different hobbies and interests and should have freedom to pursue them in the main, and opportunities for serendipitous academic learning can form in addition. Resources available for conducting 'regular' academic work well are, however, far from being in limitless supply.

15 Consider the effect on maintaining standards and assuring quality if, as in scenario (N), anyone who got nervous about their *viva-voce*, their doctoral defence, was given exemption from defending their thesis. At one SRHE Conference session in 2018, an audience participant, presumably seriously, recommended that, because of the pain so often caused to candidates, the doctorate itself be done away with. But how then could anyone who would wish to achieve such heights of intellectual flourishing do so, and how would the academic profession then be viewed?

16 For instance, I argue (Gough, 2000) for the relevance of an additional non-disciplinary dimension of community for postgraduate students which does not translate to the undergraduate level.

17 I connect this freedom with the experience of anguish (Sartre, 1958, part 1, chapter 1, pp. 17, 29–35) and, as new themes have emerged through enquiry, explore this in further writing. This is a suitable point to acknowledge my seminar and conference presentations, and the assistance audience comments have given me in developing these themes, hosted by: Society for Research into Higher Education, Philosophy of Education Society of Great Britain, Philosophy of Higher Education Conference, Researcher Education and Development Scholarship Conference, most recently the 8th Postgraduate Supervision Conference, 'Transitions, trajectories and transformations in postgraduate supervision: The times they are a-changing' (15–18 March 2022, hosted online by Stellenbosch University), and departments at my own institution; and, of course, workshops, for supervisors (on supervising) and also (for the broader group) for the UK Council for Graduate Education.

18 I do not mean to imply that practitioners assisting troubled doctoral researchers think only like this and do so cynically. But it can be easy to slip in to this mode of thinking, without 'thinking', as it were.

19 Consciousness is consciousness *of* something (Sartre, 1958, p. xxxvi: follows Husserl's intentionality thesis, which draws in turn from Brentano); likewise Aristotle's (1925 edition, Book X.4, 1175a, 22ff) point is that the pleasure in pursuing and succeeding in your interest is not simply pleasure which could also be experienced through a different pursuit but will have a character determined by that interest.

20 Indeed, students themselves seemed to receive a resource from a policy reflecting this, and saw through it, when the University of Sheffield (UK) decided to offer free pilates classes in response to students expressing frustration about the state of higher education (for them, at least), in the wake of Industrial Action taken by staff as called by the Universities and Colleges Union ("The week in higher education", *Times Higher Education*, 2506, 14 April 2022, p. 3).

References

Aristotle. (1925). *Ethica Nicomachea* (W. D. Ross, Trans.). In W. D. Ross (Ed.), *The works of Aristotle, Volume IX*. Clarendon Press.

Ayres, Z. [@ZJAyres] (2019, March 5). *Wanted to enter a poster this year on something that I think is very important and needs to be talked about more* [Tweet]. Twitter. https://twitter.com/ZJAyres/status/1102861872137674752

Becker, G. (1964). *Human capital: A theoretical and empirical analysis with special reference to education*. Columbia University Press.

Bentham, J. (1823). *An introduction to the principles of morals and legislation*. W. Pickering.

Ecclestone, K., & Hayes, D. (2008a). *The dangerous rise of therapeutic education*. Routledge.

Ecclestone, K., & Hayes, D. (2008b, December). Affect: Knowledge, communication, creativity and emotion. *Beyond Current Horizons* (online).

Eggleton, M. (2021). Emotions matter: Building emotional intelligence in children. In V. Pugh (Ed.), *A curriculum for wellbeing: Improving all aspects of wellbeing in curricula & schools*. BERA British Curriculum Forum.

Elliot, D. L., Bengtsen, S. S. E., Guccione, K., & Kobayashi, S. (2020). *The hidden curriculum in doctoral education*. Palgrave Pivot.

Engeström, Y. (1987). *Learning by expanding: An activity-theoretical approach to developmental research*. Orienta-Konsultit.

Gallie, W. B. (1955–1956). Essentially contested concepts. *Proceedings of the Aristotelian Society, 56* (New Series), 167–198.

Gough, M. (2000). Towards an understanding of postgraduate community: Wellbeing and the role of pleasure. *Journal of Graduate Education, 3*(1), 26–32.

Gough, M. (2006). Postgraduate education as a form of lifelong learning, in the context of the dimensions of economic and wider benefits. *Journal of Graduate Education, 3*(4), 116–132.

Guthrie, S., Lichten, C. A., van Belle, J., Ball, S., Knack, A., & Hofman, J. (2017). *Understanding mental health in the research environment: A rapid evidence assessment*. RAND Corporation. Retrieved March 17, 2019, from https://www.rand.org/pubs/research_reports/RR2022.html

Lane, L., Kalawsky, K., Sinclair, V., & Mellick, M. (2019). *Pinch points & good practice solutions supporting mental health & wellbeing of PGRs: A timeline of challenges to candidates' wellbeing & good-practice support initiatives*. UK Council for Graduate Education Mental Health Wellbeing Working Group. Retrieved May 20, 2019, from http://www.ukcge.ac.uk/content/publications-search.aspx

Lee, A. (2007). Developing effective supervisors' concepts of research supervision. *South African Journal of Higher Education, 21*(4), 680–693.

Lee, A. (2008). How are doctoral students supervised? Concepts of research supervision. *Studies in Higher Education, 33*(3), 267–281.

Lee, A. (2012). *Successful research supervision: Advising students doing research*. Routledge.

Levecque, K., Anseel, F., De Beuckelaer, A., Van der Heyden, J., & Gisle, L. (2017). Work organization and mental health problems in PhD students. *Research Policy, 46*(4), 868–879.

Panger, G., Tyron, J., & Smith, A. (2014). *Graduate student happiness & well-being report, 2014*. Graduate Assembly, University of California Berkeley.

Quickfall, A., Clarke, E., & Thompson, S. (2021). Wellbeing challenges and resources for ITE trainees: International comparisons. *Research Intelligence: News from the British Educational Research Association, 146* (Spring).

Sartre, J.-P. (1958). *Being and nothingness* (M. Warnock, Trans.). Methuen.

White, J. (1990). *Education and the good life: Beyond the national curriculum.* Kogan Page Ltd.

Williams, J. (2016a). *Academic freedom in an age of conformity: Confronting the fear of knowledge.* Palgrave Macmillan.

Williams, J. (2016b). Preface. In J. Williams & C. Hudson (Eds.), *Why academic freedom matters: A response to current challenges* (pp. xiii–xvi). Civitas.

CHAPTER 12

Sustainability of Doctoral Education

A Well-Being Perspective

Manuela Schmidt and Erika Hansson

Abstract

The following chapter is based on a SWOT analysis (strength, weakness, threat, opportunities) made in the literature review "Doctoral students' well-being" (Schmidt & Hansson, 2018). Despite attempts to focus on a holistic and inclusive view of the well-being of doctoral researchers – investigating both how doctoral researchers can enhance their well-being and which factors lead to lack of well-being – the results of the review suggested a rather pathological depiction of the doctoral researchers' ill-being. An update of the review is presented for 2017–2020. Based on the findings, recommendations for maintaining a sustainable approach to the well-being of doctoral researchers are presented.

Keywords

doctoral researchers – well-being – sustainability

1 Introduction

The connotations of the latest headlines in Nature's editorials covering the well-being of doctoral researchers – "PhDs: the tortuous truth" (Nature, 2019c), "Being a PhD student shouldn't be bad for your health" (Nature, 2019a), "The mental health of PhD researchers demands urgent attention" (Nature, 2019b), and "Time to talk about why so many postgrads have poor mental health" (Nature, 2018) – have a single clear theme: the increasing prevalence of mental health problems and lack of well-being among doctoral researchers. This is echoed by results from self-reported surveys showing doctoral researchers' suffering from several mental health problems and conditions caused by and/or related to doctoral education. Regardless of the country, the findings are the same (e.g., Beadle, 2020; Evans, Bira, Gastelum, Weiss, & Vanderford, 2018;

 | DOI:10.1163/9789004529304_012

Helmholtz Juniors, 2019; Levecque, Anseel, De Beuckelaer, Van der Heyden, & Gisle, 2017; Nature, 2019c). As a result, attrition and non-completion rates of doctoral researchers are peaking (Gardner, 2009; Golde, 2005; Helmholtz Juniors, 2019; Jiranek, 2010). It is well-documented that people working in academia early in their careers strive to develop strategies to maintain and enhance their well-being (e.g., Agevall, Broberg, & Umans, 2018; Schmidt & Umans, 2014). Yet doctoral education is frequently described in terms of survival, torture, peril, struggle, love-hate (hurt) relationships, fights and conflicts, burden, a battlefield and war, which makes one question whether the doctoral education is worth pursuing, and if one embarks on this journey, at what cost? It is not surprising that the current situation is referred to as a 'mental health crisis' (Evans et al., 2018) with accompanying demands for a revision of doctoral education (University Affairs, 2013).

Doctoral researchers are not alone; they find themselves in good company. Apparently the whole wide world of academia feels mentally unwell, including undergraduates, academics and non-academic university staff (e.g,. Beiter et al., 2015; Kinman & Wray, 2015; Lipson, Lattie, & Eisenberg, 2019; Tytherleigh, Webb, Cooper, & Ricketts, 2005; Winefield et al., 2003), declaring universities as 'anxiety machines' (Morrish, 2019). The well-being of all students, including doctoral researchers and staff in academia, of anyone really, is usually closely related to the well-being of the organisation, which raises the rhetorical question of what is going on in academia? Given that the well-being of academics, as well as of any other occupational group, is closely related to their productivity and the efficiency of their work (Krekel, Ward, & de Neve, 2019; Taris & Schreurs, 2009), the quality of our courses and programmes might be at risk. In the long run, this might short-circuit the sustainability of educational practices, risking structural and organisational failures on institutional levels, affecting not only the well-being of the people working there at all different levels, but also the future of the higher education system at large.

1.1 *The Concept of "Well-Being"*

Well-being is a multifaceted phenomenon. It encompasses social, cultural, physical, spiritual, and psychological dimensions among others. Two (distinct yet overlapping) perspectives on well-being have dominated the literature for a long time – well-being referring to someone's potential and true nature, and well-being based on a general idea of happiness and pleasure (Diener, 2021; Ryan & Deci, 2001; Ryff & Keyes, 1995). Well-being thus includes the presence of positive emotions (such as happiness or contentment), the absence of negative emotions (such as anxiety or depression), satisfaction, fulfilment, and positive functioning (Diener, 2021; Ryan & Deci, 2001; Ryff & Keyes, 1995).

In academia and particularly regarding doctoral researchers, interest in the concept of well-being only emerged around the turn of the century as a countermovement to the dominant focus on negatives such as stress and workload. However, a common definition of doctoral researchers' well-being is lacking. Instead, different concepts are used to operationalise or conceptualise well-being (Schmidt & Hansson, 2018), complicating the generalizability of the results and making it hard to agree on a unified concept of well-being. The well-being of doctoral researchers can be understood as comprising "various elements reflecting happiness, health and success, identified in the research literature concerning doctoral education as being affected by doctoral programme elements" (Sverdlik & Hall, 2020, p. 99). Another suggestion by Juniper, Walsh, Richardson, and Morley (2012) sees well-being as "that part of a researcher's overall well-being that is primarily influenced by their PhD role and that can be influenced by university-based interventions" (p. 565). They developed a measurement of doctoral researchers' well-being consisting of seven domains: development, facilities, home and health, research, social relations with colleagues, supervisor, and university.

2 Doctoral Researchers' Well-Being; Results from the 2018 Review

In March 2018, a systematic literature search was conducted in Web of Science, ERIC, PsycInfo and Education Research Complete looking for articles using the following keywords: well-being/wellbeing/'well being' and doctoral/PhD/student/graduate (Schmidt & Hansson, 2018). In total, 68 articles were identified but after screening, 17 articles remained, 16 of them published after 2010, indicating an increase in research on the topic recently.

2.1 *Well-Being or More Correctly, the Lack of It*

Despite our attempts to take an inclusive and holistic approach, shown by our choice of keywords, well-being was often understood pathologically, focusing on stress, exhaustion, sleeping problems, loneliness, psychological distress and depression, i.e. the lack of well-being (Schmidt & Hansson, 2018). A high number of doctoral researchers (43–56%) considered dropping out. Furthermore, about one third of the doctoral researchers experienced moderate to high emotional exhaustion, which in turn was significantly related to intention to leave academia. These results raised concerns about the general well-being of doctoral researchers a decade ago (Schmidt & Hansson, 2018).

2.2 *Stressors and Coping*

Family and friends mattered for the doctoral researchers' well-being and could be a source of general social support. Organisational as well as supervisory support were positively related to engagement in work, that in turn had positive effects on the well-being of the doctoral researcher (Schmidt & Hansson, 2018). However, social interactions and relationships did not always function as supports or as buffers to stress and instead had a dual meaning since certain relationships could also evolve from being supportive to turning into major stressors for the doctoral researchers. Also, internal struggles, individual processes, and role conflicts could be a source of stress. Furthermore, the feeling of lacking control, deadlines, limited finances and lack of time were recurring stressors in the literature (Schmidt & Hansson, 2018). Additional stressors were questions concerning what would happen after graduation as well as what to prioritise in terms of different and often opposing commitments. The stressors combined, led to less enjoyment, motivational issues, and problems finishing the dissertation (Schmidt & Hansson, 2018).

Another crucial aspect of well-being raised in the review concerned the doctoral researchers' coping abilities. The review showed that for the doctoral researchers, social support, often in the form of peer relationships was the most frequently used coping mechanism, yet coping in the form of crying and isolation was also a commonly occurring mechanism (Schmidt & Hansson, 2018). In addition, planning and exercise were mentioned by the doctoral researchers as operational coping mechanisms as well as self-reflection, yoga and compartmentalisation (Schmidt & Hansson, 2018).

3 SWOT (Strengths, Weaknesses, Opportunities and Threats)

Following Jackson, Joshi, and Erhardt (2003), the studies included in the review were subjected to an analysis identifying strengths, weaknesses, opportunities and threats when exploring the scientific work on doctoral researchers' well-being.

3.1 *Strengths – The Topic Is Trending and the Advice along with It!*

Most of the research concerning the well-being of doctoral researchers was published in 2010 and thereafter, which provides a rather recent view of the situation. The comment from Golde (2005) that research has failed to address the improvement of doctoral education is by now rather obsolete given that most of the recent studies try to give practical advice to apply in the academic setting. As the studies of the review (Schmidt & Hansson, 2018) have a wide sample variation, ranging from two to 1,760 doctoral researchers, in various academic disciplines the backdrop of the suggestions is rather robust.

Well-being can be enhanced by the development of optimal resistance strategies such as the use of daily affirmation and the use of positive thinking patterns (Shavers & Moore III, 2014). It can also be enhanced by the development of strategies to address the academic climate at large and possible discrimination issues (Schmidt & Umans, 2014). The use of supervisory contracts (Stubb, Pyhältö, & Lonka, 2012) can also help the doctoral researcher to know where he or she stands, along with the training of supervisors in mentoring, supervision and relational management (Hunter & Devine, 2016). The promotion of peer groups in the research environment such as labs but also during recreational time is another way of strengthening well-being (Haynes et al., 2012).

3.2 *Weaknesses – Argh, the Definition!*

The definition of "well-being" causes confusion as it is explained in many ways, sometimes inconsistently. It has also been mostly researched in Europe and North America, omitting most of the rest of the world. Martinez, Ordu, Della Sala, and McFarlane (2013) suggested well-being was a central component of health, much like the World Health Organization's original definition (1948) while others define it as something 'greater than health' (Todres & Galvin, 2010). Consequently, 'well-being' is also operationalised in different ways and is used both as an input measure, output measure, mediator and moderator, making it difficult to discern clear causal relationships, and consequently making the exploration of doctoral researchers' well-being difficult since it is a jumble of different factors, partially showing the complex nature of the question but also muddying the waters for a clear path forward.

3.3 *Opportunities – Expansion, Education and Equality*

Most studies of the well-being of doctoral researchers have been conducted in the field of education. This leaves a possibility to expand into fields such as psychology, management and the caring sciences. The use of theories and models from other fields might help improve the understanding of the complexity of doctoral researchers' situations and needs. If the needs are met, the well-being of the doctoral researchers would possibly improve their educational experience as well as their future success and engagement in academia.

The exploration of the education of doctoral researchers in the use of different coping strategies is also an opportunity that might lead to enhanced well-being. Strategies focusing on problems or social support have been shown to be effective in reducing stress (Carver & Connor-Smith, 2010). It is rather obvious that social support seems to be a greatly emphasised coping mechanism among doctoral researchers – so perhaps more attention should be directed at problem-focused coping.

Yet another opportunity would be to use various methods to study different doctoral programmes. Currently, there is an emphasis on the academic progress of the student, as measured by the number of publications. Monitoring not only academic progress but also the doctoral researchers' well-being could lead to expanded knowledge and subsequent change at the institutional level of academia. If well-being is heightened the number of dropouts might fall, which would reduce financial expenses for universities resulting from impaired productivity in research projects due to attrition (Golde, 2005).

Finally, the field is somewhat dominated by studies focusing on female doctoral researchers (e.g., Haynes et al., 2012; Kumar & Cavallaro, 2018; Schmidt & Umans, 2014; Shavers & Moore III, 2014), and, as earlier noted, is not very geographically diverse either. In Sweden, 46% of the doctoral researchers are women and in USA 44% of the succeeding dissertations are written by women. However, in all countries there are vast differences in the gender distribution among the different disciplines. In Finland, 76% of the doctoral researchers in the behavioural sciences are female and 71% in medicine. As for the 'hard sciences' (STEM), the numbers are the other way around. As men and women probably react and respond differently to stressors, it is of importance to give equal attention to the genders.

3.4 *Threats – Is Uniformity the Solution?*

The experiences of doctoral researchers, as well as what is expected of them, vary widely between disciplines (Stubb et al., 2012) and this might lead to an uncertain comparison. Stubb et al. (2012) reported that the reasons for interrupting one's doctorate programme differed between the faculties. Although a national agenda including all disciplines might be the best way to eliminate the discrepancies in the different programmes, the harmonisation of disciplines and countries might not necessarily enhance the well-being of the doctoral researcher.

4 The New Deal

To update and expand on the review, a new search was performed in December 2020 using the same keywords and inclusion criteria as in 2018 (Schmidt & Hansson, 2018) with the time limitation 2017–2020. A total of 63 articles were found and after reading the abstracts/articles, 16 remained. A summary of new findings is presented below.

4.1 *It's Not Getting Better ...*

The extension of the review strengthens the previous results from 2018. As before, time pressure and conflicting roles are recurring concerns stated in the literature. Furthermore, stress yet again seems to dominate the discussion in the extended new search, to the degree that it is highly anticipated (Cornwall et al., 2019), accompanied by exhaustion and depression. However, this extension also explores self-care, coping, emotions, and work-life balance even more intensively. The same applies to the role of the scholarly community and the supervisors. While women were a group given particular interest in the articles included in the review from 2018 (Schmidt & Hansson, 2018), in this extension, it appears to be shifting towards minority groups (Fisher et al., 2019; McGee, Griffith, & Houston, 2019; Miller & Orsillo, 2020; Shavers & Moore, 2019).

4.2 *Ill-Being and Mental Health Problems – The New Norm in Higher Education Institutions*

Several articles published between 2017–2020 show a growing awareness of the lack of a unified definition and understanding of the concept of doctoral researchers' well-being and its related problems (Sverdlik & Hall, 2020). They also acknowledge to a greater extent that there is a problem concerning the mental health of doctoral researchers that urgently needs to be dealt with on different levels, making ill-being and mental illness the new norm rather than an exception among doctoral researchers. The prevalence of abnormal levels of stress, depression and anxiety was 56%, 54%, and 42% respectively among a French doctoral researcher sample (Marais, Shankland, Haag, Fiault, & Juniper, 2018). The numbers from a U.S. sample looked similar (stress 38%, depression 39% and anxiety 50%) (Miller & Orsillo, 2020). However, some researchers also show awareness of the dominant negative and pathological focus of the studies in the field, suggesting a shift of focus towards positive psychology (Kulikowski, Potoczek, Antipow, & Król, 2019; Marais et al., 2018) and a more holistic approach to well-being (Yusuf, Saitgalina, & Chapman, 2020) resonating well with the recent review on the topic (Schmidt & Hansson, 2018). Thus, it may not be surprising that doctoral researchers' response to problems arising from PhD studies has been to find an even better balance for themselves by focusing on self-care and coping.

4.3 *Cultural Differences?*

There are several other issues regarding well-being related to culture. Underrepresented minority doctoral researchers report more depressive symptoms than the majority, and black female doctoral researchers report feelings of being an outsider on campus, which contributed to feelings of isolation (McGee et al.,

2019; Miller & Orsillo, 2020). Furthermore, French student well-being was seen to be specifically affected by career uncertainty, perceived lack of progress and also perceived lack of competence (Marais et al., 2018). An article exploring stress among Chinese doctoral researchers also aligns with the stories of ill-being (Wang, Wang, & Wang, 2019).

Though applicable to the wider range of doctoral researchers, imposter syndrome was particularly discussed in relation to underrepresented minorities (McGee et al., 2019; Miller & Orsillo, 2020), describing doctoral researchers as brooding over their own inadequacies, being plagued by self-doubt and beliefs that others viewed them as incompetent (McGee et al., 2019) impacting strongly on their well-being.

4.4 *Sense of Belonging and Connection*

Doctoral researchers repeatedly highlight the importance of belongingness and its impact on their well-being (Cornwall et al., 2019; Espiritu & Smith, 2020; Fisher et al., 2019; Miller & Orsillo, 2020; Yusuf et al., 2020). It comprises feeling valued, needed, accepted, significant, and 'fitting in' with the environment (Fisher et al., 2019; Miller & Orsillo, 2020). In one study, a small majority (53%) felt they belonged to the university community (Yusuf et al., 2020). Also early-stage doctoral researchers need to feel welcomed in their departments and university community, which was seen as an indicator of general departmental culture and climate (Cornwall et al., 2019). In contrast to the previous rather positive results, many doctoral researchers in Cornwall et al. (2019) described feeling a sense of isolation from the university community instead, which increased stress and loneliness (Cornwall et al., 2019).

4.5 *Mentorship*

The extended review also reveals that the experienced quality of mentorship impacts the well-being of doctoral researchers. An exploration of different 'quality levels' of supervision highlighted the need for authentic mentorship, which made the doctoral researchers feel more motivated and satisfied, which in turn led to greater performance and well-being (Al Makhamreh & Stockley, 2019). While authentic supervisors could enhance students' well-being, authoritarian styles were more likely to lead to stress and depression and were seen as toxic (Al Makhamreh & Stockley, 2019). This points to a most important issue in the exploration of doctoral researchers' well-being, namely the importance of the studies reaching more senior academics and providing them with information in relation to the well-being of doctoral researchers (Kulikowski et al., 2019). That is, there is no need to research a topic if the conclusions and suggestions for improvement do not reach an audience that has the power and authority to make the changes to enhance the current situation. The relationship with the supervisor was also identified as a stress factor by Wang et al. (2019), Cornwall et al. (2019), and Yusuf et al. (2020).

4.6 *The Issue of Time and Timing*

Time management, which can be described as having different competing commitments to be addressed at once, seems to be a difficult element for doctoral researchers to handle and a definite cause of distress and ill-being (Beasy, Emery, & Crawford, 2019). For many doctoral researchers, the work is perceived not to be turned 'on' and 'off' and then 'on' again, but rather is found to be interwoven through everyday life (Beasy et al., 2019). This could be argued as being part of the 'preparation' for working life where many occupations are interwoven through life itself, but time management might be especially challenging for younger doctoral researchers who have never attained a balanced lifestyle due to coming right out of a 'school setting' and going straight into another, in the form of a doctoral education programme. Indications of this can be found in a case study of a doctoral researcher who was at a later developmental stage in life which gave her a sense of security about herself in a way that might be fleeting for those who do not already have a family or are less 'set in their ways' (Espiritu & Smith, 2020). The doctoral researchers' ability to create a work-life balance seemed to be one of the foundations of her success, and this is also particularly true in the early years of doctoral training (Benjamin, Williams, & Maher, 2017; Cornwall et al., 2019). It might be that when doctoral researchers recognise the importance of maintaining a good work-life balance they feel more hopeful about their future and their career (Benjamin, Williams et al., 2017).

4.7 *The Duty of Academia*

Sometimes it can be hard to take responsibility over factors that one perceives as out of one's control. One of these factors is the universities' interest in the well-being of their doctoral researchers as they are in charge of maintaining a supportive environment for all their employees (Beasy et al., 2019; González-Betancor & Dorta-González, 2020). The dynamics between doctoral researchers and academia appear to be important for the enhancement of writing as well as the doctoral researchers' well-being (Beasy et al., 2019; Lonka, Ketonen, Vekkaila, Lara, & Pyhältö, 2019). Yet lack of developmental support from institutions makes it difficult for doctoral researchers to navigate in the academic landscape. The lack of compassion and respect was experienced as 'suffering for the machine', i.e. the doctoral researchers perceived the neoliberal approach of the universities as prioritised and thus, universities contributed actively to their ill-being (Beasy et al., 2019). Similar tensions were found in yet another study (Benjamin et al., 2017) when referring to 'greedy institutions', meaning universities made very high demands on the doctoral researchers, interfering with their work-life balance and well-being. Instead, researchers wanted holistic support from the institutions, not just academic support.

Structure is another important aspect of doctoral researcher well-being, that is, structure concerning the degree to which one perceives clear expectations and clear performance standards from supervisors and departments (Fisher et al., 2019). This is discussed and expanded upon by Sverdlik and Hall (2020) who state that the highest well-being among doctoral researchers is reported during the coursework phase, the most structured part of the education.

5 Let's See the Whole Picture

In sum, both our review from 2018 and the extension provided here show that studies investigating doctoral researchers' well-being in fact highlight the lack of well-being. To acknowledge and be inclusive of all the literature covering a more negative and pathological perspective on doctoral researchers' well-being, we performed yet another search in January 2021 on the terms 'stress', 'depression', 'exhaustion', 'anxiety' and 'burnout', which was limited to 2017–2020. This search resulted in 151 articles, and after reading the titles/abstracts/articles, 46 fulfilled the inclusion criteria. These results show the that the negative view dominates the literature and that its primary focus is on lack of doctoral researchers' well-being. This field could be enlarged even more also including experiences of harassment, discrimination, bullying or suicide and many more (e.g. Chemical & Engineering News, 2017; The Stanford Daily, 2019).

Although presenting an analysis of those results is beyond the scope of this chapter, we refer to a review by Hazell et al. (2020) focusing on doctoral researchers' mental health problems, such as stress and anxiety, as well as feelings of isolation, lack of belonging, and personal identity crises, which are in line with the findings presented here and in the review from 2018 (Schmidt & Hansson, 2018). The most acknowledged and cited study within this field is that of Levecque et al. (2017), who showed that 51% of the doctoral researchers in their study had at least two symptoms of poor mental health as a result of doctoral studies, the most common ones being feeling depressed or under constant stress. The study also reported that 32% of them suffered at least four symptoms, indicating a much higher risk of developing a psychiatric disorder than highly educated comparison groups (Levecque et al., 2017). And finally, Evans et al. (2018) found in their sample that 41% of doctoral researchers suffered from moderate to severe rates of anxiety and 39% suffered from depression, i.e. a six times higher risk compared to the general population, making the point of mental health problems and lack of well-being becoming the norm in higher education.

6 On a Positive Note … Suggestions for a Sustainable Doctoral Education

Most studies in the field of doctoral researchers' well-being tend to identify the researchers' struggles and, despite a plethora of research in the last few years and the growing interest, little is still known about factors positively related to their well-being (Kulikowski et al., 2019). First steps have been undertaken to shift from a negative perspective to a more proactive (e.g. Denicolo, Reeves, & Duke, 2018) or a positive psychology approach (e.g. Marais et al., 2018). Instead of 'only' eliminating the stressors in doctoral researchers' lives, a health promotion approach could also be applied focusing on positive experiences and on creating healthy work environments, and consequently making the well-being of individuals and the entire organisation more sustainable. Below we have collected some insights, as an extension of the 'opportunities' earlier listed.

6.1 *Opportunities – Expansion, Education and Equality 2.0*

- Present the doctoral researchers with authentic leadership and mentoring, genuine guidance for those in need of it and a positive and uplifting environment (Al Makhamreh & Stockley, 2019).
- Create a *culture* within the universities where the doctoral researchers, whatever their background or gender, feel valued, supported and physically as well as mentally nourished (Benjamin et al., 2017), which could facilitate the development of a sense of community and belonging (Yusuf et al., 2020).
- Normalise the discussion about mental health and well-being in the university environment (Benjamin et al., 2017).
- Institutions ought to find ways to respond to doctoral researchers' increased awareness and need for work-life balance as a way to enhance general well-being (Benjamin et al., 2017).
- Higher education institutions have the responsibility to care and create sustainable work conditions and work environments so that doctoral researchers can maintain and enhance their well-being. As previously stated, many people throughout the higher education system, including students, employees, academics and non-academics, suffer from lack of well-being and mental health problems, and this has even been described as a

pandemic of poor mental health in higher education institutions (Morrish, 2019). Kinman thus proposes a 'whole university approach' and launched in 2017 the StepChange programme[1] in the UK (Times Higher Education, 2018) to create mentally healthy and sustainable universities, stressing the need to tackle the problem holistically on all levels within academia.
- Doctoral researchers might consider and reflect upon why they want to undertake a doctoral education as those reasons affect their motivation, engagement, experienced productivity as well as their well-being

Note

1 https://www.universitiesuk.ac.uk/stepchange-mhu

References

Agevall, L., Broberg, P., & Umans, T. (2018). The new generation of auditors meeting praxis: Dual learning's role in audit students' professional development. *Scandinavian Journal of Educational Research, 62*(2), 307

Al Makhamreh, M., & Stockley, D. (2019). Mentorship and well-being: Examining doctoral students' lived experiences in doctoral supervision context. *International Journal of Mentoring and Coaching in Education.*

Beadle, B., Do, S., El Youssoufi, D., Felder, D., Gorenflos López, J., Jahn, A., Pérez-Bosch Quesada, E., Rottleb, T., Rüter, F., Schanze, J.-L., Stroppe, A.-K., Thater, S., Verrière, A., & Weltin, M. (2020). *Being a doctoral researcher in the Leibniz Association: 2019 Leibniz PhD Network survey report.* https://nbn-resolving.org/urn:nbn:de:0168-ssoar-69403-1

Beasy, K., Emery, S., & Crawford, J. (2019). Drowning in the shallows: an Australian study of the PhD experience of wellbeing. *Teaching in Higher Education, 26*(4), 602–618. doi:10.1080/13562517.2019.1669014

Beiter, R., Nash, R., McCrady, M., Rhoades, D., Linscomb, M., Clarahan, M., & Sammut, S. (2015). The prevalence and correlates of depression, anxiety, and stress in a sample of college students. *Journal of Affective Disorders, 173*, 90–96.

Benjamin, S., Williams, J., & Maher, M. A. (2017). Focusing the lens to share the story: Using photographs and interviews to explore doctoral students' sense of well-being. *International Journal of Doctoral Studies, 12*(1), 197–217.

Cameron, E., Mathers, J., & Parry, J. (2006). 'Health and well-being': Questioning the use of health concepts in public health policy and practice. *Critical Public Health, 16*(4), 347–354.

Carver, C. S., & Connor-Smith, J. (2010). Personality and coping. *Annual review of psychology, 61*, 679–704.

Chemical & Engineering News. (2017). Grappling with graduate student mental health and suicide. *Chemical & Engineering News, 95*.

Cornwall, J., Mayland, E. C., van der Meer, J., Spronken-Smith, R. A., Tustin, C., & Blyth, P. (2019). Stressors in early-stage doctoral students. *Studies in Continuing Education, 41*(3), 363–380.

Denicolo, P., Reeves, J., & Duke, D. (2018). *Fulfilling the potential of your doctoral experience*. Sage.

Diener, E. (2021). Happiness: the science of subjective well-being. In R. Biswas-Diener & E. Diener (Eds.), *Noba textbook series: Psychology*: DEF publishers.

Espiritu, E. W., & Smith, T. M. (2020). Health, wellness, and well-being of a non-traditional occupational therapy student: A case study. *Occupational Therapy in Mental Health*, 1–17. doi:10.1080/0164212X.2020.1832942

Evans, T. M., Bira, L., Gastelum, J. B., Weiss, L. T., & Vanderford, N. L. (2018). Evidence for a mental health crisis in graduate education. *Nature Biotechnology, 36*(3), 282.

Fisher, A. J., Mendoza-Denton, R., Patt, C., Young, I., Eppig, A., Garrell, R. L., ... Richards, M. A. (2019). Structure and belonging: Pathways to success for underrepresented minority and women PhD students in STEM fields. *Plos One, 14*(1), e0209279.

Gardner, S. K. (2009). Student and faculty attributions of attrition in high and low-completing doctoral programs in the United States. *Higher Education, 58*(1), 97–112.

Golde, C. M. (2005). The role of the department and discipline in doctoral student attrition: Lessons from four departments. *The Journal of Higher Education, 76*(6), 669–700.

González-Betancor, S. M., & Dorta-González, P. (2020). Risk of interruption of doctoral studies and mental health in PhD students. *Mathematics, 8*(10), 1695.

Haynes, C., Bulosan, M., Citty, J., Grant-Harris, M., Hudson, J., & Koro-Ljungberg, M. (2012). My world is not my doctoral program … or is it? Female students' perceptions of well-being. *International Journal of Doctoral Studies, 7*(1), 1–17.

Hazell, C. M., Chapman, L., Valeix, S. F., Roberts, P., Niven, J. E., & Berry, C. (2020). Understanding the mental health of doctoral researchers: a mixed methods systematic review with meta-analysis and meta-synthesis. *Systematic Reviews, 9*(1), 1–30.

Helmholtz Juniors. (2019). *Survey report 2019*. https://www.helmholtz.de/fileadmin/user_upload/06_jobs_talente/Helmholtz-Juniors/Survey_Report2019.pdf

Hunter, K. H., & Devine, K. (2016). Doctoral students' emotional exhaustion and intentions to leave academia. *International Journal of Doctoral Studies, 11*(2), 35–61.

Jackson, S. E., Joshi, A., & Erhardt, N. L. (2003). Recent research on team and organizational diversity: SWOT analysis and implications. *Journal of management, 29*(6), 801–830.

Jiranek, V. (2010). Potential predictors of timely completion among dissertation research students at an Australian faculty of sciences. *International Journal of Doctoral Studies, 5*(1), 1–13.

Juniper, B., Walsh, E., Richardson, A., & Morley, B. (2012). A new approach to evaluating the well-being of PhD research students. *Assessment and Evaluation in Higher Education, 37*(5), 563–576.

Kinman, G., & Wray, S. (2015). *Work-related wellbeing in UK higher education – 2014.* University and College Union.

Krekel, C., Ward, G., & de Neve, J.-E. (2019). Employee well-being, productivity, and firm performance: Evidence and case studies. In *Global happiness and wellbeing policy report* (chapter 5). Sustainable Development Solutions Network, Global Council for Happiness and Wellbeing.

Kulikowski, K., Potoczek, A., Antipow, E., & Król, S. (2019). How to survive in academia: Demands, resources and study satisfaction among Polish PhD students. *Educational Sciences: Theory and Practice, 19*(4), 65–79.

Kumar, S., & Cavallaro, L. (2018). Researcher self-care in emotionally demanding research: A proposed conceptual framework. *Qualitative Health Research, 28*(4), 648–658.

Levecque, K., Anseel, F., De Beuckelaer, A., Van der Heyden, J., & Gisle, L. (2017). Work organization and mental health problems in PhD students. *Research Policy, 46*(4), 868–879.

Lipson, S. K., Lattie, E. G., & Eisenberg, D. J. P. s. (2019). Increased rates of mental health service utilization by US college students: 10-year population-level trends (2007–2017). *Psychiatric Services, 70*(1), 60–63.

Lonka, K., Ketonen, E., Vekkaila, J., Lara, M. C., & Pyhältö, K. (2019). Doctoral students' writing profiles and their relations to well-being and perceptions of the academic environment. *Higher Education, 77*(4), 587–602.

Marais, G. A., Shankland, R., Haag, P., Fiault, R., & Juniper, B. (2018). A survey and a positive psychology intervention on French PhD student well-being. *International Journal of Doctoral Studies, 13*.

Martinez, E., Ordu, C., Della Sala, M. R., & McFarlane, A. (2013). Striving to obtain a school-work-life balance: The full-time doctoral student. *International Journal of Doctoral Studies, 8*(39–59).

McGee, E., Griffith, D., & Houston, S. (2019). "I know I have to work twice as hard and hope that makes me good enough": Exploring the stress and strain of Black doctoral students in engineering and computing. *Teachers College Record, 121*(6), 6.

Miller, A. N., & Orsillo, S. M. (2020). The impact of values congruity on Underrepresented Minority (URM) graduate student psychosocial functioning. *Higher Education Research and Development*, 1–16.

Morrish, L. (2019). *Pressure vessels: The epidemic of poor mental health among higher education staff.* Higher Education Policy Institute (HEPI).

Nature. (2018). Time to talk about why so many postgrads have poor mental health. *Nature,* 5.

Nature. (2019a). Being a PhD student shouldn't be bad for your health. *Nature,* 307.

Nature. (2019b). The mental health of PhD researchers demands urgent attention. *Nature,* 257–258.

Nature. (2019c). PhDs: The tortuous truth. *Nature,* 403–406.

Ryan, R. M., & Deci, E. L. (2001). To be happy or to be self-fulfilled: A review of research on hedonic and eudaimonic well-being. *Annual Review of Psychology, 52*(16), 141–166.

Ryff, C. D., & Keyes, C. L. M. (1995). The structure of psychological well-being revisited. *Journal of Personality and Social Psychology, 69*(4), 719.

Schmidt, M., & Hansson, E. (2018). Doctoral students' well-being: A literature review. *International Journal of Qualitative Studies on Health and Well-Being, 13*(1), 150–171.

Schmidt, M., & Umans, T. (2014). Experiences of well-being among female doctoral students in Sweden. *International Journal of Qualitative Studies on Health and Well-Being, 9*(1).

Shavers, M. C., & Moore III, J. L. (2014). Black female voices: Self-presentation strategies in doctoral programs at predominately White institutions. *Journal of College Student Development, 55*(4), 391–407.

Shavers, M. C., & Moore, J. L. (2019). The perpetual outsider: Voices of Black women pursuing doctoral degrees at predominantly white institutions. *Journal of Multicultural Counseling and Development, 47*(4), 210–226.

Stubb, J., Pyhältö, K., & Lonka, K. (2012). The experienced meaning of working with a PhD thesis. *Scandinavian Journal of Educational Research, 56*(4), 439–456.

Sverdlik, A., & Hall, N. C. (2020). Not just a phase: Exploring the role of program stage on well-being and motivation in doctoral students. *Journal of Adult and Continuing Education, 26*(1), 97–124.

Taris, T. W., & Schreurs, P. J. (2009). Well-being and organizational performance: An organizational-level test of the happy-productive worker hypothesis. *Work and Stress, 23*(2), 120–136.

The Stanford Daily. (2019). 'A toxic culture of overwork': Inside the graduate student mental health crisis. *The Stanford Daily.*

Times Higher Education. (2018). Half of UK academics 'suffer stress-linked mental health problems'. *Times Higher Education.*

Todres, L., & Galvin, K. (2010). "Dwelling-mobility": An existential theory of well-being. *International Journal of Qualitative Studies on Health and Well-Being, 5*(3), 5444.

Tytherleigh, M. Y., Webb, C., Cooper, C. L., & Ricketts, C. (2005). Occupational stress in UK higher education institutions: A comparative study of all staff categories. *Higher Education Research Development, 24*(1), 41–61.

University Affairs. (2013). *The PhD is in need of revision.* https://www.universityaffairs.ca/features/feature-article/the-phd-is-in-need-of-revision/

Wang, X., Wang, C., & Wang, J. (2019). Towards the contributing factors for stress confronting Chinese PhD students. *International Journal of Qualitative Studies on Health and Well-Being, 14*(1), 1598722.

Winefield, A. H., Gillespie, N., Stough, C., Dua, J., Hapuarachchi, J., & Boyd, C. (2003). Occupational stress in Australian university staff: Results from a national survey. *International Journal of Stress Management, 10*(1), 51.

World Health Organization (WHO). (1948). Preamble to the Constitution of WHO as adopted by the International Health Conference, New York, 19 June–22 July 1946; signed on 22 July 1946 by the representatives of 61 States (Official Records of WHO, no. 2, p. 100 and entered into force on 7 April 1948).

Yusuf, J.-E., Saitgalina, M., & Chapman, D. W. (2020). Work-life balance and well-being of graduate students. *Journal of Public Affairs Education, 26*(4), 458–483.

CHAPTER 13

The Role of Liminality and Reflexivity in Transformative Doctoral Learning

Shane Dowle

Abstract

It is widely accepted that progress through a doctorate is rarely straightforward. Doctoral researchers will inevitably experience numerous unsettling moments as they traverse new territory. The literature describes this experience as 'liminality' or being in-between states. Often, the experience of liminality is a precursor to a transformative moment in the doctorate, which changes how the doctoral researcher views themselves and the world. Whilst the literature is strong on the concept of liminality, less is known about how doctoral researchers pull through liminal moments to make progress. This chapter addresses that gap by arguing that reflexivity is a complementary concept to liminality because it provides an insight into (i) how doctoral researchers formulate courses of action to progress their project; (ii) what those courses of action are directed towards; and (iii) how structural components of doctoral programmes can affect progress. The conceptual discussion will be brought to life with reference to a 'river of experience' created by doctoral researchers.

Keywords

liminality – reflexivity – doctorate

> There are no safe paths in this part of the world. Remember you are over the Edge of the Wild now, and in for all sorts of fun.
>
> J.R.R. TOLKEIN

 | DOI:10.1163/9789004529304_013

1 Introduction

It is widely accepted that doing a doctorate is rarely straightforward. Instead, the doctoral experience is imbued with uncertainty because there are no safe paths that guarantee a successful outcome. Doctoral researchers will inevitably encounter numerous challenges as they traverse new territories, which can be experienced as disorienting, disquieting and disheartening. The literature conceptualises those unsettling moments by using the theory of liminality.

Liminality is well documented in the research literature about the doctoral experience. It describes doctoral researchers who are undergoing a process of becoming. In other words, a doctoral researcher experiencing liminality will find themselves between states – they are not who they once were, and neither are they the person they will become. Whilst the experience of liminality is often unsettling for the doctoral researcher, it can be a precursor to a transformative breakthrough moment. Those breakthroughs are critical for making progress and can lead to fundamental changes in how the doctoral researcher views both themselves and the world.

Given that it is almost impossible for a doctoral researcher to avoid experiences of liminality, it is surprising that the literature offers few theories of how a doctoral researcher pulls through liminal moments to make progress. This chapter addresses that gap by drawing on the concept of reflexivity, as defined by Archer (2007). The chapter argues that reflexivity is a useful complementary concept to liminality because it provides an insight into (i) how doctoral researchers formulate courses of action to progress their project; (ii) what those courses of action are directed towards; and (iii) how structural components of doctoral programmes can affect progress.

The first section of the chapter discusses how the concept of liminality has been used to understand the doctoral experience. In the second section, the case is made for using reflexivity as a complementary concept to liminality. In the third section, the conceptual discussion is made more vivid by drawing on a 'river of experience' from a workshop on doctoral completions. The chapter then concludes by offering some thoughts on how to protect reflexive time in the context of the accelerated academy and global pandemic.

2 Liminality – There Are No Safe Paths in This Part of the World

Liminality is a spatial concept that originated in the anthropological work of Turner (1974). The positionality of those experiencing liminality is described as being "ambiguous, neither here nor there, betwixt and between all fixed points of classification" (Turner, 1974, p. 232). The concept of liminality can be usefully applied to understand how doctoral researchers experience the learning process throughout a doctorate. So much of the doctorate is uncertain and there are no safe paths that guarantee a successful outcome for the research project. The doctoral researcher spends a lot of time tangled up in working through wicked and complex problems, whilst the overall shape, contribution and destination of the project are not yet known to them. Also, the doctoral researchers themselves can undergo a significant transformation during their doctorate. As Keefer (2015) acknowledges: "liminality in this domain refers to the in-between period where one is no longer who previously existed, nor has yet developed into the independent researcher or expert practitioner" (p. 18).

Whilst experiences of liminality can be incredibly unsettling for doctoral researchers, they are often regarded as a necessary precursor to a transformation in how they perceive themselves and the world. Kiley (2009) and Kiley and Wisker (2009) have identified how liminality precedes the crossing of concept thresholds that can transform doctoral researchers' relationships with knowledge and the knowledge creation process. According to those authors, it is through the experience of liminality that doctoral researchers develop deeper, more complex, and more sophisticated understandings of argument, theory, knowledge creation, analysis, and research paradigms. Dowle (2020) also identified how liminality can precede transformations in relationships, particularly in how doctoral researchers view themselves in relation to significant others in their networks. Elsewhere, Winstone and Moore (2016) have highlighted the link between liminality and identity negotiation. Their research with doctoral researchers who also work as Graduate Teaching Assistants (GTAs) informs how doctoral researchers engage in identity malleability and oscillation between different identities throughout their doctorates.

The discussion so far has focused on the inner turmoil that a doctoral researcher might encounter when experiencing liminality. Helpfully, the research literature has also identified some of the signs of liminality. Kiley (2009), for example, highlights how doctoral researchers may appear stuck on a problem, make very slow progress and also engage in mimicry of the behaviour of others. Keefer (2015) adds that doctoral researchers who become withdrawn and isolated, experience a drop in confidence, or who experience a perceived misalignment between themselves and research might also be in a liminal state.

Experiences of liminality can, of course, be distressing and even lead to withdrawal from the doctorate (Breier, Herman, & Towers, 2019). Yet liminality can also be a strangely exhilarating, intriguing and enticing space in which the prospect of new understanding is dangled. The concept of 'heavenly hell' explored in the next Chapter is relevant here. Wisker and Bengsten (2019) have also likened this experience to the Gothic. Here, normality becomes unsettled, but it offers a seductive portal into a different way of seeing the world.

In summary, the literature reinforces the idea that there are no safe paths through a doctorate. The concept of liminality has been widely and helpfully deployed to theorise what happens in the doctoral learning process when doctoral researchers encounter uncertainty. Liminality is understood to be potentially transformative because it can precede transformations in doctoral researchers' relationships with knowledge, relationships with others and even their identity.

Given the centrality of liminality to the experience of doctoral-level learning, it is surprising that more attention has not been given to how experiences of liminality can be scaffolded, and progress supported. In the next section, I argue that the concept of reflexivity complements liminality because it provides clues for how doctoral researchers come through experiences of liminality.

3 Reflexivity – You Are over the Edge of the Wild Now, and in for All Sorts of Fun

Reflexivity is a potentially empowering concept when applied to the experience of doing a doctorate because it positions the doctoral researcher as an active agent in their learning experience (Farrell, Oerton, & Plant, 2018). As other scholars have noted, it is through engagement with reflexive practices that doctoral researchers develop sophisticated critiques and understanding of their positionality in interpreting data to generate new knowledge (Alvesson & Sköldberg, 2009). Reflexivity can also act as a mechanism through which doctoral researchers make sense of their changing identities, moments of new becomings, and how the sense of self is re-formed (Fox & Allan, 2013; Taylor, 2010). Reflexivity can even enable sophisticated strategies for connecting academic research to practice (Farrell et al., 2018). In short, it is through the development of a capacity for reflexivity that doctoral researchers can take control of their research projects, make sense of emerging identities, and can direct their research towards making a difference in the world.

Reflexivity is full of promise and potential. It empowers the doctoral researcher to negotiate liminal moments and to make the most of their doctoral experience. But given that reflexivity is a largely internalised and deeply personal process, it can be difficult for supervisors, researcher developers and administrators to get an insight into what happens during the multiple reflexive moments that doctoral researchers experience. If we are to understand how doctoral researchers use reflexivity to formulate courses of action, then it is necessary to understand how reflexivity works.

One of the most insightful accounts of reflexivity has been developed by Archer (2003, 2007). For Archer (2003), reflexivity refers to our internal conversations. In other words, it is about the conversations we have with ourselves that might involve mulling over a problem, planning something, imagining, deciding, reliving, prioritising, imaginary conversations with others, budgeting and clarifying. Reflexivity also acts as a mediator between structure and agency, as Archer (2007) summarises: "reflexivity is the regular exercise of the mental ability, shared by all normal people, to consider themselves in relation to their (social) contexts and vice versa. These deliberations form the bases on which people determine future courses of action" (p. 4).

Reflexivity is by no means uniform. Archer (2003) identified four principal reflexive modes: (i) communicative reflexivity – which requires dialogue with others to make sense of internal conversations; (ii) autonomous reflexivity – where individuals draw on previous experiences and specialist knowledge to make sense of internal conversations; (iii) meta-reflexivity – where individuals are reflexive about their own reflexive practices; and (iv) fractured reflexives – those whose power to hold internal conversations about the self and society has been suspended.

Regarding the doctoral experience, Rainford (2016a, 2016b) points out that reflexive practices are unlikely to be neat. Instead, doctoral researchers employ multi-modal and hybridised forms of reflexivity as they encounter novel challenges within the doctorate. Rainford's (ibid.) autoethnographic accounts provide compelling evidence about how different forms of reflexivity are drawn on in response to liminal moments. One example given is how social media, such as Twitter, operate as expressions of communicative reflexivity through which the input of others is drawn on to navigate critical incidents.

Other research supports the notion that reflexivity is a difficult, complex, and ongoing process. In their dialogic account of the doctoral experience, Fox and Allan (2013) show that reflexivity was crucial for navigating liminal moments such as grappling with belonging in the academy, trying to make sense of theory and, also, dealing with the vicissitudes of personal life. Again, both authors draw attention to how reflexivity is not a linear or neat process but involves a "fragmented, dynamic and partial" (p. 111) experience.

The scholarship on reflexivity and the doctorate, although limited, provides an insightful glimpse into the cognitive processes through which doctoral researchers navigate liminal moments. It invites us to consider the social and structural factors that impinge on doctoral researchers' deliberations. It also focusses attention on how doctoral researchers exercise agency to make progress with their projects and own personal development.

In the next section, I draw on a case study 'river of experience' that was created during a workshop run by the author. The 'river of experience' will be used to bring to life the interactions between liminality and reflexivity. It will also highlight the impact of structural factors in the doctorate on progress and provide some clues about how doctoral researchers exercise agency to win through liminal moments.

4 Liminality and Reflexivity in the Doctorate – An Example

This section draws on a case study 'river of experience' that was created during a workshop on doctoral completions run by the author – see Figure 13.1. 'Rivers of experience' are a creative research method rooted in constructivist research philosophy and designed to elicit incidents and experiences that are particularly significant to a person. The technique was first devised by Pope and Denicolo (1990) and further developed in Denicolo and Pope (2001). The procedure for using the method is described in some detail in Cabaroglu and Denicolo (2008).

The 'river of experience' method is very simple to use and yet very powerful for eliciting rich accounts of how people make sense of critical incidents that occur along life journeys (Bradley-Cole & Denicolo, 2020). In this case, workshop participants were asked to draw their 'river of experience' by envisaging

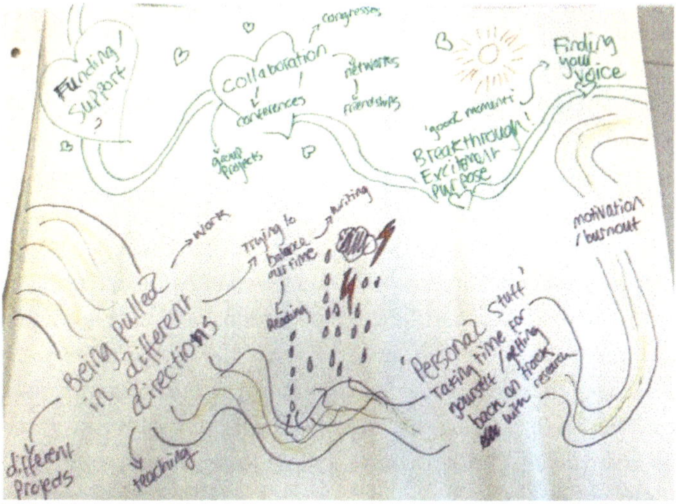

FIGURE 13.1 Doctoral researchers' river of experience

their own doctorate as a meandering river and to note against each bend in the river on their diagram an experience that was significant to them and affected their progress. Participants then joined together in small groups to discuss their rivers. Figure 13.1 is the outcome of that joint discussion.

In Figure 13.1, participants mapped out two tributaries to their river. The tributary at the top of the diagram depicts the factors that were mostly positive in affecting their progress. The tributary at the bottom describes the inhibitors of progress. Starting in the top left corner, the doctoral researchers described the importance of securing funding in enabling them to undertake a doctorate at all. Access to a funding package was critical in making the doctorate a viable option but, in discussion, it emerged that participants had varied levels of support from their funding packages. Some had funding to cover their tuition fees, others had a stipend to live on as well as funding for their fees, and others had partial awards. In all cases, all funding packages were time limited. Whilst having access to some financial support meant that doctoral researchers in the workshop were able to embark on their doctorates, the monetary value of the funding package and its duration were a source of considerable anxiety for many. All were grateful for the financial support, but grants are barely adequate to make ends meet anyway (Deem & Dowle, 2020). Doctoral researchers reported how they needed to take on additional paid employment to meet basic living costs and they also expressed disquiet about the competitive labour market they would enter after the doctorate, especially if they desired an academic post (McAlpine & Emmioğlu, 2014). These conditions created a dilemma for researchers. They needed to pack in lots of enrichment activities during their doctorates to enhance their CVs and to balance this against the exigencies of their own projects, always with one eye on the ticking clock. Access to funding, then, was seen as both an enabling factor for their research (without the funding their doctorates simply would not have happened) but it was also perceived as a structural factor that exerted extra pressure to complete within, typically, three years and constrained the time available to engage with necessary enrichment activities.

Consequently, for these participants, the doctoral experience was perceived as a time pressured, juggling act. The time pressure frequently pushed participants into a liminal space, as depicted in the bottom left-hand corner of the river. Here doctoral researchers drew attention to how the core of their projects, in this case reading and writing, had to be balanced against other income generating work commitments, teaching responsibilities and other projects with which they were involved. Those pressures created a sense of being pulled in several different directions at once. Reflexively, they reported engaging in a constant and continuous act of prioritisation, re-prioritisation and planning to squeeze lots of activities into a compressed period. One element of this, which they found very challenging, was prioritising time for themselves and for keeping their projects on track. This created the curious effect of sometimes pushing the research project itself into a liminal space, whilst other activities swallowed up chunks of time. It is a vivid depiction of how the contested ideas of what a doctoral education is (explored in Chapter 2 of this book) create concrete dilemmas and challenges for doctoral researchers themselves. Even more concerning was how this pressure also led to a serious risk of experiencing burnout or other mental health condition. The experiences of this group were consistent with concerns about the mental health of doctoral researchers as reported elsewhere (Levecque, Anseel, De Beuckelaer, Van Der Heyden, & Gisle, 2017). This brings into sharp focus the challenges that doctoral researchers face when trying to meet the demands that the doctoral process makes of them. The time pressure is so acute that it can create the structural conditions for compromised wellbeing, unless doctoral researchers are pro-actively supported and empowered to put their health first.

On a more positive note, the tributary at the top of the diagram draws attention to how liminality can be successfully overcome when communicative reflexivity is used. In this case, Figure 13.1 draws attention to the value of collaborations and interactions with other researchers. Specifically, doctoral researchers discussed how they directed their actions to attending conferences and congresses; working on group projects; and developing professional networks, from which, in many cases, supportive and long-lasting friendships emerged. Doctoral researchers noted numerous benefits of engaging with communities and emphasised the communicative aspect. They highlighted how interactions with others offered the opportunity for problems to be voiced, discussed, and played with, and how others' input provided a scaffold for working through the problem and finding possible solutions. The networks that doctoral researchers formed with others also acted as a protective factor and helped to reinforce doctoral researchers' resilience and heighten their commitment to seeing the doctoral process through (McCray & Joseph-Richard, 2020).

Figure 13.1 also draws attention to how acting reflexively through periods of liminality can lead to a transformation in a doctoral researcher's relationship with knowledge creation and their own identity. In the top right-hand corner of the diagram, doctoral researchers describe the effects of experiencing breakthroughs in their research. Those breakthroughs were experienced as reinvigorating and reignited the sense of excitement, purpose and value (Bryan & Guccione, 2018) of their doctorates. For these doctoral researchers, the most transformative outcome was in finding their own voice as researchers. Finding their voice was a significant milestone in their own identity trajectories and often the culmination of hybridised reflexive moments and took place over a long period of time. It built on communications and interactions with significant others; it included hours of working with bricolages of materials and texts and chipping away at an idea until a way through could be gleaned; and it also drew on numerous meta-reflexive, internal conversations as doctoral researchers consciously considered how they were thinking about their particular research projects, and the meaning of the doctoral experience more broadly.

In summary, Figure 13.1 provides an informative insight into the how doctoral experience is peppered with liminal moments and how reflexivity is one way through which liminal moments can be traversed and transformations can result. This example is particularly adept at bringing into focus how structural factors can impact on how doctoral education is experienced. In this case, the doctoral researchers were grateful for the funding they had access to, but it was stark how varied the funding packages were and also how the typical three-year duration of funding created a sense of acute time pressure. It was also clear from the example how the contemporary doctoral experience comprises so much more than the thesis and research project. Now, doctoral researchers have a wealth of opportunities to engage with. Whilst these are enriching and valuable, they are sometimes undertaken because of necessity, either to fortify a CV or to bring in much needed extra income. These pressures can be experienced as liminal moments, even to the point where doctoral researchers feel that they themselves have been pushed to the edges of what is manageable. Linked to these liminal moments, Figure 13.1 also highlights how acting reflexively through the doctorate can help doctoral researchers to pull through liminality with transformative effects. The example shows how constant planning and re-prioritising activities to make the most of a compressed doctoral experience is essential. It also emphasises the importance of doctoral researchers being empowered to make time for themselves and be supported in healthy working practices to avoid burnout. Also, the importance of communicating with other researchers and developing networks helps to enrich the doctoral experience as well as facilitate problem solving. In the end, it is reflexive practices that can bring doctoral researchers to transformative moments and underpin shifts in their identity to the point where their own, individual, and unique voice emerges.

5 Conclusion – Protecting and Scaffolding Reflexive Time

In this chapter, I have explored the complementary concepts of liminality and reflexivity. Whilst the concept of liminality focusses on ambiguity, in-betweeness and sense of not yet having arrived that pervades much of the doctoral experience, reflexivity offers some insights into how doctoral researchers can pull through liminal moments. An example 'river of experience' brought to life the interaction between liminality and reflexivity. Of note was the time pressure in the doctoral process as well as how hybridised forms of reflexivity are enabled by engaging with networks (communicative), working at a problem (autonomous), and conscious consideration how doctoral researchers think about their particular projects and finding meaning in the doctoral experience (meta).

At the time of writing, the experience of time pressure in the doctorate has been amplified by the impact of the Covid-19 pandemic. There are many reports highlighting the difficulties that doctoral researchers have faced during the pandemic as a result of social distancing measures and local and national lockdowns. These include no, or very limited, access to research facilities and/or participants for projects; increased caring responsibilities for dependents as schools have closed and other support services have been reduced and, of course, the very real risk of contracting Covid-19 and becoming unwell. The situation has forced doctoral researchers to make some difficult decisions about the scope of their projects and has added to the juggling act, especially in light of the limitations of bridging funding (Davis, Quinn, & Weale, 2020).

This presents a conundrum. In this chapter, I have argued that reflexive practices can enable doctoral researchers to pull through liminal moments and make progress with their doctorates, often with transformative effects for the individual doctoral researcher. But reflexivity takes time. Doctoral researchers reported acute time poverty in normal circumstances, which has been exacerbated by the global pandemic. This raises the question of what actions can be taken to protect and scaffold time for reflexivity? The following suggestions are adapted from a PhD thesis on the topic of timely completion (Dowle, 2020):

- *Plan, but plan flexibly*: Doctoral researchers and supervisors are encouraged to think carefully about what adds value to the doctoral experience and the doctoral researcher's career aspirations. This helps with identifying the enrichment activities that are most beneficial, allowing them to be spread over the duration of the doctorate. The project itself also benefits from having a plan in place with clear objectives and milestones built in. However, plans should be regularly reviewed and include time for doctoral researchers to work through wicked problems. They should also be realistic and take into account the disruption caused by the pandemic.
- *Embrace the joy of the process*: There is no doubt that doing a doctorate requires a lot of hard work and that there is a lot of pressure on the doctoral researcher. However, it is important not to lose sight of joy in the research process. It is helpful to recall why the decision was taken to do a doctorate in the first place and to recognise the changes that doctoral researchers have undergone in the process. Celebrating and recording little victories along

the way can also sustain doctoral researchers through the process and reinforce a sense of self-efficacy.

- *Take care*: Time away from the doctorate can be as productive as time directly engaged in the research project. Taking holidays and regular breaks are good tactics for maintaining a healthy work-life balance and a sustainable pace of activity.
- *Connect and communicate*: Opportunities to connect with others, especially other doctoral researchers who are likely to be experiencing similar problems, are a rich source of support and guidance. They can help with overcoming research problems, providing advice and also to gauge progress. It is perhaps more important than ever in the pandemic that those networks are nurtured to combat experiences of isolation. Regular contact and communication with supervisors is also important to make sure there is a shared awareness and strategy for dealing with threats to progress caused by the pandemic.
- *Use professional support*: No doctoral researcher should ever feel that they are alone during the doctorate. There are lots of avenues of support for doctoral researchers, supervisors, and professional services staff including Doctoral Schools, counselling services and programme directors. Between them, these support networks can provide expert guidance and support on a range of different problems that the doctoral researcher might experience.
- *Identify opportunities for funding and/or registration extensions*: In the context of the global pandemic, some universities and funders have been able to provide additional bridging support for doctoral researchers. These might be in the form of funding extensions (UKRI, 2020) and/or thesis deadline extensions. There are also hardship funds in most universities for doctoral researchers who are experiencing severe financial difficulties. Identifying what support is available and when the doctoral researcher can avail themselves of that support is helpful for clarifying the real deadlines and planning. Any additional financial support can also provide a lot of relief to doctoral researchers grappling with the added time pressures created by the pandemic.

In conclusion, it is very unlikely that a doctoral researcher can pass through their doctorate without experiencing liminality. As captured in the quotation that opened this chapter, 'there are no safe paths' through the doctorate – it is inherently risky and uncertain. However, reflexivity can enable doctoral researchers to navigate liminal moments and to make progress with transformative results. Some suggestions have been provided to help protect reflexive time and scaffold reflexive practices. It is hoped that this will enable doctoral researchers to feel more secure when 'over the Edge of the Wild' and that it might even lead to 'all sorts of fun'.

References

Alvesson, M., & Sköldberg, K. (2009). *Reflexive methodology: New vistas for qualitative research* (2nd ed.). Sage.

Archer, M. S. (2003). *Structure, agency, and the internal conversation.* Cambridge University Press.

Archer, M. S. (2007). *Making our way through the world: Human reflexivity and social mobility.* Cambridge University Press.

Bradley-Cole, K., & Denicolo, P. (2020). *Constructivist coaching: A practical guide to unlocking potential alternative futures.* Routledge.

Breier, M., Herman, C., & Towers, L. (2019). Doctoral rites and liminal spaces: academics without PhDs in South Africa and Australia. *Studies in Higher Education, 45*(4), 834–846. doi:10.1080/03075079.2019.1583727

Bryan, B., & Guccione, K. (2018). Was it worth it? A qualitative exploration into graduate perceptions of doctoral value. *Higher Education Research & Development, 37*(6), 1124–1140. doi:10.1080/07294360.2018.1479378

Cabaroglu, N., & Denicolo, P. (2008). Exploring student teacher belief development: An alternative constructivist technique, snake interviews, exemplified and evaluated. *Personal Construct Theory and Practice, 5*, 28–40.

Davis, N., Quinn, B., & Weale, S. (2020, November 15). PhD students fear they won't finish in time as UKRI curbs extensions. *The Guardian.* https://www.theguardian.com/world/2020/nov/15/phd-students-fearful-after-funding-body-ukri-curbs-extensions

Deem, R., & Dowle, S. (2020). The UK doctorate: History, features and challenges. In P. Altbach, H. de Wit, & M. Yudkevich (Eds.), *Trends and issues in doctoral education worldwide: An international research inquiry.* Sage.

Denicolo, P., & Pope, M. (2001). *Transformative professional practice: Personal construct approaches to education and research.* Whurr.

Dowle, S. (2020). *Retheorising doctoral completions: Exploring the role of critical events, structure and agency* [Ph.D.]. Royal Holloway, University of London, Egham.

Farrell, C., Oerton, S., & Plant, E. (2018). Doing a doctorate in business administration: The case for critical reflexivity. *The International Journal of Management Education, 16*(3), 370–379. doi:10.1016/j.ijme.2018.06.002

Fox, A., & Allan, J. (2013). Doing reflexivity: Moments of unbecoming and becoming. *International Journal of Research & Method in Education, 37*(1), 101–112. doi:10.1080/1743727x.2013.787407

Keefer, J. M. (2015). Experiencing doctoral liminality as a conceptual threshold and how supervisors can use it. *Innovations in Education and Teaching International, 52*(1), 17–28. doi:10.1080/14703297.2014.981839

Kiley, M. (2009). Identifying threshold concepts and proposing strategies to support doctoral candidates. *Innovations in Education and Teaching International, 46*(3), 293–304. doi:10.1080/14703290903069001

Kiley, M., & Wisker, G. (2009). Threshold concepts in research education and evidence of threshold crossing. *Higher Education Research & Development, 28*(4), 431–441. doi:10.1080/07294360903067930

Levecque, K., Anseel, F., De Beuckelaer, A., Van Der Heyden, J., & Gisle, L. (2017). Work organization and mental health problems in PhD students. *Research Policy, 46*(4), 868–879. https://doi.org/10.1016/j.respol.2017.02.008

McAlpine, L., & Emmioğlu, E. (2014). Navigating careers: Perceptions of sciences doctoral students, post-PhD researchers and pre-tenure academics. *Studies in Higher Education, 40*(10), 1770–1785. doi:10.1080/03075079.2014.914908

McCray, J., & Joseph-Richard, P. (2020). Towards a model of resilience protection: Factors influencing doctoral completion. *Higher Education, 80*(4), 679–699. doi:10.1007/s10734-020-00507-4

Pope, M., & Denicolo. (1990). Adults learning – teachers thinking. In C. Day, M. Pope, & P. Denicolo (Eds.), *Insights into teachers' thinking and practice*. Routledge.

Rainford, J. (2016a). Becoming a doctoral researcher in a digital world: Reflections on the role of Twitter for reflexivity and the internal conversation. *E-Learning and Digital Media, 13*(1–2), 99–105. doi:10.1177/2042753016672380

Rainford, J. (2016b). Making internal conversations public: Reflexivity of the connected doctoral researcher and its transmission beyond the walls of the academy. *Journal of Applied Social Theory, 1*(1), 44–60.

Taylor, C. A. (2010). More than meets the eye: the use of videonarratives to facilitate doctoral students' reflexivity on their doctoral journeys. *Studies in Higher Education, 36*(4), 441–458. doi:10.1080/03075071003714115

Turner, V. (1974). *Dramas, fields and metaphors: Symbolic action in human society.* Cornell University Press.

UKRI. (2020). *Review of extensions for students impacted by Covid-19.* https://www.ukri.org/wp-content/uploads/2020/11/UKRI-11112020-ReviewOfExtensionsForStudentsImpactedByCovid-19.pdf

Winstone, N., & Moore, D. (2016). Sometimes fish, sometimes fowl? Liminality, identity work and identity malleability in graduate teaching assistants. *Innovations in Education and Teaching International, 54*(5), 494–502. doi:10.1080/14703297.2016.1194769

Wisker, G., & Bengtsen, S. (2019). *Towards Gothic-influenced approaches to doctoral journeys and supervision: Challenging conformity, destruction and despair, releasing and shaping creative energies* [Paper]. SRHE: Creativity, criticality and conformity in higher education, Newport.

CHAPTER 14

This Could Be Heaven, or This Could Be Hell

Exploring the Complexity Experienced by Swedish Doctoral Researchers from a Workplace Perspective

Marie-Louise Österlind

Abstract

The situation for Swedish doctoral researchers has been described as a 'heavenly hell'. Many are satisfied with their education and have a good relationship with their supervisor. Still, there are also problematic aspects of life as a doctoral researcher which at the worst can lead to illness and/or dropping out. A similar dualism exists in studies at the international level.

This chapter aims to explore the complexity experienced and handled by Swedish doctoral researchers from a workplace perspective. It reveals some of the greatest difficulties and proposes means to cope with them. The arguments presented are based on previous research, personal experience and empirical data from qualitative questionnaires and interviews. Here, leaders of doctoral education and policymakers are provided with examples from which to develop and enhance their doctoral researchers' working conditions in order to minimise work-related illness and attrition, stimulate creativity and passion, and encourage flexibility to cope with the rigors inherent in research. The special circumstances caused by the ongoing Covid-19 pandemic are noted. The theoretical starting-points of the measures suggested are the Demand-Control-Support Model and relational pedagogy.

Keywords

doctoral researcher – work conditions – work-related illness – Demand-Control-Support Model – relational pedagogy

1 Introduction

Many of the doctoral researchers educated at Swedish universities develop into researchers and teachers, while others become business leaders or heads

 | DOI:10.1163/9789004529304_014

of public organisations and authorities. The quality of research education and the work conditions of doctoral researchers thus carry great weight not only for the individuals but for society at large. The situation for Swedish doctoral researchers has been oxymoronically described as a 'heavenly hell'. Most are satisfied with their education and have a good relationship with their supervisors. Still, there are also problematic aspects of their situation which at worst can lead to illness and/or attrition (Swedish Higher Education Authority, 2016).

This chapter explores the complexity experienced and handled by Swedish doctoral researchers from a workplace perspective. The questions posed are: what are the greatest difficulties and what can/should be done to deal with these? The exploration is based on reports from Swedish governmental organisations and trade unions, previous research, in conjunction with personal experience and qualitative empirical data. A portrait composed from the empirical material illustrates the doctoral researchers' situation. I hope to provide leaders of doctoral education and policymakers with examples from which to develop and enhance their doctoral researchers' working conditions. This should help them to minimise work-related illness and attrition while stimulating creativity and passion as well as promoting flexibility to cope with the rigours inherent in normal research.

The special circumstances caused by the ongoing Covid-19 pandemic added to the challenges faced by all concerned. The theoretical starting-points of the measures suggested are the Demand-Control-Support Model and relational pedagogy.

2 Being a Doctoral Researcher – A Heavenly Hell

A heavenly hell is how the complex situation experienced by many Swedish doctoral researchers has been described by Anna Ilar (2017), the then chairperson of the Doctoral Candidate Section of the Swedish Association of University Teachers and Researchers (SULF). A similar dualism is found in international studies of doctoral researchers' conditions: *love and hurt* (Woolston, 2017); *fear and joy, commitment, and anguish* (Woolston, 2019).

2.1 *This Could Be Heaven*

Being a doctoral researcher in Sweden has several advantages compared to some other countries. Research education is free of charge and the doctoral researchers must primarily be employed as doctoral candidates (The Swedish Higher Education Ordinance, SFS 1993:100). They are covered by the social insurance system and are entitled to both sickness and parental benefits. Their working conditions are regulated under the Swedish Work Environment Act (SFS 1977:1160) with the purpose of preventing occupational illness and accidents and to otherwise ensure a good work environment. Studies have shown that many of them are satisfied or very satisfied with their education and that they have a good relationship with their supervisors (Swedish Higher Education Authority, 2016; Union of Civil Servants, 2021). At best, they are able to devote four to five years of their lives to learning more about their special interest. They are part of a productive collegial context, where they develop professionally and personally, with support from one or several supervisors. They participate in conferences and are introduced to the international research community.

Many Swedish doctoral researchers report feeling privileged and associate their work with freedom, independence, creativity, good career chances and possibilities to contribute to social development (Källhammer, 2008; Åström, 2008; Swedish Higher Education Authority, 2016; Union of Civil Servants, 2021). This agrees well with how good and healthy work is construed by people with an academic education (Aronsson, Bejerot, & Härenstam, 1999).

The heavenly aspect of life as a doctoral researcher has in previous interviews (Österlind & Denicolo, 2019) been expressed as follows:

> Those were the best days of my life! I spent all my time doing research on what interested me most! (Professor, male)

> I'm not typical. I had a very good time. Everything was fine. (Recent PhD graduate, female)

2.2 *And This Could Be Hell*

The 'heavenly' dimension is contrasted by a darker dimension which, if uncontrolled, can lead to a private 'hell'. This dimension includes high or very high demands and stress levels, unclear or contradictory goals and expectations, lack of acceptance, acknowledgement and support from supervisors and other members of the research collective (Källhammer, 2008; Swedish Higher Education Authority, 2016), high workload, fragmented tasks and lack of time (Holmström, 2018). Many doctoral researchers (43%) state that they devote 40–59 hours a week to their research studies and projects, 5% that they work more than 60 hours per week and 58% that they have worked or studied even when sick. In this group experiencing 'hell', women are overrepresented.

The situation seems particularly hard for female doctoral researchers. They report worse work conditions, higher stress levels [women: 59%, men 50%], poorer wellbeing and higher discrimination [women: 23%, men 4%] (Swedish

Higher Education Authority, 2016). Women are also overrepresented in long-term sickness absence (Källhammer, 2008). Those who work on their own, without belonging to a research group, have lower work satisfaction, which it is said also applies more to women than to men (Holmström, 2018). This may be an unexplored discipline-based factor.

The supervisor is by far the most important person to those experiencing doctoral research education. Supervisors are expected to provide support and help to develop independent researchers. It is therefore very serious that 27% state that deficiencies in supervision shortcomings have to a high or very high extent impeded their research and dissertation work. Quite a few (22% of the women; 17% of the men) have felt the dependence on their supervisor troublesome. Nearly a fifth (18%) have experienced a lack of interest on the part of the supervisor. In spite of this, only 11% have changed or considered changing their supervisor (15%) (Swedish Higher Education Authority, 2016).

The work conditions described above may, if prolonged, lead to depression and a state of exhaustion, especially if individualised and normalised (Swedish Higher Education Authority, 2016). They may also contribute to the fact that a relatively large number of doctoral researchers do not complete their degree within the stated time. For example, as many as 31% of the doctoral researchers had not completed their doctorate eight years after being registered to a four or five year long doctoral programme, and the overall attrition rate is estimated to be over 25% Insufficient supervisor support is the most frequently mentioned reason for dropping out (40%) followed by loss of motivation (37%) and deficient psychosocial work environment (28%) (Dryler, 2012). Even if dropping out is unsatisfactory in many ways, it may for the individual doctoral researcher be the best (or only) way of avoiding long-lasting work-related ill health.

This is not unique for Sweden. High dropout rates, delay, and dissatisfaction among PhD students are common problems in doctoral education (Ryan, Baik & Larcombe, 2021). A recent global survey of more than 5000 doctoral researchers shows that over 25% were concerned about their mental health. More than 10% had sought help for anxiety and depression (Woolston, 2019).

3 What Is It Like to Be a Swedish Doctoral Researcher Today? Doctoral Researchers' Voices

Board members of the Doctoral Candidate Section of the Swedish Association of University Teachers and Researchers were asked in 2020 to reflect as expert witnesses on the following areas from personal experience and their overall knowledge:

1. What is it like to be a doctoral researcher? What are the joys and the difficulties?
2. What type of help and support would be desirable compared to what you are able to get if you need it?
3. What improvements in doctoral researchers' work conditions are most urgent?

Four people answered in writing via a digital questionnaire with open questions and the fifth person via a voice-recorded telephone interview. The answers were analysed thematically. To bring life to the material and give voice to the participants, the result of the analysis is presented below in the form of a doctoral researcher portrait, combining the most frequent descriptions from the data.

3.1 *Portrait of a Doctoral Researcher*

It is a very mixed situation to be a doctoral researcher. One day you feel great, and everything is fine, the next day everything is awful and you feel generally depressed.

The pressure is very high. In my field writing a compilation thesis is mandatory. The time limit of my employment in combination with the insecurity of what I produce adds to the pressure. I don't know whether I will achieve a publishable result until I have already spent a couple of months to design and implement an experiment.

I have nothing to compare with. I have never had another job. This is such a unique work situation. Talking about it is hard. It is too complex. My family and friends cannot understand why I work during weekends and holidays without being paid. It is really hard to balance your private life with doctoral studies and with working in a research project. The whole academic world is extremely stressful and limitless. Your role models that you look up to, are similarly stressed, in the midst of it all, so you imitate an unhealthy behaviour. Or, they say one thing but do another.

The relationship with the supervisor is highly asymmetric. As a doctoral researcher you are powerless. What help you can get to cope with disagreements and difficulties depends on things like who is the director of studies for research education. Several times I have told myself: If I just manage to stand it now, I can quit later.

In theory there is always help available, but in practice you are passed on from one person to another without receiving any help. If you're suffering from mental illness, it is difficult enough to contact one person and worse to be redirected. Nobody seems to have the overarching responsibility for how we feel and for our work situation. The supervisor is seldom the best person to turn to. It does not feel as if the university trains supervisors and research group leaders enough in this respect. The help we can get is not always relevant or objective. This is especially problematic for international doctoral researchers because they are not familiar with the system.

What we really need is a kind of comfort zone where we can discuss our problems, the stress and the anguish about our studies without having to be afraid of being misunderstood or judged.

4 How Can the Difficulties Be Understood and What Should Be Done to Come to Terms with Them?

Doctoral researchers are entitled to good work conditions. In Sweden, universities' legal responsibility for creating good work conditions for their employees and students is regulated in the Swedish Work Environment Act (SFS 1977:1160), whose overarching aim is to prevent occupational illness and accidents and to otherwise ensure a good work environment (Ch.1, §1). Several of the difficulties experienced by doctoral researchers receive special focus in the Organizational and Social Work Environment Provisions (AFS 2015:4), which monitor knowledge requirements, aims, workload, work hours and discrimination harassment. In common with other countries, the Rector or Vice Chancellor has the ultimate responsibility for the work environment. Heads of Department or the equivalent usually have delegated responsibility, but the director of studies for research education, research leaders and supervisors are expected to be responsible for observing problems, taking adequate measures, and following them up.

The irregularities existing within the 'hellish' dimension need to be addressed to minimise the risk of serious work-related ill health. Just as good work conditions lead to increasing efficiency and improved performance, they are also essential for research quality.

The theoretical basis of the measures suggested below is derived from the Demand-Control-Support Model (Karasek & Theorell, 1979; Johnson & Hall, 1988) and from relational pedagogy (Aspelin, 2017).

4.1 *Demands, Control and Support*

What demands individuals are exposed to and to what extent they can exert control over the conditions of work are the starting point of the well-known

Demand-Control-Support Model (Karasek & Theorell, 1979; Johnson & Hall, 1988). High demands in combination with low influence and limited control over one's own work situation lead to a tense work situation where the risk of work-related stress and poor health is great. If, on the other hand, individuals enjoy a high degree of self-monitoring and can use their knowledge to cope with the high demands, the possibilities for active engagement in the work situation increase. Although this appears to be stimulating, there is a risk that the individual works too much and thus impairs the chances of recovery. If this goes on for a long time, the health effects may again be negative. Such potentially negative effects can be lessened if the individual has good social support at the workplace. This may function as a stress buffer and result in a healthy work situation.

The Demand-Control-Support Model is a general model focusing on the individual. It has been criticised for not taking into consideration the contextual factors that play a decisive role for how well those organisational changes function that are intended to achieve improved health and increased wellbeing (see e.g., Sparks & Cooper, 1999). Used in academic contexts, the model has demonstrated that work demands, control and supervisory support are predictive of both job strain and job satisfaction (McClenahan, Giles, & Mallett, 2007). The predominant focus on the individual in the academic world tends to weaken the social support more than usual in workplaces of other types (Källhammer, 2008).

If translated to the situation of doctoral researchers, this would entail that good and healthy work can be achieved, given that high but clear and reasonable demands are matched with a high degree of self-monitoring and good social support from supervisors, fellow doctoral researchers, and colleagues at large. Such a student-centred approach could increase individual well-being and organisational sustainability (Schmidt & Hansson, 2018). This may, however, be difficult to achieve given the individualistic and competitive academic culture. Even more so when taking into consideration the special circumstances caused by the ongoing Covid-19 pandemic which involves social isolation to prevent infection. Under any work circumstances this would lead to concerns about mental health.

4.2 *The Importance of Relationships for Learning and Development*

Relational pedagogy starts from the idea of the human being as a relational being, who learns, develops, and grows in relation to others. Education and learning are regarded as relation-oriented processes where the individual's interpersonal encounters are of great importance (Aspelin, 2017).

The relationship with the supervisor(s) is often regarded as crucial for the doctoral researcher's advancement and chances of development (Mainhard,

Van Der Rijst, Van Tartwijk, & Wubbels, 2009; Duke & Denicolo, 2017). A good doctoral researcher-supervisor relationship heightens the former's satisfaction and reduces the risk of dropping out (Rooij, Fokkens-Bruinsma, & Jansen, 2021). It can also stimulate the doctoral researcher's creativity (Whitelock, Faulkner, & Miell, 2008).

The importance of relationships and support was a recurrent theme in the interview I conducted with a professor emerita and a very experienced supervisor. Another relevant theme was trust in the doctoral researcher's capacity for development and 'success'. This also includes having realistic expectations of what the doctoral researcher is supposed to achieve and when. This contributes to clarifying their mutual expectations about process and responsibilities. The following is the response to a question about what helps make a good supervisor-researcher relationship. Both the doctoral researcher and the supervisor must be genuinely interested in the topic. It enables 're-enthusing' one another, making them both dedicated towards a common goal.

> They need to be honest with each other. Make an agreement about this. If a supervisor considers that the doctoral researcher has not achieved what was agreed on, the supervisor must say so. It is important to build a strong and confident connection, so that each can support the other, and with the supervisor also accepting criticism from the doctoral researcher. It also involves the supervisor daring to cut the umbilical cord in a timely manner. That is the most important thing of all. (Professor Emerita)

4.3 *Contextual Factors*

Several studies of the doctoral researchers' conditions and difficulties focus on individuals. The supervisor's importance for their progress and wellbeing is frequently emphasised. Still, some studies weigh in contextual factors of decisive importance for both parties, such as: research being a highly challenging work with unpredictable and nonlinear progress (Juniper et al., 2012); academic competition and performance cultures that make healthy work difficult or impossible (Deem, 2020); and a politico-economic context where both supervisors and doctoral researchers find themselves in tension between reforms based on managerial logic from the business world and professional academic logic (Pettersen, 2015).

There are, however, more recent studies suggesting a change of the academic culture as a long-term sustainable solution to improve the work conditions of doctoral researchers and others (see e.g. Duke & Denicolo, 2017; Deem, 2020; Ryan, Baik & Larcombe, 2021). The latter suggest a challenging and comprehensive change based on the doctoral researchers' own suggested improvements. This demands a work culture that is welcoming and inclusive, directed towards cooperation and understanding, as well as a research community that appreciates its members and their wellbeing, not just their productivity and performance. In conclusion they state: Without doubt, this will be the most challenging – but perhaps the most important of the HDR [Higher Degree by Research] suggestions to implement (Ryan et al., 2021, p. 13).

5 Conclusions

The problematic aspects of the work conditions of doctoral researchers as described above must be confronted and dealt with. In the short-term, department heads must ensure that doctoral researchers' work conditions are included in the systematic work environment management (Organizational and Social Work Environment Provisions AFS 2015:4Eng), comprising examination, risk assessment, measure-taking and evaluation. The objective should be to make reasonable demands, providing a high degree of self-monitoring and good support from supervisors and colleagues. To aid this continuing professional development for supervisors and research leaders should take place regularly.

A long-term sustainable improvement of work conditions within academia (for both doctoral researchers and supervisors) would require more far-reaching changes on the contextual level, entailing a shift from a competition-oriented culture to a culture oriented towards cooperation and support. Cultural changes of this type may be hard and time-consuming to achieve but, if they are successful, they could contribute to beneficial work conditions in which doctoral researchers (and graduated PhDs) can attain their full potential. One example is the comprehensive change that has been carried out at the Belgian top ranked Ghent University. Ghent replaced their quantitative evaluation system with a more holistic five-year model built on individual goals and feedback reports, with an increased emphasis on coaching. The paradigm shift was announced in a press release: "Ghent University is deliberately choosing to step out of the rat race between individuals, departments and universities" (Redden, 2019).

6 Conclusive Personal Reflection

I have written this chapter from the perspective of someone has seen both sides of the situation. Some time ago I was admitted as doctoral researcher at a Swedish university. My doctoral research years were a heavenly hell, like those described above. I loved doing research, found most courses interesting, had a doctoral employment at a university college; I had good doctoral researcher fellows, belonged to a good research environment and received support from an external mentor, now a fellow book editor, who introduced me into the international research networks to which I still belong.

I and my three doctoral researcher fellows from the college had the same supervisor and assistant supervisor. After each supervision session we felt so mortified that it took several weeks to regain a reasonable balance. The situation did not improve until we took courage and demanded new supervisors. Only then did we realise how supervision could and should be, and that we were not the ones at fault.

The repressive and anguish-provoking seminar culture prevailing at that time in our research venue made us tremble before each seminar and fear the occasions when we ourselves were to make presentations. The conversation order was hierarchic. The tone was often hard and sometimes condemnatory. In contrast, the supportive and productive seminar culture in the multi-scholarly research environment to which I belonged at the university college, where I had my doctoral employment, made me experience every seminar as a learning opportunity. Everybody was given space and voice independent of academic standing.

Support from others was of crucial importance throughout this extensive period. That is what stopped me from giving up and dropping out. The PhD dissertation defense took place in 2013 at the university college which had continually provided support and good contexts. Since then, I have joined in with colleagues in an endeavour to at least maintain that standard and improve on it, both in our own institution and more generally. My experience has provided special motivation while the Covid problems have added to our challenges.

Acknowledgement

I would like to acknowledge the support provided by Professor Pam Denicolo during my doctorate and beyond.

References

Aronsson, G., Bejerot, E., & Härenstam, A. (1999). Healthy work: Ideal and reality among public and private employed academics in Sweden. *Public Personnel Management, 28*(2), 197–215.

Aspelin, J. (2017). In the heart of teaching: A two-dimensional perspective of teachers' relational competence. *Educational Practice and Theory, 39*(2), 39–56. https://doi.org/10.7459/ept/39.2.04

Åström, E. (2008). *Frihetens pris – ett gränslöst arbete: en tematisk studie av de akademiska lärarnas och institutionsledarnas arbetssituation.* Swedish National Agency for Higher Education [Högskoleverket].

Deem, R. (2020). Rethinking doctoral education: University purposes, academic cultures, mental health and the public good. In S. Cardoso, O. Tavares, C., Sin, & T. Carvalho (Eds.), *Structural and institutional transformations in doctoral education* (pp. 13–42). Palgrave Macmillan.

Dryler, H. (2012). *Rapport 2012:1 R Orsaker till att doktorander lämnar forskarutbildningen utan examen – en uppföljning av nybörjarna på forskarnivå läsåren 1999/2000 och 2000/01.* Swedish National Agency for Higher Education [Högskoleverket].

Duke, D. C., & Denicolo, P. M. (2017). What supervisors and universities can do to enhance doctoral student experience (and how they can help themselves). *FEMS Microbiology Letters, 364*(9). https://doi.org/10.23865/hu.v8.1138

Holmström, O. (2018). Ensamarbetande doktoranders perspektiv på forskarutbildning och doktorandtillvaro: Ämnesmässig ensamhet, den informella socialisationens kraft och erkännandets betydelse. *Högre utbildning, 8*(1), 14–29.

Ilar, A. (2017). *Intervju i SVT Nyheter/Vetenskap 2017-11-06. Enkät visar: ofta himmelsk helvete att börja forska.* https://www.svt.se/nyheter/vetenskap/enkat-visar-ofta-himmelskt-helvete-att-borja-forska

Johnson, J. V., & Hall, E. M. (1988). Job strain, work place social support, and cardiovascular disease: A cross-sectional study of a random sample of the Swedish working population. *American Journal of Public Health, 78*(10), 1336–1342.

Juniper, B., Walsh, E., Richardson, A., & Morley, B. (2012). A new approach to evaluating the well-being of PhD research students. *Assessment & Evaluation in Higher Education, 37*(5), 563–576. doi:10.1080/02602938.2011.555816

Karasek, R., & Theorell, T. (1990). *Healthy work: Stress productivity, and the reconstruction of working life.* Basic Books.

Källhammer, E. (2008). *Akademin som arbetsplats: hälsa, ohälsa och karriärmöjligheter ur ett genusperspektiv* [Licentiate dissertation]. Luleå technical university.

Mainhard, T., Van Der Rijst, R., Van Tartwijk, J., & Wubbels, T. (2009). A model for the supervisor–doctoral student relationship. *Higher Education, 58*(3), 359–373. https://doi.10.1007/s10734-009-9199-8

McClenahan, C. A., Giles, M. L., & Mallett, J. (2007). The importance of context specificity in work stress research: A test of the Demand-Control-Support model in academics. *Work & Stress, 21*(1), 85–95. doi:10.1080/02678370701264552

Organizational and Social Work Environment Provisions (AFS 2015:4Eng).

Österlind, M.-L., & Denicolo, P. M. (2019). *Should I stay or should I go? – A further exploration of Swedish doctoral researchers' "heavenly hell"* [Paper]. Annual Research Conference, Newport, Wales.

Pettersen, I. J. (2015). From metrics to knowledge? Quality assessment in higher education. *Financial Accountability & Management, 31*(1), 23–40.

Redden, E. (2019). Ghent University, in Belgium, embraces new approach to faculty evaluation less focused on quantitative metrics. *Inside Higher Education.*

Ryan, T., Baik, C., & Larcombe, W. (2021). How can universities better support the mental wellbeing of higher degree research students? A study of students' suggestions. *Higher Education Research & Development.* doi:10.1080/07294360.2021.1874886

Schmidt, M., & Hansson, E. (2018). Doctoral students' well-being: A literature review, *International Journal of Qualitative Studies on Health and Well-Being, 13*(1), 1508171. doi:10.1080/17482631.2018.1508171

Sparks, K., & Cooper, C. L. (1999), Occupational differences in the work-strain relationship: Towards the use of situation-specific models. *Journal of Occupational and Organizational Psychology, 72*, 219–229. doi:10.1348/096317999166617

Swedish Higher Education Authority [Universitetskanslersämbetet]. (2016). *Rapport 2016:18. Doktorandspegeln 2016 – en enkät om studenternas studiesituation.* Stockholm.

Swedish Higher Education Ordinance, SFS 1993:100.

Swedish Work Environment Act [Arbetsmiljölagen] (SFS 1977:1160).

Union of Civil Servants [Fackförbundet ST]. (2021). *Hur mår doktoranden? En rapport från Fackförbundet ST och SFS doktorandkommitté om forskarstuderandes psykosociala arbetsmiljö.* https://st.org/rapport-hur-mar-doktoranden

van Rooij, E., Fokkens-Bruinsma, M., & Jansen, E. (2019). Factors that influence PhD candidates' success: the importance of PhD project characteristics. *Studies in Continuing Education, 43*(1), 48–67. doi:10.1080/0158037X.2019.1652158

Whitelock, D., Faulkner, D., & Miell, D. (2008). Promoting creativity in PhD supervision: Tensions and dilemmas. *Thinking Skills and Creativity, 3*(2), 143–153.

Woolston, C. (2017, October 26). A love–hurt relationship. *Nature, 550*, 549–552.

Woolston, S. (2019, November 14). PhD poll reveals fear and joy, commitment and anguish. *Nature, 575*, 403–406.

CHAPTER 15

Epilogue

Continuing to Focus on the People Involved in Doctoral Education

Pam Denicolo, Marie-Louise Österlind and Britt-Marie Apelgren

The origins of this book predated the onset of the Covid-19 pandemic, but the chapters emerged and were completed during the first phase and, meanwhile, yet another new variant was identified. It seems that people globally are having to become more resilient to the stresses that living with this threat to existence produces. Resilience can be defined as the ability to adapt successfully in the face of adversity.

Especially in relation to doctoral researchers, resilience is a word whose interpretation and impact has undergone some metamorphosis in recent years. Authors in this book have noted the rise, especially over the last twenty years, of interest in student well-being that paralleled similar concerns about the welfare of workers more generally. Yet, as several of our fellow contributing authors have noted, the doctoral process is of necessity already replete with challenges, intellectual, physical, and emotional, because all its participants are working at the boundaries of knowledge with risks aplenty to eventual success. As learning and working conditions converge, as they do for both staff and doctoral researchers, further challenges emerge. Early in the millennium those of us working with doctoral researchers were discouraged from mentioning resilience as a necessary or useful aptitude for those undergoing a doctorate on the grounds that it could be seen as placing an added burden on them when we should be relieving their stresses. Now, as we complete this book, workshops, and other training to build resilience are burgeoning, for researchers and their teachers/supporters.

Although being demanding is the very nature of the doctorate and confronting challenge is its core activity, we, the contributing authors, recognise a duty of care to our researchers and colleagues, and to ourselves. As chapters in this book demonstrate, escalating changes in the policies and systems of higher education and threats and precarity in its wider environment add to obstructions to the wellbeing of all doctoral participants. Despite that, these chapters have also presented a range of opportunities to transform the context of and support for those engaged in doctoral study. In this concluding chapter we

 | DOI:10.1163/9789004529304_015

review the main challenges then collate and evaluate the potential opportunities rehearsed by our colleagues.

Paradoxes abound in this education sector. When employers questioned the readiness for employment of those who had spent several years concentrating on resolving an extremely specific research issue, the response was to provide additional skills training to help researchers become more adaptable to different work environments both within and outside the university sector. Although the rubric contended that these skills also contributed to improved research ability and outcomes, nevertheless this training added to the demands on the time of the researchers and the skills of their supervisors. When other staff were recruited to aid researcher development then new working relationships between staff had to be negotiated. Simultaneously, demands from funding bodies, as a result of governmental pressure, included not just researchers with improved skills but research products that had readily discernible, clearly argued impact. This shift of focus led to a need for both academic staff and their researchers to work across disciplinary boundaries and, indeed, to liaise increasingly with other professions and industry, again adding to workloads and stretching intellectual stamina.

Undoubtedly there are many benefits to working collaboratively with others, extending communities of practice, as have been rehearsed within these chapters, yet maintaining such communities also demands time and skill, and presents yet another contradiction for those involved. Again, we are faced with a Janus-faced word since collaboration, with positive constructs such as teamwork, co-operation, and alliance, can also be viewed as consorting with the enemy. In very many respects, academe is rife with competition: institutions compete for esteem, to gain funding and students; individual academics and researchers also seek singularity of esteem to attract students and funding for their research as the main ways to gain promotion or even to gain a permanent contract. Indeed, research careers have always entailed a degree of insecurity but the growth of casualisation in the sector has exacerbated that precarity at a time when staff and researchers are also facing the challenges to skill and stamina of remote working during the pandemic.

Many of our authors have alluded to the diversity and patchiness of support within and between institutions and countries for the professional development of staff. Although it has long been assumed (mostly wrongly) that the proven ability to gain a doctorate conferred on staff numerous abilities (such as skill in teaching, managing people and finance, negotiating with external bodies, etc.), few academic doctors have been prepared for dealing with the escalating pace of change in today's universities as well as the wider environment. While other respected professions, for instance medical doctors and pharmacists, lawyers, and psychologists, involve a requirement to regularly update theory and practice through continuing professional development, it seems that staff in academia cannot expect that support as a matter of course. Authors in this book, and those whose work they reference, from disparate national and cultural contexts, provide strong evidence to support the conundrum that those very institutions whose main purpose is to teach and to conduct research, neglect the need for their own staff to reflect on practice and seek out new ideas and skills.

On the other hand, most of our authors mention, and indeed celebrate, the passion and persistence that researchers at all levels bring to their work, at least initially. Harnessing those attributes to support individual and collegiate agency appears to be useful in developing and maintaining well-being. However, this should not be seen as an excuse to add to the traditional, inherent pressure on those engaged, at whatever level, in doctoral work. It seems that recent policy and procedure changes in the wake of the Bologna agreement, such as skills training and wider collaboration, despite original intentions to improve the doctoral process paradoxically bring with them additional burdens. In academe, while remaining flexible internally to adapt to external developments, there is a requirement to be alert to the potential negative repercussions.

A case in point is the response to the need to isolate because of the Covid-19 pandemic. Worldwide staff and researchers responded creatively to the then extraordinary circumstances. Staff developed, almost synchronously, online workshops, debates, tutorials and examinations and their own skills of e-learning and e-teaching, so different to those required in face-to-face work. Often this involved doubling up lessons providing both online and in person versions to different student groups, and frequently required 'working from home' with all its trials of inadequate equipment and managing the family while maintain a professional role. Researchers modified, sometimes radically, their research methods and/or focus to accommodate restrictions, learning themselves the skills of e-learning. As we write, it is both clear that 'new norms' have been established as the immediate expectations of institutional leaders were raised about capacity and resilience of researchers and their supporters. Already there are signs of growing dissent emerging in the sector. Our authors propose instead that carefully thought-out plans be devised, and structures improved to make best use of the new skills to reduce the excessive burdens unexpectedly imposed globally on the people in academia.

Serendipitously, just as we were 'putting this volume to bed', Professor Dame Sarah Gilbert gave her Dimbleby Lecture, Vaccine vs. Virus: This race, and the next one. In it she explains clearly to the UK public how and why the vaccines were developed so quickly without loss of rigour – down mainly to well-practised research methods, well established networks, and bravery in following unanticipated opportunities. She contrasted this to the normal process of university research – when more time and energy must be devoted to the constant competition for funding than to the research itself. After a decade of pointless pontificating about health and climate matters from pompous, populist politicians, denigrating experts, we hope this demonstrates a turning tide.[1]

In it she emphasises that one potential advantage that has emerge from this situation is that communication has been improved between individuals and groups within and between disciplines and countries so that policies, procedures, standards, and support systems for research and researchers (including the doctorate) can be more readily compared, with discrepancies noted and addressed when useful, productive ideas are shared. We hope that this book contributes to that process by providing readers the opportunity to compare and contrast their own experience of doctoral education, recent and ongoing, with that of the widely dispersed chapter contributors. We see it as demonstrating the dearth of research on improving the experience of researchers and their supporters, motivating coordinated collaboration to develop systems that demonstrably acknowledge that the people within them matter.

Note

1 You may be able to find a full transcript online as the 44th Dimbleby Lecture: https://www.ox.ac.uk/news/2021-12-07-professor-dame-sarah-gilbert-delivers-44th-dimbleby-lecture

Appendix: Terminology and Conditions

Inevitably as the doctorate was adopted and developed in geographical regions, indeed influenced by the range of universities within a region, different terminology and customs/practice emerged. Although increased communication between institutions globally has led to some commonality or at least recognition of where comparability exists, readers might find it helpful to consult the summary below of main variations in terminology and expectations about rules and procedures related to the doctorate in the range of locations represented by our authorship.

Terminology and conditions	Country examples
Fees	UK
No fees	Sweden
Doctoral researchers as university employee	Sweden
'Collective agreements' in place negotiated between employers and unions	Sweden
'Advisor' is term for main supporter	USA
'Supervisor' is term for main supporter	UK, Australia
The doctorate is primarily a research-focused degree	UK, Sweden, Australia
The doctorate has a substantial, required taught component	Sweden, USA
'Thesis' is term for the written product	UK, Australia
'Dissertation' is term for the written product	USA
Compilation of papers also used as a written product	Sweden, UK, Australia (optional)
Monograph is term for the written product	Sweden
Open viva	Sweden and other European countries
Closed viva	UK, Australia (when an oral examination is required)
Normally no viva	Australia (but some universities now require one)
Fixed maximum term	Sweden, UK
Open ended	Several European countries, but reducing
'Professor' used to denote any academic	USA
'Professor' used to denote the highest academic title	UK, Sweden, Australia

Index